GERSHOM SCHOLEM

Gershom Scholem

Master of the Kabbalah

DAVID BIALE

Yale

UNIVERSITY

PRESS

New Haven and London

ALSO BY DAVID BIALE

Gershom Scholem: Kabbalah and Counter-History

Hasidism: A New History (with David Assaf, Benjamin Brown,
Uriel Gellman, Samuel Heilman, Moshe Rosman, Gadi Sagiv,
and Marcin Wodziński)

Norton Anthology of World Religions: Judaism (editor)

Not in the Heavens: The Tradition of Jewish Secular Thought

*Blood and Belief: The Circulation of a Symbol
Between Jews and Christians*

Cultures of the Jews: A New History (editor)

Eros and the Jews: From Biblical Israel to Contemporary America

CONTENTS

CONTENTS

THIRTY-FIVE YEARS after his death, Gershom Scholem (1897–1982) continues to cast a long shadow over the world of Jewish thought. During his lifetime, he won wide acclaim for unearthing the sources of Jewish mysticism and messianism that other historians, convinced that Judaism was primarily a religion of reason, had ignored or despised. By restoring myth to Judaism, Scholem offered a radical new definition of his subject: the Jewish religion consists of paradoxes and contradictions, the rational and the irrational. Judaism has no dogmatic "essence" but is rather made up of whatever Jews have done or thought, no matter how outlandish or even demonic.

Scholem's study of Jewish history thus broke out of the narrow confines of academic scholarship to provide a revolutionary way of thinking about Judaism. It is perhaps for that reason that at a time when the stars of other thinkers, famous in their day, such as Martin Buber and Franz Rosenzweig, have somewhat faded, Scholem has come to inhabit a brighter place in the Jewish firmament, as a luminary who continues to speak to us today. In 1973, when the English translation appeared of his monumental biography of Shabbatai Zvi (*Sabbatai Sevi*), the messianic figure from the seventeenth century, the reviews of the book, as one commentator has noted, had already diverged from the controversy that the Hebrew edition aroused in 1957. The reviewers of the English edition spent far less time discussing Scholem's subject—few were competent to do so—than talking about Scholem himself. He had become the subject.

Scholem also transcended the world of scholarship for other reasons. When he published his memoir *From Berlin to Jerusalem* in 1977, he put his stamp on a powerful narrative of modern Jewish history: by rejecting his bourgeois German Jewish roots and embracing Zionism, Scholem moved his idiosyncratic life choices from the margins to a central story. The German Jews, he alleged, had lived an illusion that was the "German–Jewish dialogue," and only those few who became Zionists saw through this illusion. However, Scholem's Zionism was anything but conventional, so his critique of the movement that brought him to Palestine in 1923 made his position both more interesting and more challenging. He defended the right of the Jews to create their own society yet criticized Zionism for failing to truly renew Judaism.

It is perhaps for all these reasons—intellectual, political, and cultural—that Scholem's star has never faded. Remarkably, in the year that this book is making its appearance, no less than five other books dealing in whole or in part with Scholem's biography are being—or have been—published (see the bibliographical note). This is more than at any other time since Scholem's death and begs for an explanation. Certainly, as contemporary Zionism confronts a deep political and moral crisis, Scholem's earlier reflections on the price that messianism might exact from modern Jewish nationalism seem apposite, even if formulated in a different reality. And his argument for an inclusive definition of Judaism also has resonance in an age when the battle between secularism and Orthodoxy has reawakened throughout the Jewish world. And so it is that contemporary writers of different persuasions find him urgently relevant.

In this book I do something that has not yet been done with respect to Scholem. The reader will find here an account of his life with an attempt to understand him from within. By using diaries and letters, I have tried to enter into his inner life and view him not only as a thinker and writer but also as a human being. At the same time, I have engaged with his most important writings in an effort to integrate them into his life. As such, this is the study of an extraordinary thinker: not an ethereal intellectual but a fully embodied person, filled with passions and paradoxes, much as he described Judaism itself.

GERSHOM SCHOLEM

1

Berlin Childhood

BERLIN, 1897. The city is exploding with commerce and culture, a far cry from the tiny Prussian capital of Frederick the Great. Between 1849 and 1871, when it became the capital of Bismarck's unified Germany, its population doubled, to 825,000. But the city was scarcely fit to serve as the capital of a new European power. In the 1870s, the socialist leader August Bebel noted that "waste water from the houses collected in gutters along the curbs and emitted a truly fearsome smell."[1] Within a few decades, however, city planners, engineers, and public servants would transform this primitive backwater into a gleaming, modern metropolis.

By 1897, the population of Berlin had again doubled, to 1.7 million. A year before, work had begun on a modern subway system, to be completed in 1902, which would take its place alongside an extensive network of street trams. Museums, opera, and theater crowned a rich cultural life. And the new Reichstag building, completed in 1894 with its impressive dome, sent a clear message of Germany's place in the modern world.

The Jews were an integral part of Berlin's landscape at the end of the nineteenth century. When Moses Mendelssohn had entered via the Rosenthaler Gate in 1743, there were only about 2,000 Jews in the city. By 1871 the number had risen to 36,000. They had won most of their civil rights in mid-century, but with the emancipation of all German Jews in 1871, they were now the full equals of their Christian neighbors (they were, however, still barred from holding academic chairs as well as high offices in government and the military). In business, the professions, and the arts, in particular, they were represented often beyond their numbers in the population. By 1897, the Jewish population of Berlin had swollen to 110,000, the second-largest Jewish community (after Vienna) west of Warsaw. The community boasted recently built Reform synagogues, often in the "Moorish" style, but there were relatively few of the Orthodox Jews more commonly found in the rural communities farther east.

All was not, however, entirely well for these generally prosperous, highly Germanified Jews. During the great depression of the 1870s, a new, racial anti-Semitism emerged that took its place alongside older religious and Enlightenment hostility to the Jews. Adolf Stoecker, the Kaiser's court preacher, gave voice to some of these sentiments. For the first time, political parties whose main platform was anti-Semitic competed for seats in the Reichstag, although they were generally unsuccessful.

In response to these attacks, most Jews took refuge in their German identity and argued that the best response was to relinquish not only the orthodox religious markers of Judaism but also presumed Jewish "traits." Thus, in 1897, the year with which we begin, Walther Rathenau, scion of Germany's foremost electrification company, wrote a scathing polemic titled "Hear, O Israel," in which he attacked his coreligionists for "[your] unathletic build, your narrow shoulders, your clumsy feet . . . [your] wheedling subservience and vile arrogance."[2] Rathenau did not advocate conversion, since the baptized Jews would take these same traits with them into the church, a belief that echoes arguments of the racial anti-Semites. Despite the overtones of self-hatred in his essay, Rathenau resolved to remain Jewish. But he did not embrace the new Zionist movement, also a product of the year 1897. Like Rathenau, the Zionists were determined to transform the physical and behavioral characteristics of the Jews into *Muskeljudentum* (muscular Judaism), in Max Nordau's phrase. For Rathenau, though, the Jews needed to solve their problems—for which he, like many Zionists, blamed the Jews themselves—within Germany.

On December 5, 1897, the same year that Rathenau published his diatribe and Theodor Herzl convened the first Zionist Congress, a fourth—the youngest—son, named Gerhard, was born to Arthur and Betty Scholem. The Scholems were a family of printers who had been resident in Berlin for three generations. The family originated in Glogau, Silesia, the vast area east of Berlin, conquered by Frederick the Great in 1742, and the original heartland of many of the Jews who ultimately came to Berlin in the nineteenth century. The name Scholem was a highly unusual family name among European Jews, although it was not uncommon as a first name (derived from the Hebrew for "peace"). In fact, Gerhard Scholem's great-great-grandfather was named Scholem ben Elias. When, after 1812, the Prussian Jews were required to take last names, Scholem ben Elias's widow, Zipporah, indicated that she wished to be called after the personal name of her late husband—Zipporah Scholem—and thus was the family name born. Her son Marcus Scholem moved to Berlin early in the nineteenth century and married the daughter of a Dutch Jewish merchant. Gerhard's grandfather, born in 1833, was named after Scholem ben Elias (his own grandfather), as was the Jewish custom, and thus bore the amusing name of Scholem Scholem. However, in a sign of

Jewish acculturation, this family forebear took the German name Siegfried in the 1850s in order to signify his enthusiasm for the operas of Richard Wagner.

Siegfried's son Arthur Scholem was an Anglophile who had spent a year in London in the 1880s working in the printing trade with relatives. Upon his return to Germany, he joined his father's printing business, but the two did not get along, and in 1891, Arthur opened his own shop. In 1890, he married Betty Hirsch and had four sons with her in rapid succession. When Gerhard was born, the family lived on the banks of the Spree canal on Friedrichsgracht, but in 1906 they moved a mere fifteen hundred feet to Neue Grünstrasse. Arthur's print shop was a short walk away. The neighborhood, not far from the city center, was favored by many bourgeois Berlin Jews, but those who achieved greater wealth than the Scholems, such as the family of Gerhard's friend Walter Benjamin, moved to the city's burgeoning western suburbs of Charlottenburg and Grunewald. Nothing remains of the Scholem family house on either street since Allied bombing, the Russian army invasion of what would become East Berlin, and Communist urban planning obliterated virtually all of the buildings on both streets.

Arthur Scholem was a bourgeois German Jew typical of his generation. He had dropped out of gymnasium (high school) and did not benefit from a university education, although a younger brother went on to study medicine, a sign of the family's rising fortunes. One generation removed from Jewish practices, Arthur had little regard for the Jewish religion: he went to work on Yom Kippur and made a point of not fasting. On Shabbat, he would light a cigar and utter a cynical blessing over tobacco. Like Franz Kafka's father, whom that writer describes as passing on an "insignificant scrap of Judaism"[3] to his son, Arthur Scholem had little interest in a Jewish identity for his children. But he socialized primarily with Jews, a common pattern even among Jews who had converted to Christianity.

Kafka noted in his letter to his father (which was never delivered) that Hermann Kafka was a typical representative of the generation of Jews who had migrated from the relatively devout countryside to the cities. Judaism for them was a matter of childhood nostalgia, not something that they practiced often or believed in strongly. They expected their children to show deference to occasional symbols of Judaism, but their own lack of conviction set a bad example. When Franz Kafka became interested in Judaism, which we might have expected to have given him something in common with his father, the opposite occurred: the father treated his son's new interest as one more sign of his ineptitude.

Arthur Scholem was even farther removed from the Judaism of the Silesian countryside from which his ancestors hailed, and, as we will see, his reaction to his own son's Jewish commitments was as hostile as that of Kafka's father. He did don a top hat and accompany Gerhard to synagogue for his bar mitzvah, but he deliberately scheduled it for just before his son's fourteenth birthday, perhaps as a way of establishing a distance from the Jewish tradition toward which he still felt it necessary to make a gesture. As was common among such assimilated German Jews, the Scholems had a Christmas tree, which they explained to themselves as a symbol of German culture. When Gerhard became a Zionist, he found a picture of Theodor Herzl under the tree on Christmas morning. The present was evidently not meant to be ironic. Surprisingly, though, given his indifference to Judaism, when his son Werner married a non-Jewish working-class woman, Arthur cut off all relations with him, as if to say that intermarriage was a boundary he dared not cross.

Arthur evidently inherited a volcanic temper from his father and, in turn, passed it on to his son Gerhard. The similarity between father and son may well account for the future rocky relations between them. Starting in his forties, Arthur suffered from a worsening heart condition that would ultimately kill him at age sixty-one. As a result, his wife, Betty, who worked in the print shop keeping the books, increasingly took over its management. To judge by Gershom Scholem's memoir *From Berlin to Jerusalem*, and by the copious letters Betty wrote to her son over some three decades, she was a highly talented and cultured woman, whose temperament was the opposite of her husband's. As opposed to Arthur, she was not averse to throwing in an occasional Yiddish phrase, although she was no more religious than her husband. Because of Arthur's illness, he was not able to accompany her on the trips to the Swiss Alps that she loved. As a result, she often traveled with her youngest son. And despite Gerhard's annoyance with his mother's irenic nature, she seems to have been able to calm his volatile outbursts. As will become evident, this couldn't have been easy.

Gerhard was tall and lanky, with prominent protruding ears, which caused him no end of teasing in school. He was already showing his brilliance as a child. An autodidact from an early age, he skipped his schoolwork while still earning outstanding grades. Possessed of overweening self-confidence, he could be brusque and overbearing. Yet he was anything but a loner. He was garrulous and sociable, with many lifelong friends.

The four Scholem sons provide a remarkable snapshot of the political options embraced by the German Jews of the late imperial period. The oldest, Reinhold, became a fervent German nationalist, even more assimilationist than the father, and he never gave up his views, even though Hitler forced him to flee to Australia. The second, Erich, followed in the rather middle-of-the-road path of the father. He and Reinhold took over management of the print shop, and he, too, ended up in Australia, where Betty Scholem joined her two oldest sons for the last years of her life (she died there in 1946). The third son, Werner, took a left-wing turn: he became a radical socialist even before the First World War, affiliated with the rump anti-war movement of the German Social Democrats, and after the war joined the German Communist Party, becoming one of its most prominent deputies in the Reichstag in the early 1920s.

Gerhard was closer to Werner than to his two older brothers, who had already left home by his teen years. Werner, whose temperament appears to have been as stormy as his younger sibling's, turned Gerhard into a socialist for a period of time, taking him to café meetings of young workers and, after the outbreak of the war, to clandestine antiwar gatherings. Although they would ultimately part company over Marxism and Zionism (in a long letter from September 1914, Gerhard explained why he couldn't embrace historical materialism), the bond between the two youngest Scholem sons was enormously influential for Gerhard's early formation.

The year 1911, when Gerhard was thirteen, marked the turning point in what was otherwise a conventional Berlin Jewish childhood. Jewish children received perfunctory religious education in the context of their public schooling. Gerhard's teacher, Moses Barol, was a highly learned Russian Jew but a rather unsuccessful pedagogue. Yet Barol may have changed the future of Jewish scholarship when he showed the class a three-volume abridgement of Heinrich Graetz's *History of the Jews*. Although Gerhard would later take great issue with Graetz, he was captivated by the passionate style with which the nineteenth-century historian related the story of the Jews. Graetz led him to discover many other Jewish books in the Berlin Jewish Community Library and also to undertake with his friend Edgar Blum to learn Hebrew. Barol provided the lessons for a few months, but then Gerhard took the study up on his own with the passionate intensity that would characterize all his intellectual endeavors.

In his first diary entry, dated February 17, 1913, he noted that since his bar mitzvah over a year earlier, "I am orthodox and hate Lindenstrasse [the address of the Reform synagogue] where I was bar mitzvah [he writes the abbreviation B.M. in Hebrew characters]."[4] He began to attend the small Orthodox

7

Alte Synagoge, which was a twenty-minute walk from his house. By 1912 or 1913, he had also begun to experiment with keeping the tenets of Jewish law. And he soon joined a small circle studying Talmud with Isaac Bleichröde, the learned great-grandson of the German Jewish scholar Akiba Eger.

This passion for Judaism soon combined with another lifelong passion: bibliophilia. Rummaging in used bookshops, Scholem began to build a library of Judaica and German literature and philosophy. So important was this endeavor that when he came to write his memoirs near the end of his life, he was able to note with precision when and where he had purchased certain books. His diary records a particular fascination with the authors of modern anti-Semitism, in particular Wilhelm Marr (who invented the term *anti-Semitism* in 1879) and Houston Stewart Chamberlain, whose *Foundations of the Nineteenth Century* was one of Hitler's later inspirations. Scholem studied these books with great diligence. Naturally, he rejected their ideas as pure invention, but he allowed that the bourgeois Berlin Jews might have been happy if the anti-Semites' fantasies of Jewish power had actually been true.

Among Scholem's earliest acquisitions were books by Zionist authors: Theodor Herzl, Ahad Ha'am, Nathan Birnbaum, and Max Nordau. This first romance of Zionism through the written word soon took on more active form when his brother Werner introduced him in 1912 to the Jung Juda Zionist youth group, which met in the Tiergarten railway station. Although Werner would abandon Zionism a few years later, introducing Gerhard to this group was a service to the movement for which it still owes him thanks.

Not surprisingly, Gerhard was unable to keep this new interest in Judaism and Zionism to himself and provocatively threw it in his father's face at the family table. The result, also not surprisingly, was stormy arguments as Arthur scathingly rejected both of his sons' ideological experimentations. In a bitter diary entry from early 1913, Gerhard wrote that if he were Werner, he would have fled the family home "ten times over" since "with us, nothing more remains of the Jewish family."[5] Werner did, in fact, depart for Hannover that fall, and Gerhard's wish to escape his father's table was fulfilled a few years later, if not at his own initiative. Arthur may well have seen Gerhard's activities as a deliberate attempt at generational rebellion, and no doubt it was. He would never fully comprehend that Gerhard was prepared to make his life choices based on these early Jewish interests: what might have started as mere adolescent rebellion became something altogether more serious. However, to complicate the picture, when Gerhard produced his first translation from Hebrew into German—the biblical book Song of Songs—Arthur printed it in a beautiful limited edition in his print shop. This would not be the last time that Arthur expressed pride in his son's scholarship, even if mingled with criticism, via his printing press.

As divergent as Zionism was from the prevailing atmosphere in the Scholem home, it was not as alien as it might have seemed. Gerhard's favorite uncle was Theobald Scholem, who was Arthur's brother, ten years his junior. Theobald had lively academic interests in ethnography and history but was not able to gain a higher education since family reasons forced him, with another brother, to take over their father's print shop. He was a passionate Zionist, and his shop published the young movement's main German newspapers. Although Theobald was probably not the major inspiration for Gerhard's Zionism, Jewish nationalist ideas must have been in the air at family gatherings, even as the butt of jokes at Theobald's expense. In addition, Theobald's wife, Hedwig, who was also a Zionist, read Gerhard's Zionist writings with great interest. She learned some Hebrew and even exchanged letters with Gerhard in that language. Theobald and Hedwig, with their daughters Dina and Eva, emigrated to Palestine after the Nazis came to power.

What did it mean for a young German Jew, who had little firsthand experience of anti-Semitism and whose future prospects in Germany were bright, to embrace Zionism a decade and a half after Theodor Herzl burst onto the world stage? For many central European Jews, Zionism meant an assertion of national pride and dignity in an atmosphere of growing nationalism. But it did not mean a commitment to the Jewish tradition, at least no more than for other acculturated German Jews, nor did it mean any interest in decamping to Palestine. Gerhard and his comrades in Jung Juda took a more radical path. They resolved—and many of them fulfilled the resolution—to leave Germany as soon as they finished their education. And they did so out of a profound sense that Zionism meant refashioning their Jewish identities, renewing a Judaism that, in their view, had calcified in its German incarnation. Zionism and Jewish renewal for these teenagers meant the same thing. What they sought was not a Jewish state—we will see that Gerhard only reluctantly embraced political Zionism many years later—but rather a cultural renaissance based in the Hebrew language and Jewish sources.

Both Judaism and Zionism stood in diametric opposition to Arthur Scholem's instinctive devotion to a liberal, nonreligious German Jewish identity, and that is certainly one major reason why Gerhard embraced them as a rebellious adolescent. But his turn to these radical alternatives, although clearly marked by personal idiosyncrasies—there were few other German Jews (Aunt Hedwig was one) who actually learned Hebrew!—was also an expression of a larger, generational revolt. Gerhard belonged to the generation of German Jews who would far exceed their fathers and mothers in terms of education and for whom the Weimar Republic would ultimately open up professional opportunities largely or partially blocked in the prewar Second Reich. Much more secure in their Germanness than their parents, who still felt the need to prove their belonging, they were freer to rebel, turning to political radicalism and cultural experimentation in place of bourgeois conformism. Given the greater opportunities available to Jews in Weimar Germany, the decision to leave for Palestine was particularly radical.

But this rebellion was often accompanied by anguished struggle. As Franz Kafka wrote to Max Brod about those who took up literary creation in German: "Their hind legs were bogged down in their fathers' Judaism, while their front legs could find no new ground. The resulting despair was their inspiration."[6] For Gerhard Scholem, the search for new ground, also at times marked by despair, would ultimately lead to Palestine, the Hebrew language, and the search for the hidden sources of Judaism.

Scholem's early search for an authentic Jewish identity was linked to the overwrought neo-Romanticism that swept up German youth at the time. The philosophy of Friedrich Nietzsche and the poetry of Stefan George promised stirring alternatives to the rational bourgeois culture of late Wilhelmine Germany. And the Wandervogel youth movement, with its celebration of nature and youthful camaraderie, found its Jewish analogue in the Zionist Blau-Weiss. Most young Jews did not see their salvation in such Jewish alternatives, but those who did participated in larger trends among the youth of Germany at the time.

Because Gerhard and his comrades in the Jung Juda group associated their Zionism with a renaissance in Judaism, at the beginning of 1914 they joined the Berlin youth branch of the Agudat Israel, the Orthodox movement founded in 1912 in Kattowitz, in the Prussian province of Silesia. Although the eastern European Jews who established the Agudah intended it as an Orthodox response to Zionism, it seems that the Berlin branch must have lacked this ideological dogmatism, for it is hard to imagine our fervent young Zionists having anything to do with an anti-Zionist party. The Berlin branch's promise to teach Hebrew may have been an initial motivation.

Gerhard was chosen to be a member of the leadership, but his romance with Orthodoxy was short-lived. In May 1914, the executive of Agudat Israel accused Scholem and his comrades of "not being true to the law." Harry Heymann, a member of Jung Juda, declared that he and his group were resigning, and Gerhard followed up with a letter to the same effect, the first missive that appears in his collected correspondence. Interestingly, at no point did this controversy revolve around the Agudah's rejection of Zionism; rather the conflict centered on Orthodoxy. In his diary, Gerhard notes, "A month later, I left Orthodoxy. It wasn't an easy decision. It excited quite a stir. Now to switch over to Martin Buber with full sails, also to socialism."[7]

In his later memoirs, Scholem claims that his main interest in the Agudah was a young woman named Jettka Stein, whom he helped with her schoolwork, but when his romantic advances were rebuffed, he left the Orthodox organization. There is some contemporaneous evidence for this account. Stein appears in his diary more than half a year later; he was clearly still infatuated with her. And two years after that he confessed to his diary that she was the only reason he attended synagogue. Some forty years later, Stein appeared at a lecture he gave in Tel Aviv; she too had immigrated to Palestine, where she became an English teacher.

But whatever Stein's role might have been in attracting Scholem to Orthodoxy or causing him to reject it, his resignation from Agudat Israel must have been a personal crisis of both religious faith and organizational involvement. In the same diary entry in which he reports his resignation, he relates that he has also withdrawn from the Jung Juda leadership, saying that he's "finished with organizations. People laugh at me." That this self-evaluation was close to the mark receives confirmation from an incident that took place nearly a decade later, when the philosopher Hans Jonas saw Scholem for the first time in a meeting debating whether the Blau-Weiss youth movement and the organization of Jewish university students should merge. Jonas describes him interrupting the speakers, waving his huge hands like a big bird, and shouting at the top of his lungs. Scholem's doctrinaire manner and argumentativeness no doubt made him a difficult comrade, even at age sixteen.

Having abandoned Orthodoxy (at least for a time—he would return to it episodically), Scholem now turned to the prophet of Jewish renewal who did not demand obedience to the law. This was Martin Buber, arguably the most influential Jewish thinker in central Europe in the first decades of the twentieth century. Although raised by his grandfather in a partially traditional setting, Buber broke with religious Judaism and joined the Zionist movement in 1898, affiliating with its cultural faction. In 1902 he became the editor of *Die Welt*, one of the Zionist newspapers printed in Theobald Scholem's shop. Buber combined a neo-Romantic, *völkisch* philosophy with a fascination with Hasidism. In the first decade of the twentieth century, he published collections of the tales of Rabbi Nahman of Bratslav and of the Baal Shem Tov, the founder of Hasidism. The purpose of these books was to demonstrate that Judaism contained within it forces for spiritual renewal. Thus, Buber's cultural Zionism—as opposed to that of other writers of his time—was not hostile to religiosity, although he decisively rejected what he called "official Judaism."

Between 1909 and 1911, Buber delivered in Prague three lectures, which were published under the title "Three Addresses on Judaism." These lectures became the inspiration for Zionist youth in the German-speaking world since they offered a vision of Judaism that was the opposite of the liberal, assimilationist culture of the German Jews. Here was a call to elevate myth above reason, the Orient over the Occident, and a subterranean, vitalistic tradition over the legalism of the rabbis.

Buber's Hasidic stories and his philosophy of Jewish renewal had a profound effect on the young Gerhard Scholem, especially, it seems, after his brief flirtation with Orthodoxy. The entries in his diary from 1913 through 1915 are shot full of such Buberian expressions as "der Gott von Erlebnis" (the God of lived experience). In one of his letters to Werner from September 1914, he counters Werner's historical materialism by referring to what he had clearly read in Buber's Hasidic tales: "You have perhaps once heard of a mystical sect among us Jews, the Hasidim in Galicia, who teach socialism *sans phrase*. They stand on the soil of unity and myth, which is life." And quoting from Buber's "Three Addresses": "Before the gates of Rome sits a leprous beggar and waits. He is the Messiah . . . and for whom does he wait? For you!" Buber thus pointed the way for Gerhard to an authentic Judaism that combined messianism and socialism without reducing the first to Orthodoxy or the second to Marxism. Werner, on the other hand, dismissed Buber as a "coffeehouse anarchist."[8]

For Gerhard, this was hardly a pejorative. In his 1914 letter to Werner, Gerhard was already offering anarchism as an alternative to his brother's Marxism. He had for a few years been reading anarchist writers like Peter Kropotkin, and he also came to know Gustav Landauer, the highly original German Jewish anarchist who was murdered during the short-lived Bavarian Socialist Republic in 1919. Landauer taught an ethical and communitarian form of anarchism that was also deeply mystical. Although Scholem declared that "I, Gerhard Scholem, do not stand on the soil of anarchism, even if I greatly honor Gustav Landauer," he was, in fact, gravitating toward an anarchism that might be combined with both Judaism and Zionism. Landauer's *A Call for Socialism* made a particular impression.[9]

In a diary entry from January 1915, he demanded, following Landauer, revolution, not reform. This revolution would overturn the family and the authority of parents. It would also revolutionize Judaism and Herzl's Zionism, which Scholem now regarded as a sell-out. The true Zionism was anarchism, a break from Europe and embrace of the Orient. In a different entry, he married this anarchism to the philosophy of Nietzsche: his goal was to write a *Judenzarathustra*.

Landauer was close to Martin Buber, and Buber also called himself a religious anarchist, another way in which Scholem and Buber were similar, even if they ultimately parted ways. On January 27, 1915, the Berlin branch of Jung Juda held a discussion of Buber's philosophy. Scholem gave a prefatory lecture in which he celebrated Buber as the generation's true prophet. Unlike Ahad Ha'am, the standard-bearer of cultural Zionism whose advocacy for Hebrew culture Scholem also admired, Buber preached revolution rather than gradualism. And unlike Herzl, who called for a *return* to Judaism (albeit not to Orthodoxy), Buber demanded "a *renewal* of Judaism." By uncovering the sources of Hasidism, Buber had shown the young generation that Judaism possessed the forces of myth and mysticism that the renewal of Judaism required. Against the rationalism of the West, Buber called for the Jews to align themselves with "the creative peoples of the Orient."[10]

Despite this lecture delivered to the Jung Juda group, Scholem's relations with his comrades, already rocky, as we have seen, reached a crisis in May 1915. The result of this crisis was the extraordinary long diary entry of May 22, which reveals a great deal of the inner turmoil, as well as the megalomaniacal aspirations, of the seventeen-year-old Scholem. Written in the third person, as if to prepare the ground for his future biographer, the entry starts with some lines about his hardworking but otherwise prosaic family. Remarkably, it was not his father who came in for the most scathing criticism but his uncle Theobald, who, although unnamed, had to be the object of Gerhard's scorn for the idealistic and scholarly airs that he put on in order to impress his nephew. This is not a little surprising since Theobald, as both a Zionist and an intellectual manqué, was closer to Gerhard than was Arthur, but perhaps Theobald represented for him a bourgeois version of his aspirations, a version that he needed to overcome.

After this attack Scholem describes how he came to embrace Herzl's Zionism, which led him to immerse himself in the writings of the Orient. He quickly became disillusioned with the lack of "soul" in Herzl's writings but believed that he could find what he was seeking in other books. He attests here that his bibliophilia reached virtually manic proportions as he swallowed books at an incredible speed, becoming known as a "bookworm and scholar." However, his comrades in Jung Juda soon made fun of him as a "big walking conversational lexicon" and as "Scholem the Buberian." He came to see these erstwhile companions as abandoning the great spiritual search to which he was devoted and settling instead for a kind of quotidian rationality: "So wondered the wounded youth greatly and as he also recognized their soullessness, he set forth on his own way to Zion."[11]

This individual path to Zion was bound up with Buber, to whom he then devotes a lengthy section of the diary entry. Indeed, a few weeks before this entry, Scholem notes in his diary, "I'm back in the mood for Buber. I'm in a deep Buberian spirit," and conceives of writing Buber a long letter (although he evidently did not do so). A week later, the long letter had turned into a plan for a whole book on Buber, although he concedes ignorance about Buber's biography. It is Buber, he says, who has come to awaken the somnolent Zionists who only felt themselves united by historical memory and "the demonic power of racial instinct." In their place, Buber found beauty and spiritual renewal in the despised Jews of the East, in Hasidism. He conveyed this truth "not only as he found it, but as he found it in himself" (Buber's imaginative retelling of Hasidism, which Scholem salutes here, would later become one Scholem's main criticisms of Buber).[12]

Then the entry takes an astonishing turn. Buber may have proclaimed Jewish renewal, but he was not himself the redeemer: "He only wanted to prepare the way for one greater who would come after him." Who was this? Scholem answers:

> The young man . . . believed deeply that the soul of Judah wandered among the nations and in the Holy Land, awaiting the one presumptuous enough to free it from banishment and from the separation from its national body. And he knew in his depths that he was the Chosen One. . . . And the dreamer whose name also signifies that he is the Expected One [is] Scholem, the Perfect One [a wordplay on *Scholem* and *shalem*, "perfect," "whole"]. It is he who must equip himself for his work and begin forcefully to forge the weapons of knowledge.[13]

Scholem thus understood his feverish thirst for the Hebrew language and Jewish books as weapons in the messianic mission for which he believed himself destined. This may also explain his reading of the New Testament, and especially the Gospel of Mark, books one might not immediately associate with the renewal of Judaism. But perhaps the messianic impulses of early Christianity fed his lonely fantasies of a singular historical vocation.

Neither his messianic pretensions nor his wounded rejection of his Jung Juda comrades would persist for long. While he clearly continued to consider himself a figure of world historical proportions, he made only a few hints later to claims like this one. On the contrary, on September 19, he told his diary that he no longer considered himself the Messiah. But the deflation of this role went hand in hand with severe doubts about Zionism. Indeed, the diary entry is marked by deep melancholy, even depression. He admits that since early April, he had entertained periodic thoughts of suicide. While the messianic episode preceded and followed by suicidal thoughts might suggest that he was cycling between ecstasy and depression, we should be hesitant to offer a clinical diagnosis based on a few diary entries. Nevertheless, we will see that throughout his life Scholem was capable of extraordinarily intensive work punctuated by episodes of withdrawal, lethargy, and even depression. The cures to which the family doctor, his uncle Georg, repeatedly sent him may have been a response more to his psychological states than to physical illness.

By his eighteenth year, Gerhard Scholem had already declared the intellectual and political commitments that would guide him into adulthood. Ravenously devouring books, he devoted himself not to a single field but to the broad philosophical tradition that was the heritage of young German intellectuals of his age. In later years, when he had become a historian of Kabbalah, he would remain deeply informed by the philosophical reading of his youth. Side by side with these more general interests, he taught himself Hebrew and began to delve deeply into the Jewish literary tradition, starting with the Bible and extending through the Talmud and medieval texts. This commitment to Hebraism was part and parcel of his commitment to Judaism, although exactly in which form remained uncertain. And, finally, his Jewish commitment was inseparable from Zionism. All these early commitments were now to be tested in the crucible of the First World War.

2

The Abyss of War

THE GREAT WAR, as it came to be called, burst like a summer thunderstorm over the European continent in July and
August 1914. After the Austrian archduke was assassinated in
Sarajevo on June 28, the Habsburg government issued an ulti-
matum to Serbia as the pretext for going to war. Although Serbia accepted nearly all the far-reaching demands, Russia had
meanwhile mobilized its army, sending it to the German border. Demonstrations for and against war swept the streets of
Berlin. On August 1, the Kaiser's government announced the
mobilization of the German army and the Kaiser himself, appearing before his subjects, declared, "I recognize in my Volk
no more parties. Among us there are only Germans."[1] As if in
reaction to this patriotic message, the controversy over the war
of late July gave way in August to a wave of military enthusiasm.
Although not everyone succumbed to it, some liberals such as
the patron of the arts Harry Kessler now declared themselves

conservative nationalists. The Social Democratic Party, which had opposed war and had sworn to uphold internationalism over national interests, voted for credits to fund the mobilization. None of these tumultuous events merited a mention in Gerhard Scholem's diary for a simple reason: he and his mother were high in the Swiss Alps from mid-July to mid-August. The family doctor had prescribed solitude, an intimation of a nervous disorder that would play an increasingly prominent role in the next few years (the previous year, 1913, had also involved a four-week "cure"). In mid-August, the young Scholem wrote a rambling, feverish entry in his diary that cryptically mentions a *Kriegslärm* (war ruckus) but is otherwise silent on the guns of August. Instead, he ruminated on the mystical allure of the high mountains and glaciers and offered scathing observations on the tourists whose Bible was the red Baedeker guidebook. Against these laughable bourgeois, he proposed an alternative: Shabbatai Zvi, the seventeenth-century Messiah, who spoke out loud the four-letter name of God and yet was not struck down by lightning. This act of religious heresy associated with messianism seems to have grabbed Scholem's attention, almost certainly from his reading of Graetz's history, in which the nineteenth-century historian tells the story. Did he identify with Shabbatai as a messianic figure? The diary entry is not definitive, but in light of his messianic outburst of the following year, we cannot discount the possibility. Either way, this was the first and earliest reference to a figure who would play an outsized role in Scholem's personal and professional future.

Upon his return to Berlin, he found the city in the thrall of war fever. But not everyone. Gustav Landauer opposed the war, as did Werner Scholem, who associated himself with the radical faction of the Social Democrats that rejected it, a faction that included Karl Liebknecht and Rosa Luxemburg, who were murdered in January 1919. Werner took his younger brother to clandestine meetings of war resisters and was probably instrumental in influencing Gerhard to embrace radical opposition. Gerhard was soon to fashion his own objections to the war in Zionist terms.

On February 5, 1915, the *Jüdische Rundschau*, the main organ of the German Zionists, published an article by Heinrich Margulies, a Zionist writer and later director of Israel's Bank Leumi, in which he passionately proclaimed that the Zionists should support the German war effort not just as Jews but even more as Zionists. Echoing Martin Buber's language, Margulies argued that the war provided "the secret of community." Margulies was later to break with Buber and, like Scholem, would immigrate to Palestine in the 1920s. But although Margulies would eventually prove himself a "real" Zionist, Scholem led the charge against his article by writing a response and soliciting fifteen of his friends, including his brother Werner, to sign the statement. This letter to the editor denounced Margulies and rejected on Zionist grounds any loyalty to Germany or any of the other combatant states. For the sixteen signatories, mostly drawn from the ranks of Jung Juda, Zionism meant rejection of the war (it is unlikely, however, that Werner signed his brother's letter on Zionist grounds). The letter was shown to Arthur Hantke, the president of the Zionistische Vereingung für Deutschland (German Zionist Federation), who, although sympathetic to its sentiments, feared that its publication might lead to the banning of the federation. In a meeting with Gerhard and two of the other signers, Hantke seems to have persuaded the young Zionists to withdraw the letter, and it was never published (we know its content because Scholem transcribed it into his diary).

But the unpublished letter had dramatic consequences for its author. He took it to the gymnasium to solicit the signature of his friend Edgar Blum. Another student filched it from his briefcase and showed it to the school authorities, who, after a monthlong investigation, decided to suspend Scholem for his antiwar activities. This action, rather than outright expulsion, allowed him to take the *Abitur* examinations without graduating. And so, only a few months after his seventeenth birthday he found himself free of school, and since he had rarely exerted himself there in any case he seems to have experienced few regrets (his father, however, was anything but amused). Taking advantage of an arcane Prussian law meant for intellectually unsuccessful aristocrats, he was able to enroll in the University of Berlin without a high school diploma. So began his academic career, with courses in philosophy and mathematics.

Blocked from inveighing against the war in the *Jüdische Rundschau,* Gerhard and his Jung Juda comrade Erich Brauer decided to publish their own underground newsletter, which they named *Die blauweisse Brille* (Blue-White Spectacles). The name suggested both a Zionist (blue and white) perspective on the war and also a dig at the Blau-Weiss youth movement. Scholem had gone on a number of hikes with the Blau-Weiss, but rejected their purported Zionism as a sham. This hostility toward the mainstream Zionist youth movement would later influence much of his political activity within German Zionism.

Die blauweisse Brille came out three times in the summer and fall of 1915. The two youths contrived to print their newspaper as a lithograph in Arthur Scholem's shop without his knowledge (it seems that one of the workers must have eventually revealed to Arthur what was transpiring under his nose, because in the spring of 1916 further publication became impossible). Scholem wrote much of the copy, while Brauer, who would become an ethnographer in Mandatory Palestine, contributed the graphics. In the first issue, Gerhard denounced the Jewish youth movement (the Blau-Weiss) as "Jewish movement without youth, Jewish youth without movement, youth movement without Judaism." He also penned a rather puerile antiwar poem with the refrain "It was the war!" (*Es war der Krieg!*), whose first two stanzas proclaimed:

Out of the Infinite
In front of you a star rises
Far beyond space and time
You believe that it carries you
You gave yourself to it solemnly,
It was the war!

But it did not lead
As you believe in seeing
Its sparks rising
To the light of the primordial world
It was only a chimera
Which passed through the world
It was the war![2]

The poem goes on to suggest that the war is a game launched by God but devoid of discernable meaning, certainly not the mystical meaning that others have assigned to it.

In the second issue, Scholem made his Zionist criticism of the war even more explicit: "Does the way to Zion lie through the capitals of Europe? We want to draw the line between Europe and Judah: my thought is not your thought, my way is not your way." True Zionists had to reject the war. The nationalist fervor that gripped Europe in those years had nothing to do with Zionism, which Scholem wanted to keep free of militarism and blind patriotism.

In June 1915, shortly before publishing the first number of *Die blauweisse Brille*, Scholem made the acquaintance of Walter Benjamin, a student of philosophy and literature five years his senior. This was to be one of the most decisive relationships of his life. He had first encountered Benjamin in the fall of 1913 at a meeting of youth movement activists and was struck more by his peculiar and intense way of speaking—Benjamin stared at the ceiling while speaking as if from a script—than by what he later admitted was Benjamin's tortuous argument. A year and a half later, they ran into each other again at a discussion group and at the university library. They began to visit each other and to converse deeply about books—they were both compulsive bibliophiles—and about ideas. Like Scholem, Benjamin had broad intellectual interests that spanned European philosophy and literature. And like his new friend, he had a particular penchant for the esoteric, for subterranean ideas that went against the mainstream.

The friendship with Benjamin is especially significant for understanding Scholem's later reputation not just as a scholar of Judaism but as a twentieth-century thinker with a global reach. Even as he immersed himself in Jewish sources—the Bible, the Talmud, and medieval Jewish thought—he read widely in many fields. The interplay between his Jewish and non-Jewish interests, between the "particular" and the "universal," explains how a scholar of arcane Jewish mystical texts could break out of his seemingly narrow field to speak to a much broader audience. And in many ways, Walter Benjamin was the first member of that audience.

Benjamin had been active in the youth movement of the educator Gustav Wyneken but not in the Zionist youth movement, toward which he maintained an ambivalent attitude. In fact, one of the mysteries of the Scholem-Benjamin friendship, immortalized in Scholem's memoir *Walter Benjamin: The Story of a Friendship,* is that Scholem, who was passionately, even dogmatically committed to Zionism, would adopt a non-Zionist like Benjamin as his closest friend. Benjamin repeatedly professed interest in Zionism but was never able or willing to fully embrace it. Certainly, there were deep intellectual affinities between the two men, but as would become evident, their affective affinity went equally deep. Nonetheless, their differences over Zionism and Benjamin's rather manipulative personality both raise questions, which probably cannot be answered, about the real foundation of their friendship.

Benjamin was inalterably opposed to the war, and, with

Scholem present one day in the fall of 1915, consumed large quantities of coffee before his army medical examination to induce an attack of nerves. The trick worked, and Benjamin won a deferment, as would Scholem two years later. So the two also shared a radical antiwar politics, and it was only in later years, after Scholem immigrated to Palestine and Benjamin became a kind of Marxist, that their political paths parted.

Benjamin also expressed vehement criticism of Martin Buber, against both his philosophy of mystical experience and his support for the war. It seems that Benjamin was crucial in turning Scholem from a Buberian Hasid to a *misnogged* (the term used historically to define opponents of Hasidism). Benjamin argued that Buber represented "female thinking," whatever that meant, probably in reaction to Buber's mysticism of experience. Benjamin opposed Buber's *Erlebnis* (a mystical "lived" experience) with a less mystical form of experience, for which he employed the German word *Erfahrung*. Scholem would adopt his friend's version. In July 1916, Benjamin also wrote a letter to Buber declining an invitation to contribute to Buber's new journal *Der Jude*. The letter is quite opaque, but one thing is clear: Benjamin's objection to Buber was not primarily political—that is, Buber's support for the war—but rather centered around a philosophy of language. It was to be on both political and philosophical grounds that Scholem, too, would come to reject Buber.

As early as December 1914, Buber had delivered a Hanukkah address in which he hailed the war as generating an experience of mystical community. Scholem had evidently not been aware of Buber's stance when he enthusiastically lectured the Jung Juda group in January 1915 on Buber's Zionist philosophy. But after the row over the Margulies article and Scholem's suspension from school, he discovered that Margulies was an associate of Buber's. His relationship to his spiritual idol now entered into a state of crisis.

The same day as the messianic diary entry from May 1915, Scholem penned the following poem:

> Martin Buber, who found the expression
> For the deepest longing of the millions
> Of our brothers, who live in darkness
> *Our* Buber has turned away.
> On the loud paths of history
> You have betrayed those who crowned you;
> In the cries of war and heroic deeds
> You have suddenly seen other visions.
> The prophet of Old-New Land lends his word to the war
> Bows to the land which we have left,
> Goes with those, whom Jung-Juda hates
> One way to "Victory."[3]

In light of this poem, it now becomes clear that Scholem's proclamation of himself as Messiah was wrapped up in the crisis of his relationship to Buber. The older man had become John the Baptist to his Jesus of Nazareth, a necessary forerunner but not one capable of fulfilling his eschatological role. Yet, as we shall see, Scholem's view of Buber was never so simple as mere rejection and replacement.

In the first issue of *Die blauweisse Brille* from the summer of 1915, Scholem and Erich Brauer published a caricature of Buber by Brauer along with a parody of his writing. A copy made its way into Buber's hands, and he reacted, surprisingly, by inviting the two young Zionists to visit him at his home in the Zehlendorf neighborhood of Berlin. Scholem describes this meeting in his memoirs (he mistakenly dates it to March 1916). In his account, Buber was exceedingly gracious, and "listened seriously to my speeches without indicating that he had changed his opinion—while Brauer, who was a very shy man, kept silent."[4]

It is likely that Scholem's later account of this meeting turned it into an altogether more polite conversation than it actually was. Given what we have already learned about the young Scholem, he was brash to the point of rudeness, talking incessantly and brooking no disagreement. Raphael Buber, Martin's son, described one meeting between the two from a later date. He saw a gangly young man storm into his father's study and shout at the top of his lungs. When the unruly visitor stormed out, the father had to restrain the son from assaulting his guest. "That man," said Buber, "is named Gershom Scholem and he is destined to become a great scholar."[5]

But Buber didn't take this volcanic act lying down either. In 1916, Scholem submitted an article on the Jewish youth movements for publication in Buber's *Der Jude*. When the two met in December, Buber criticized it severely as utterly negative and lacking in positive proposals. Scholem was clearly taken aback and wrote petulantly in his diary that Buber had refused to engage in a real dialogue with him. He accused Buber of being able to speak only "out of his system," as if Buber were the more dogmatic of the two.[6]

In the spring of 1916, Buber published an essay in the first issue of *Der Jude* titled "Die Losung" (The Password), which stated in even bolder terms the connection between his mysticism of experience and the war. Yet as vehemently as Scholem railed against both Buber's philosophy and his politics, he nevertheless saw Buber as a potentially sympathetic addressee or, perhaps, an adversary worth convincing. In a July 1916 meeting in Heppenheim (where Buber had moved earlier in the year), he told Buber about the letter he had organized against Heinrich Margulies's pro-war article and how it had gotten him suspended from school. Since Margulies's article was shot through with Buberian expressions, it is hard to fathom just what Scholem intended by highlighting for Buber his opposition to it. In subsequent years, he met frequently with Buber and also carried on a lengthy correspondence with him; once he began to study Kabbalah, he shared the fruits of his research with Buber. It might not be an exaggeration to say that the intellectual support he could never win from his father, he sought from Buber. But his desire for approval from the older man simultaneously provoked stormy rebellion.

In the summer of 1916, Scholem wrote at times feverishly in his diary about Buber. These entries demonstrate Buber's absolute centrality for the young Scholem trying to chart his own course toward both Judaism and Zionism. At the beginning of August 1916, he wrote in one of his most outlandish statements: "Astronomy is the teaching of the inner laws of Zionism. The *Three Addresses on Judaism* is not as Jewish as the *Theoria motus corporum coelestium* [Theory of the Motion of Celestial Bodies] of Gauss, the builder of Zion. Buber is a mystic, the greatest of all mystics, but . . . the Messiah will be an astronomer."[7] A few weeks later, he wrote that Buber lacked mathematics and, consequently, he was not the prophet of the Messiah! Since Scholem himself was at that time studying mathematics, including mathematical astronomy, it would appear that he was once again entertaining thoughts of himself as the savior of the Jews. By improbably turning the mathematician Carl Friedrich Gauss into a Zionist, he was evidently expressing the wish that his own academic studies might have redemptive meaning.

For Scholem, Buber was a teacher who "taught the truth, but taught it falsely." In the fall of 1916, he wrote to his friend Edgar Blum that he had thought much about Buber over the previous summer and resolved "that I must be and am fundamentally opposed to him." Buber's movement was a sham because its ideology was founded in Erlebnis. Ahad Ha'am—the prophet of cultural Zionism—was truly Jewish and thus the only one who "stands in Zion." Buber, on the other hand, was spiritually in Heppenheim. His "dangerous and pernicious" way led not to Zion but to Prague (that is, to the Buberian circle in Prague).[8]

We are now, of course, far from the controversies over the

Great War. But because for Scholem, as for some other young Jews, Buber's mysticism had become the chief philosophical underpinning for the war, to reject the latter meant to reject the former. For Scholem, authentic Judaism could only be realized in Zion, and Zion could only be redeemed by authentic Judaism. Buber betrayed both by his teaching of a mysticism of experience and by his support for the war. His call to realize this Erlebnis in the present moment, rather than the utopian future, turned his mysticism into "the wasteland of the Ghetto."[9] Scholem rejected Buber's Zionism just as he rejected the Zionism of the Blau-Weiss youth movement, which took much of its inspiration from Buber: both could realize their aspirations in *Galut* (exile or diaspora) outside of history rather than within it in Zion. His later argument that Buber's approach to Judaism was ahistorical had its roots in this rejection of Buber's mysticism of experience. And already in these early ruminations, he had adopted the nonmystical experience of "tradition." Tradition is what develops within history, while mystical experience must remain mired in the present moment.

Scholem's attack on Buber took public form in a debate that ensued in Siegfried Lehmann's Volksheim, a club for young Jews from eastern Europe. Scholem attended a speech by Lehmann in September 1916 and engaged in a fiery argument with the speaker. He made Lehmann a proxy for Buber. Lehmann's talk, he said, was delivered in "Buberdeutsch." Buber's interpretation of Hasidism, as conveyed by Lehmann, was a form of "aesthetic ecstasis," whose goal was to make Hasidism acceptable to bourgeois Jews. Lehmann's version of Hasidism was devoid of actual Hasidic sources, privileging beauty over truth. In light of Scholem's frontal assault on Lehmann, it is ironic that this ostensibly Buberian aesthete immigrated to Palestine in 1927 and founded the Ben Shemen Youth Village there, thus contributing greatly to the practical Zionism that Scholem purported to advocate against him.[10]

In these thoughts, delivered orally at the Volksheim, written down in his diary and in a long letter to Lehmann, the eighteen-year-old Scholem sketched out *in nuce* the main lines of attack that he would adopt against Buber in two landmark essays in the 1960s and that would inform his own very different approach to the study of Judaism. According to the young Scholem, Buber believed that Hasidism represented "subterranean" Judaism because he hated the Judaism that was "aboveground," that is, the rabbinic tradition. Buber sought to detach Hasidism from this rabbinic scaffolding and celebrate it as a movement of revolution *against* Judaism. For Scholem, both the subterranean and the "terrestrial" dimensions of Judaism were necessary. Deeply engaged for several years in the study of Talmud, he was groping toward an inclusive definition of Judaism in which myth and law, the irrational and the rational were all equal parts of the complex dialectic of tradition. As opposed to the Buberians, Scholem advocated studying Hebrew and *all* the textual sources of Judaism.

Scholem's intemperate performance in the Volksheim had an unexpected consequence: Franz Kafka's fiancée, Felice Bauer, was present and reported on Scholem's arguments to Kafka. Kafka wrote back endorsing Scholem's position in his characteristically paradoxical way: he agreed with Herr Scholem because Scholem was one of those who demanded too much and therefore accomplished nothing. When, fifty years later, the correspondence between Kafka and Bauer was published, Scholem was both astonished and pleased. In fact, shortly after the contretemps with Lehmann, Scholem read Kafka's parable "Before the Law," first published in a Jewish newspaper in 1915 and later included in Kafka's posthumous novel *The Trial.* The parable, in which a man in search of the law never gets beyond the first door, made an enormous impression on him and pointed to the possibility of a kind of secular mysticism.

The war, which was always close to the surface of these

intellectual debates, was anything but an abstraction. By the spring of 1915, all three of Gerhard's brothers were in uniform. When they returned home for Passover, Gerhard apparently made some sarcastic, antinationalist statements in response to his parents' pride in their older sons' service. Arthur responded by canceling the Passover Seder and declaring, in response to Gerhard's opposition to the war on Jewish grounds, that after the war he would resign from the Jewish community. But the war took a more direct toll on Gerhard. When one of Werner's closest friends died in combat, he wrote despairingly in his diary, "Send the old men to the war, so that they beat each other to death, but do not rob us of young blood."[11] In March 1916, Werner himself was wounded in the foot in an offensive on the Russian front. And two of Gerhard's closest friends from school and Jung Juda, Harry Heymann and Edgar Blum, both fell in action.

With universal conscription the order of the day, Gerhard could not hope to avoid his own encounter with the German military machine. In his memoir, he depicts the process as a relatively rapid one: he was called up to the draft board, feigned psychosis during a few weeks in a medical hospital, and was discharged. Oddly, he says there that he does not wish to speak further about the incident, perhaps hinting that there might be more to say.

In fact, the process lasted more than a year and a half and involved two spells of actual service in uniform and an extended stay in a military hospital. In the autumn of 1915, with his eighteenth birthday looming in December, he decided to do something for which he had criticized Werner at the beginning of the year: enlist rather than wait to be drafted, in order to avoid being posted to the infantry, with its horrendous casualty rate. In late November, his father, exuding patriotic pride, accompanied him to the train to Lower Saxony, where Gerhard began basic training. He does not appear to have suffered unduly and even found a comrade from Berlin with whom he could exchange jokes. But he was put on leave after exhibiting signs of "neurasthenia" (the fin-de-siècle name for what we today call "stress") and claiming to have fainted during long marches. In December, he was examined again, and, after reporting that he had been sent for cures for neurasthenia three times previously, he was given a medical deferment.

Did he fabricate these symptoms, as he later claimed? His uncle Georg, the family doctor, evidently thought that the diagnosis of neurasthenia was accurate because in the spring of 1916 he confirmed that his nephew was suffering from a bad case of nerves (we recall that Georg had sent him for rest cures several times). Significantly, he attributed Gerhard's malady to excessive reading—not the rigors of military training—and prescribed, as Gerhard wrote to Harry Heymann, quoting the doctor, that "you shouldn't touch a book for six months, moreover you shouldn't do anything other than eat, sleep, and go for walks, blow off a semester at the university, and go on a journey for the summer from the end of May for four months."[12] For once, Arthur Scholem was solicitous of his youngest son and agreed to support a long, bucolic rest in the mountain village of Oberstdorf im Allgäu from June 20 to the end of July. Arthur must have taken his physician brother's diagnosis seriously.

Some of the letters that Gerhard wrote during this long vacation suggest that he was hardly at rest. He boasted to Erich Brauer that he had fifteen to twenty regular correspondents (at the end of his life, he left tens of thousands of letters for his archive) and complained when Brauer was too cheap to send him more than a postcard. He also corresponded with Martin Buber and sent Buber his long, critical essay on the Jewish youth movement, which he had been working on for a year and a half. On the same subject, he wrote scathingly to Brauer about the Berlin-Lichtenberg Zionist youth group, which was insufficiently Zionist for his taste. Of their leader, Albert Baer, he says,

"His memory should be for a blessing, his name will be wiped out [then in Hebrew: *yemach shemo*]. That's what I have to say about the Jewish youth movement. I've lent them Buber. Na!" And then, maniacally, "We must open up our mouths! Don't sleep! [double underlined]. I hope and believe that you will find comrades for the struggle and for the ideology. Upwards! For fourteen days I've been in a true ecstasy for our cause."[13] If one symptom of his illness was hyperactivity and grandiosity, Oberstdorf does not seem to have cured it.

Upon his return to Berlin in the fall, Scholem again enrolled in courses at the university in mathematics and philosophy, but it was becoming clear to him that despite his mathematical talents, others were much more gifted. By now he was trying his hand at translations from biblical Hebrew, including the Song of Songs and the book of Lamentations.

On October 26, he wrote to Blum describing these activities, including "browsing obscure Kabbalistic texts." He noted how little had been written about interpretation, tradition, and the question of language in Judaism, all themes that would loom large for him in later years. He was now studying the philosophy of mathematics rather than mathematics itself and had come to the cryptic conclusion, echoing his earlier statement on Gauss as a Zionist, that "for me, Zion and mathematics are identical things and astronomy is the inner law of Zionism."[14]

As to Blum's detailed account of battles on the Russian front, which had filled his friend's letter from the previous month, he responded—insensitively, given the challenges Blum faced in the trenches—that "the problem of the war no longer exists for us who are Zionists in the most serious sense." But the letter to Blum was returned to sender: more than two weeks earlier, Blum had been wounded in the pelvis and on November 1 he died of his wounds. Scholem noted these facts in his diary and confessed that he was unable to offer any words of consolation to Blum's mother since the death of his best friend was the frightful work of the devil brought to perfection. He then went on to meditate darkly about the absence of divine grace and justice in the world.[15]

In January 1917, Werner, who was in Halle recuperating from his wound, took part in an antiwar demonstration on the Kaiser's birthday. He was arrested and charged with treason, although the charge was reduced to the still serious one of insulting the Kaiser (lèse majesté). Gerhard immediately realized that he too could become a target of the police since he possessed incriminating letters from Werner. He quickly gathered up his papers and deposited them at the house of his Jung Juda friend Harry Heller.

However, punishment for his antiwar views would come not at the hand of the law but at the hand of his father. Gerhard seems to have ventured a defense of Werner at the family dining table, which caused a stormy confrontation. On February 15, although he was living at home, Arthur sent him a letter ordering him to leave the house as of March 1 and giving him one hundred marks, after which he would be totally cut off (Arthur had also cut off Werner). In this letter and a follow-up missive in May, Arthur recommended that Gerhard volunteer for civilian service with the War Office so that "this will teach you what gainfully earned bread tastes like and real work will do your arrogance a world of good. What you call work is only a game."[16] The problem that Arthur had with his two youngest sons was not just their lack of patriotism, which was bad enough, but their frivolous forgoing of gainful employment for political and intellectual pursuits. In Gerhard's case, as he pointed out in a letter a few months later to his Aunt Käte, who sent him some money, the main issue was his Zionist activities. In this correspondence, Arthur gave voice to what was often the complaint of Jewish businessmen toward their sons who turned away from commerce for loftier pursuits. Arthur's anxieties over the vagaries of making a living were not abstract: in August 1916 his shop went bankrupt. So he may well have projected his own economic fears onto his profligate sons.

Before the March 1 deadline Gerhard found lodging in a pension run by a Frau Struck, which housed a group of Jews from eastern Europe (Ostjuden), among them the future president of Israel, Zalman Rubashov (later Shazar), whom Scholem had met earlier. Rubashov, who had made a study of aspects of the Sabbatian movement, evidently played a major role in directing Scholem's interest to this historical episode, although his own study of the subject would begin a decade later. In his memoirs, Scholem waxes nostalgic over the Pension Struck and the cult of the Ostjuden which he found there. The reality, though, as revealed in his diary, was less rosy. He complains of the noise, his fellow boarders and, above all, his landlady.

It was also in this period that Scholem became friends with the Hebrew writer S. Y. Agnon (who would win the Nobel Prize in Literature in 1966). He watched Agnon in the reading room of the Jewish community thumbing through the card catalogue. When he asked what he was looking for, Agnon replied with mock naïveté: "For books I haven't read."[17] This would be the start of a long friendship, sometimes marked by competition and even hostility. Scholem was clearly intrigued by Agnon's deep roots in the Jewish tradition but also by his skeptical and ironic relationship to it. Scholem translated one of Agnon's early stories into German and would later write several articles that are still considered classics in the explication of Agnon's writing. Agnon responded tongue in cheek with several fictional characters based loosely on Scholem himself.

Although the Pension Struck was less than an ideal domicile, Scholem had other worries. In March 1917, the army again declared him fit for battle and in May gave him his marching orders. On June 18, Rubashov accompanied him to the barracks in Berlin, and he was then dispatched for duty in a reserve infantry battalion in Allenstein, in East Prussia. Of his military activities, he reports very little, although a photograph from the period shows him in uniform with his unit. The soldiers were evidently forbidden to fraternize with the local population, visit the town or even pick blueberries in the woods: "So we run around the woods like idiotic sheep, making dirty jokes and contenting ourselves in this manner."[18] The one soldier in his barracks who refused to indulge in vulgar jokes and curse words was Gustav Steinschneider, a grandson of Moritz Steinschneider, one of the founders of the nineteenth-century "Science of Judaism," against which Scholem would later write a number of fierce polemics. This was the beginning of his friendship with Gustav. Other members of the Steinschneider family would be important to Scholem later in life.

Within a few weeks of his arrival in Allenstein, Scholem developed disturbing symptoms: fainting spells and severe anxiety (in several letters, he blamed a shaking hand for his bad handwriting). He was relieved from training and put in charge of delivering the mail and inspecting the soldiers after they used the latrine to make sure they disinfected themselves. His fellow soldiers began to make fun of him for his illness and made anti-Semitic remarks behind his back. But they evidently developed a healthy fear of him, since one of the symptoms of his illness seems to have been violent outbursts in which he threatened to harm whoever got in his way. Here was a physical manifestation of the verbal aggression for which he had already developed a fearsome reputation among the young German Zionists.

During this period, he carried on an intensive correspondence with his Jung Juda comrades Heller and Brauer, and with his new friend Werner Kraft, who would become a noted literary critic and join Scholem in Jerusalem after the Nazis came to power. Gerhard now signed his name regularly "Gerschom Schalom" in either Latin or Hebrew characters. He seems to have adopted the biblical "Gershom" at least half a year earlier, perhaps to signify how alien he felt in Germany (the name *ger sham* literally means "an alien there").

On July 25, he was hospitalized in the psychiatric ward of the military hospital and put under observation by the doctors, all of whom, he wrote, were Jewish. He exclaimed in a letter: "The devil can kiss my ass if I am shipped back to the infantry from here." He was supposed to remain there for six weeks, but on August 11 he reported to Kraft that he would soon be released: "I consider my release as a victory of my psychological efforts, which have cost me enough." A few days later, he wrote to Heller in Hebrew, so as to evade the censor, and announced that he had fooled the doctors by faking his illness.[19]

Once again, we are confronted with the question of whether Scholem, like Thomas Mann's famous "confidence man" Felix Krull, really put one over on the Allenstein psychiatrists. If so, he was playing a dangerous game. Had they judged him to be faking, he could have stood trial for dereliction of duty and drawn a long prison sentence. The German military did recognize conscientious objection by pacifists, but many military doctors considered it a kind of mental illness. Such objectors could find themselves hospitalized long-term, which might have become Scholem's fate as well, even though he did not claim to be a conscientious objector. In Scholem's case, the chief psychiatrist diagnosed a disturbance in his relationship with his parents, especially his father, as the cause of his "illness," which manifested itself in a "visionary state." He gave Scholem a diagnosis of *dementia praecox*, the nineteenth-century term for what we today call adolescent schizophrenia, met with Arthur Scholem, and persuaded him that he needed to take his son back in order to address the disease. Arthur seems to have been sufficiently shaken to agree to reconcile with Gerhard.[20]

The diagnosis of schizophrenia seems puzzling since Scholem exhibited few of the features that we associate with that disease. However, it happens that we know who the chief psy-

chiatrist at Allenstein was: Karl Abraham, one of Freud's foremost disciples and the one with whom Freud confessed to a "racial" kinship. Although in Abraham's writings about dementia
praecox he typically placed more emphasis on a disturbed relationship with the mother, he might have seen Scholem's case as
a variant type. He also saw an overlap in causation between dementia praecox and hysteria, the latter corresponding much
better to Gerhard's fainting spells and shaking hands. However,
the "visionary state" (perhaps his messianic hallucinations?) that
Scholem described to Abraham might suggest the paranormal
voices of schizophrenia. It seems unlikely that Scholem knew
who the chief psychiatrist was, apart from his Jewish origins, so
he was extraordinarily lucky to have landed in the care of a
Freudian and to have exhibited symptoms that might be attributed to family dysfunction. By avoiding charges of malinger-
ing, on one hand, and hospitalization, on the other, he seems to
have threaded the needle in winning a discharge. He was hardly
the only person to do so, however: we recall that Walter Benjamin overdosed on caffeine as a way of getting out of the draft
and others in Scholem's circle also sought medical deferments.

Since the military medical records from Allenstein have
disappeared (possibly destroyed when the Red Army overran
East Prussia in January 1945), we cannot examine Abraham's
thinking about his case. It is hard to imagine that a psychiatrist
of his experience could be totally fooled. We have already seen
ample evidence of a nervous disorder of some kind including
violent mood swings. Perhaps Scholem was simply exaggerat-
ing symptoms that were already present. Or perhaps Abraham
recognized how extraordinary his patient was and, whether out
of Jewish sympathies or not, went out of his way to arrange for
his discharge.

While he was in the hospital, Scholem's Buber obsession
continued. By 1917, Buber had retreated from his support for
the war and was also beginning to abandon his mysticism of ex-

perience for the dialogic philosophy he would make famous in *I and Thou* (1923). But one wouldn't know it from reading Scholem's diaries and letters. His vitriol continued to mount. From his hospital bed, he wrote to Werner Kraft about Kraft's declaration that he "hated" Buber. Scholem replied that he shared Kraft's "hatred," calling Buber "demonic" and "anti-Jewish." But he took Kraft to task for rejecting Judaism because he could not stand Buber. Buber did not represent Judaism, despite the pedestal on which many of their generation placed him. Scholem claimed that his own immersion in Jewish texts had demonstrated to him how little Buber stood within the tradition. In other words, Buber endangered Jewish renewal because many young acculturated German Jews took him as the embodiment of authentic Judaism. Once they came to reject him, they ended up rejecting Judaism *tout court*. Scholem made it clear without saying so that if Kraft was looking for an embodiment of Judaism, it could be found in Scholem himself![21]

In the fall of 1917, now discharged from the military, he wrote, "In the last period—it is already quite a long time—I have been in continual unconditional enmity against Buber. I have a hundred difficult objective and personal objections to him." Buber was not a mystic but a mystical author: "Buber is a false teacher, he teaches the truth, but he teaches it falsely." By November, his earlier plan from 1915 to write a biography of Buber had metamorphosed into its opposite, a plan to write a refutation of Buber's whole corpus: "One must write a thorough critique of all of Buber's books: from Rabbi Nahman to the most recent scandal [referring to Buber's recently published *Ereignisse und Begegnungen*]. The whole lot of it. In his books, the abyss, which has swallowed Buber up, finds expression or opens up."[22] Scholem's complex relationship with Buber, marked equally by admiration and aversion, had started over the question of the war. But if his 1915 poem proclaimed, "It was the war!," little could he imagine then that this political battle would mushroom into a philosophical rivalry that would shape his emerging sense of himself as a Jew and as a student of Judaism.

At the same time that Scholem struggled with Buber—or, more accurately, his image of Buber—he continued his related struggle against the German Zionist youth movement. His first public volley beyond the hardly public *Blauweisse Brille* appeared in the first issue of Buber's *Der Jude* in 1916 while the second appeared the following year in the Blau-Weiss's own newsletter. Scholem was thus hardly afraid to attack his enemies on their own turf. The gist of his critique was that no Zionist youth movement was possible without knowledge of Hebrew and immersion in Jewish sources. Members of the Blau-Weiss took his criticism seriously, and it provoked a broad public debate. His opponents accused Scholem, with some justification, of an elitist and utopian attitude. Certainly, few were intellectually equipped to follow his lonely path. But there were those who recognized that his attack on the assimilationist tendencies in the Blau-Weiss was not off the mark. Some of his erstwhile targets, like Heinrich Margulies, ended up adopting his position.

Scholem's close brush with the First World War came to an end in August 1917, although his final discharge did not come until January 1918, with permission to leave the country granted in the spring. In the meantime, with a mutual decision that he should not return to his father's house, he took up university studies in Jena. But the emotional rollercoaster which had characterized his encounter with the military now came to dominate his romantic and intellectual life.

A sign of that turmoil was a decision that he took at the end of November 1917 to translate a series of Hebrew laments into German, starting with the biblical book of Lamentations and sections of Job. These translations remained in manuscript, but in 1919 translations of several medieval laments appeared in *Der Jude*. In essays that Scholem wrote in his diary, we learn that he considered Hebrew laments to convey the essence of the Hebrew language, which was wrapped up in silence (there are striking echoes of Walter Benjamin's 1916 essay on human and divine language). To translate these quintessential Hebrew texts into German was, for Scholem, a "farewell present" of a Zionist to the German language of his youth. But lamentations drew him in particular, in part because of the epochal destruction of the war, and in part as reflections of his own emotional state: the melancholy of a young man ready to say "good-bye to all that."

3

Scholem in Love

In October 1917, shortly after his brush with the military, Scholem transcribed a letter into his diary in which he reported that only when he had established his true way could he "have the greatest experience of my life: to come into absolute, splendid relationship with one man, who has influenced my life not by his teaching, but by his being, by the awe in which I hold him to this day. This man was not a Zionist and came perhaps first through me to Judaism." But the "deepest, the absolute Judaism spoke in him, without his having a sense of it."[1] There is little doubt that this man was Walter Benjamin.

In the more than two years since they had become friends, Scholem's relationship with Benjamin had developed beyond an intellectual companionship into something much more intense. Where Scholem would have stormed against anyone who did not profess Zionism or Judaism, in the case of Benjamin, the "deepest, the absolute Judaism spoke in him," and it was this insight that led Scholem to believe that he could convert him to Zionism. When Benjamin later became an idiosyncratic Marxist, Scholem would insist that the true Benjamin was Jewish, even though Benjamin's invocation of Jewish sources was episodic and largely superficial (as Scholem himself noted, much of what Benjamin knew about Judaism he got from Scholem).

A few months later, in a diary entry written on his twentieth birthday, Scholem relates that, sitting in his room alone, clearly pensive if not depressed, he received a brief letter from Benjamin: "Today midday, as I was just sitting and always thinking about Walter and yearning for him and wondering why he doesn't write, then a short express letter arrived from him." This letter, he says, made him happier than anything in his life. Benjamin had written in appreciation of his response to an essay of Benjamin's on Dostoyevsky's *The Idiot*. Despite what might seem the purely intellectual nature of this missive, Benjamin made clear that he had severed his ties with most people, but not Scholem, with whom he was now in the deepest affinity. Scholem wrote in his diary, "Walter, dear Walter, I thank you out of my deepest soul, so deep that I will never be able to express this thanks."[2] A half-year later, he returned to Benjamin's letter and called its ten lines "the only perfect letter I have received in my life."[3] And sixty years after that, he included the full text of Benjamin's letter in *From Berlin to Jerusalem*, although he removed the reference to the gushing emotions of his response, emotions which nevertheless clearly continued to affect him for the rest of his life.

It is hard to avoid the possibility that Scholem and Benjamin's friendship had a homoerotic component. This speculation finds some support in a strange incident that Scholem relates in *Walter Benjamin: The Story of a Friendship*. In September 1921, he and Benjamin journeyed to a remote village in the Rhön Mountains and spent two days in a house belonging to their friend Ernst Lewy. He describes the almost Gothic atmosphere there: "There was something uncanny about his [Lewy's] wife . . . she had the attracting power of a swamp, the magic of an orchid, and the sucking and frightening quality of a clinging vine. . . . Mrs. Lewy dominated her husband in a strangely quiet way. The atmosphere was an enchanting one and affected all of us."[4]

Benjamin and Scholem were housed in a large room with a huge double bed. When they awoke in the morning, Benjamin said to Scholem, "When I opened my eyes just now, if you had been a girl lying there, I would have thought that I was the bishop of Bamberg" (the previous owner of the house). Scholem makes no comment on this strange remark but immediately goes on to discuss Benjamin's proposal for a journal to be named *Angelus*.[5]

It is hard to know what to make of this odd incident, and we should refrain from considering it explicitly sexual. But there is something in the awkward way Scholem felt compelled to tell the story that suggests his own unease, which was not great enough to cause him to suppress the story but still sufficient for him to refuse his readers any commentary. In later years, Scholem came to reflect on the emotional nature of his relationship with Benjamin and Benjamin's then-wife, Dora: "Was it (as it sometimes seems to me in retrospect) that three young passionate, gifted people who were almost completely dependent on one another and were seeking the road to maturity had to use one another as release mechanisms in the private sphere? Were there in this 'triangle,' of which we were unaware, unconscious emotional inclinations and defenses that had to be discharged but which we were not able to recognize in our 'naiveté,' that is, owing to our lack of psychological experience? I could not answer these questions even today." Later, he reported Dora's diagnosis of her husband that "Walter's intellectuality impeded his libido."[6] He also asked other women who knew Benjamin how they viewed him, and they all testified that he was not attractive to them as a man. One said that for her and her female friends, he did not even exist as a man. And yet Benjamin had many female lovers in his abbreviated life. His attraction to them apparently lay in his unique intellect and way of conversation. This, in fact, seems to have been true for Scholem as well, but it is peculiar that he felt moved to interview Benjamin's female friends on the question of his sexuality.

What is the relevance of such emotional questions for understanding an intellectual like Gershom Scholem? Are they merely biographical curiosities or might they shed light on the remarkable achievements as a historian of Jewish mysticism for which he is justly famous? A common perception of Scholem sees him as a scholar laboring in ivory tower solitude to uncover sources of Jewish history unknown or neglected. Nothing, however, could be farther from the truth. Two souls dwelled within his breast: the dispassionate ascetic and the passionate lover. It is said that real meaning of *Zohar* (the name of the most important book of medieval Jewish mysticism) is "Eros." If so, then Scholem's passionate engagement with the *Zohar* and the other mystical texts he would end up studying was a form of *amor dei intellectualis* (intellectual love of God), but this same passion governed his relations with people.

In addition, while we may think of him as a lone wolf, in fact Scholem's Zionism, like that of many young people of his generation and the next, was profoundly collective and often bound up with romantic infatuations as well. It was expressed in passionate debates among his comrades in Jung Juda, many of whom—those who survived the war—immigrated to Palestine. And, as one might expect among such ardent young people, ideology often led to romance and vice versa. Scholem was anything but immune from this dialectic.

As his feelings about Walter Benjamin show, the young Scholem was at times confused about relations between the sexes. In a muddled diary entry, also from October 1917, he declared that the spheres of men and women are different. The public is not the sphere of women: "I wish not to see them there. I am not a feminist (*Frauenrechtler*)."[7] A few weeks later, he offered the following—at times contradictory—meditation on love:

> Jewish love—and I love jewishly—is not like goyish love. Jewish love does not perform magic. Indeed, it could do this—and here lies its abyss. This is the essence of seduction. The order [*Ordnung*] of love means that two people encompass the world, if they are intended for each other. Friendship does not encompass the world. I don't believe that one can stand in relation to a girl in any other way than in the relationship of love. Man is only intended for one woman . . . although one perhaps loves more [than one]. Friendship with a woman is either an injured relationship or a swindle. How can one have a friendship with a woman when one can only know a woman through love?[8]

"Abyss" (*Abgrund*) was one of the most common words in the young Scholem's vocabulary, and though it might seem to be a negative term, at times he seemed to embrace it.

He was preoccupied with the role of women in Zionism and the renewal of Judaism. In July 1918, he wrote a series of ninety-five theses for Walter Benjamin's birthday in conscious imitation of Martin Luther's famous ninety-five theses (he never actually delivered them to Benjamin). Among them: "There is no female Torah" (no. 29); "There is no female Zionist who would not be unhappy [a response to the philosopher Hermann Cohen's sardonic statement that the Zionists were boys who just wanted to be happy]" (no. 47); and "There is a category of German Jewesses who lack nothing [to become] a Zionist than a husband" (no. 48).[9]

These statements, which often verge on misogyny, do not tell the whole story. His early writings contain contradictory sentiments. In July 1917, he wrote to his Jung Juda friend Aharon Heller from the military psychiatric ward in Allenstein, appending a postscript to weigh in on what he calls a "matter of the greatest importance" in their youth movement: "*What are the objections against women in Jung-Juda?* There are girls (Grete Brauer, for example, or others I [can] think of) who want the same as we [men] and work towards it. *Must our Bund exclude them?*"[10] The "Bund" refers here to an idea from the previous summer when a meeting of the Jung Juda took place in Obertsdorf, where Scholem was resting on the orders of his family doctor. There he conceived the idea of a *Bund der Eifer,* or "band of the zealous."

Some months later, having been released from the army, he returned to this theme in his diary, at times blatantly contradicting himself. Right before the entry in which he denies that he is a feminist, he insists that more women must be included in Jung Juda, because "we mustn't demand that we isolate ourselves and because they need our support." They should take part in the work of rebirth in their way. "Otherwise people would have to say that we leave women outside our organized movement, and that would be completely false for us."[11]

As early as two years previously, he had put this position into effect. In 1915 he exchanged a series of letters with a Julie Schächter, a member of the Jung Juda group who had leveled a rather devastating—one might even say "Scholemesque" —critique of Scholem's own role in the movement. She attacked him for a surfeit of words and paucity of action, just the kind of critique he liked to make of the Blau-Weiss: "We need healthy, pithy [*kernig*] Jews. . . . Healthy, simple men with iron will and the courage to act. Dive deeply into Jewish knowledge. This will give power and freshness, which we Jews possess, but which we have lost and [need to] win again."[12] She called on Scholem to lead the group to become *Menschenmaterial.*

Scholem obviously took her critique seriously and used the opportunity to develop his own Zionist philosophy, agreeing with Schächter that there was too much idle talk among the

Zionists. He concluded by telling her that his comrade Erich Brauer had wanted to strike her from the list of subscribers to *Die blauweiss Brille* but he had insisted on keeping her. Despite her "ill-tempered theoretical disagreement" he regarded her as a "dear comrade."[13]

Julie Schächter disappears from view, but other women both inside and outside the Zionist movement took her place. I have already noted his infatuation with Jettka Stein in 1914 and 1915. The Scholem Archive at the National Library in Jerusalem also contains letters from 1915 and 1916 from a schoolmate named Stephanie Rothstein, who developed an infatuation with Scholem and wrote to him in increasingly intimate tones. She reported her embarrassment when her mother discovered letters from him to her, letters that have not survived. Unlike Stein, Rothstein does not appear in Scholem's memoir. But other women do.

During the academic year 1917–1918, when Scholem was at Jena, he befriended a remarkable array of women. Since most of the men were in the army, women made up the overwhelming majority of students in the German universities, a majority that Scholem seemed to greatly enjoy. He taught them Hebrew and endlessly discussed philosophy and Zionism with them. Among these women were Käthe Hollander, from a baptized family who had returned to Judaism; Toni Halle, whose sister married Scholem's friend Werner Kraft and who later went on to direct a progressive high school in Tel Aviv; and Valeria Grunwald, a medical student of Hungarian origins.

In his diary, Scholem fumes against another female student, Grete Kramer, who refused to continue Hebrew lessons with him on the grounds that he frightened her. His reaction more or less confirms her opinion: "And I am an idiot! Why did I get involved with this girl, even though she was the cheeriest. . . . She doesn't want—this reptile—to learn Hebrew, because she would have to do it with me and because she is afraid of me, so she says." He calls her a "lame idiot" and "dimwitted," but as if to show that he has no hard feelings, he notes five days later that he went to her house for Shabbat dinner.[14]

Perhaps the most striking of these women was Grete Lissauer, whom Scholem met in 1916 at the University of Berlin in lectures by Ernst Troeltsch. In *From Berlin to Jerusalem*, he describes her as thirty-five years old and the wife of a professor of medicine who had been called up by the military: "What attracted my attention was not so much her striking dark beauty and bearing as the notes—protesting against Troeltsch's somewhat too 'cultivated' presentation—that she dashed off in a large passionate script, using an enormous number of exclamation points and question marks. The expression on her face reflected her emotions as effectively as the expressionistic explosions in her notebook." From Scholem's diaries, it becomes clear that he developed an adolescent crush on Lissauer. They argued about philosophy, but Scholem clearly found her attitude toward Judaism highly challenging. She introduced him to Max Fischer, a Jew who had converted to Catholicism, prompting him to write Fischer a letter which, he claimed, "was not only to him, but instead ought to be directed to all modern *acherim* [a Talmudic term for heretics] and thus also to Frau Grete Lissauer."[15] Lissauer did not convert to Christianity, but she later separated from her husband, became a Communist, and died in Moscow in the mid-1920s.

Yet another woman to whom he appears to have been attracted was Katharina Gentz. He describes her as the first non-Jewish woman with whom he became friendly, which tells us something about the relative social segregation of even highly acculturated families like the Scholems. Gerhard's brother Werner married a non-Jewish working-class woman, Emmy Wiechelt, which, as we have seen, caused Arthur Scholem to cut off relations with his third son. Gerhard presumably was not thinking of Emmy, with whom he was rather friendly, when he singled out Gentz as the first Gentile woman of his acquaintance.

Gentz was seven years older than Scholem, but he considered her the most impressive student at Jena. She had a fine bearing and "the face of a noble damsel from medieval times." However, she was unapproachable, and the young Scholem only managed to strike up a conversation with her by pushing her coal cart up the hill to her apartment, which led to an invitation to tea. The adjectives he uses to describe her suggest the spell she cast over him: "She exuded an indescribable tranquility and her great reserve masked an immense human openness."[16] A diary entry from December 18, 1917, confirms this retrospective memory and suggests that much of Gentz's spell lay in her Germanness: "Only a German can be like that."[17] This attraction must have been deeply confusing to Scholem in light of his angry proclamations that he no longer considered himself German.

All these relationships were passionately intellectual but were hardly lacking in erotic energy. Scholem also found an avenue for expressing erotic feelings in his passion for Jewish texts. As we have already seen, one of his earliest literary endeavors was a translation of the Song of Songs, which his father published in a beautiful limited edition in 1915. Scholem translated this biblical text twice more, although the two subsequent translations were never published. But his diary also contains a rumination dated May 26, 1917, on the Song of Songs. There he rejects the traditional allegorical reading of the love poem in favor of a literal one: "The love of the Song of Songs is true love." Human love is the true task of Jewish lovers, a love that Scholem here describes as "deep spirituality."[18] Thus, Judaism, spirituality, and love were intimately bound up with one another.

Around the same time as he wrote this fragment, Scholem increasingly began focusing his romantic desire on another woman, Grete Brauer, whom he mentions parenthetically as an example of a girl whose ideology was equal to that of the boys in Jung Juda. Grete was the sister of Erich Brauer. We'll follow this story rather carefully since it is the central, if unacknowledged, chapter in Scholem's *annus amoris*, 1918, when his youthful infatuations would yield to a more mature relationship.

Grete Brauer was five years Scholem's senior, but in one letter he notes that she is, "thank God, much younger than her age."[19] He seems to have spent time with her from as early as the fall of 1916. She was a member of the Blau-Weiss, and Scholem had thrown himself into a single-minded campaign to convince its members to resign on the grounds of the organization's insufficient commitment to what he called "radical Zionism." In 1917, he toured the country, haranguing groups of Jewish students in the Blau-Weiss and noting with pride whenever anyone announced his or her resignation. Members of Jung Juda who had left the Blau-Weiss he called Scholem's people or Scholem mystics, which gives us a vivid picture of how politically active he was in those years and the way he fancied himself as a kind of leader. In May 1917, he went for a walk in the forest with Erich and Grete, noting afterward that Grete had begun to think along the lines of Scholem and his friends. And he adds that "she is the first girl whom I have befriended honestly."[20] On October 10, he gleefully announces to his diary that Grete has succumbed to his importuning and is now officially out of the Blau-Weiss.

However, Scholem's relationship with Grete was not only political. The next month, he reported a deep conversation with her about knowledge and gender. He had come to the important realization that women had a different relationship to knowledge from that of men. Women lacked the ability that men had to communicate their knowledge, which posed the most important problem in what he calls "the metaphysics of gender" (*Metaphysik der Geschlechter*). Yet, we must not conclude that this is another example of Scholem's misogyny, for he says that only idiots think that women cannot gain knowledge and even greater idiots have founded anti-feminism on this belief. He calls such attitudes "metaphysical heresy."[21]

A month later still, in the diary entry on Walter Benjamin's birthday letter, he notes that the letter had renewed his faith in God. He then mentions two other friends who have also renewed his life: Werner Kraft and Grete Bauer. By February 1918, his feelings have intensified. Now he tells his diary that he wants to have an honest talk with her and address her with the familiar "Du." If she does not reciprocate, he will establish a distance from her. And then, in a baffling comment, he says, "My inner order of life must be changed. I am not worthy of Walter."[22] Might this mean that expressing love for a woman threw doubt on his love for Walter? A week later, in the same vein: he must escape the atmosphere of "relationships" in which he lives. The only relationship that he could see continuing was with Grete, but it was apparently dead. Of course, his relationship with Walter was totally different: "It stands at the center of my life, he and no one else."[23]

But was the relationship with Grete Brauer dead? He evidently did not believe so because he wrote her a letter expressing his feelings. Interestingly, he did not preserve a copy of this crucial letter, as was his practice with other important letters. On March 5, Brauer answered him, saying that she could not give him what he needed. Cryptically, she says that she is "in an abyss of mourning" and cannot establish bridges to others.[24] Two days later, he answered her with a long, floridly romantic letter. The more locks and walls she erects around herself, the more certain he is that he can reach her "aloneness" (*Einsamkeit*). He claims that he will not resort to rhetoric, since language is holy for him. Oddly for a love letter to a woman, he refers several times to his feelings for Benjamin: "You are as old as Walter, and yet the years that you have before me have filled me with a completely different feeling."[25] He refers also to his translation of David's biblical lament for Jonathan, which he had given her the previous December, a peculiar text if one wishes to declare a heterosexual love. Clearly, Benjamin continued to cast a long shadow over his emotional life.

Within the letter are allusions to a disturbed mental state (at one point he calls it *Irrtum*, "fallacy") that had afflicted him for a long time, perhaps even as long as a year and certainly since he had been in Jena. For the past fourteen days he had been in a deep depression, a condition expressed by David's lament. He clearly believed that Grete had the power to save him from this malady: "The pure power of your existence is that which has kept me healthy in this whole time in the deepest sense and has prevented the burning fervor in which I have lived and [still] live from burning out." He concludes: "My love, I count the hours until your answer."

On March 11, Brauer wrote asking him to come to Berlin since what she had to say could not be put in letters. Nevertheless, she made her intentions plain: she regretted that she would cause him pain, but she was living under a "law" from which she could not free herself (like her "abyss of mourning," this "law" remains shrouded in mystery). It was not within her power to give him what he wanted: "I am not the person who can help you as you want. I want to be your friend as I was until now; more than this it is not possible for me to give you."[26] On March 14 he wrote in his diary: "Today a miracle took place: I've read Goethe [as if?] for the first time in my life. This too was the result of 'the Greteschen letter,'" thus eliding Gretchen in Goethe's *Faust* with Grete Brauer.[27]

Scholem resolved to go to Berlin to put an end to what he called "these unspeakably awful weeks." In a postcard also written on March 14, to his friend Werner Kraft, he says that he "lives above an underground explosion and flies next perhaps to an explosion in Berlin." On March 16, he wrote a desperate letter to his Jung Juda friend Aharon Heller, asking to stay with him in Berlin. Scholem needed to come urgently, but his finances were in terrible shape, and he had no money for a hotel. He was also in poor health: "Es geht mir sehr schlecht." But above all, Heller must keep his visit secret since his parents must on no account find out about it. What transpired during this secretive visit is unknown, but in a letter to another woman, to whom we shall shortly return, he refers to freeing himself—using the same language as earlier—with an "abysmal explosion."[28]

To judge by references to Grete Brauer over the next year, however, it seems that he had not freed himself at all. The afterlife of this first true love was much longer than its life. In April 1918, he wrote her a puerile poem titled "Farewell to a Young Girl," which, despite his feelings for Grete, he seems to have recycled later and sent to another adolescent flame. In it he laments the prospect of immigrating to Zion alone: love and ideology were clearly bound up with each other. In October 1918, now in Switzerland, he wrote in his diary as if he had become the young Werther of another of Goethe's works: "I think all the time of Grete. If I should die tonight, I would die with the thought of dying for her. I think night and day of her." And there may even have been echoes of his feelings much later: in 1920 he included in his diary a letter, probably never sent, which was meant for Brauer. In the letter he raises the question of whether Zionism can ever lead to a collective "we," but even though the content appears ideological, the failure of his relationship with Brauer surely lurks beneath the surface. The same year, he wrote her another poem that he saved in his archive.[29]

In a melodramatic twist, Grete Brauer ended up marrying the same Aharon Heller with whom Scholem stayed during his failed trip to Berlin. Heller went on to become one of the leading doctors in Palestine and the State of Israel, where he founded Beilinson Hospital in Tel Aviv. In a cryptic note in the expanded Hebrew edition of *From Berlin to Jerusalem*, Scholem says that Heller broke off relations with him when they were both in Palestine and that this was "the greatest puzzle of my life."[30]

Could this rupture have had something to do with Grete Brauer? We will never know, because Scholem excised her totally from his memoir, as if she had never existed, an astonishing decision given the rich detail he provided for his youth otherwise. It was as if the pain that her rejection of him caused remained so great that he could not bear to recount it sixty years later.

On May 4, 1918, with the permission of the German military authorities to leave the country, Scholem departed for Switzerland. In his later memoirs he describes his sense of "euphoria" in crossing the border. It is in fact possible that this euphoria was not only because he was leaving Germany behind, but also because he was closing the page on the "abysmal explosion" of his relationship with Grete Brauer. He was going to live in close proximity to Walter and Dora Benjamin. He had clearly transferred his feelings about Walter to Dora, keeping a picture of the two of them on his desk in Jena (he was the only nonrelative to attend their wedding in April 1917). When their son Stefan was born, he was overwhelmed with joy, as if the boy were his own son or, perhaps, brother (the psychological complexities cannot be unraveled here). Oddly enough, though, it was not until 1921, long past the Swiss period, that he began to address Walter and Dora with the familiar *Du*, even though he was on that basis much earlier with other friends, such as Werner Kraft, as well as his comrades from Jung Juda, where such informality was part of the movement's ideology.

He initially moved to a room in the village of Muri, outside Bern, where Walter and Dora were living. There he and Walter devised a satirical "University of Muri" that spoofed German universities. The two now picked up the intense conversations they had abandoned when Walter and Dora left Germany for Switzerland the previous July. Yet the Swiss ménage à trois was less than a success. Walter and Dora had screaming arguments, which Scholem was forced to witness. He also came to realize that both Walter and Dora were fundamentally amoral, which disturbed him greatly. Dora accused Scholem of causing disruption in their family, at times resorting to letters written in the name of their infant son Stefan. Her accusations hint that Scholem himself might have done his share of shouting. These scenes went on for over a year after he came to Switzerland. His friendship with Walter Benjamin certainly continued—albeit with many crises—but his utopian ideas of what it would mean to live with Walter and Dora were shattered.

Once again, we need to wonder about the nature of his relationship with Walter, which was able to survive such crises. It was as if Scholem had fallen under Walter's spell, a spell that Benjamin seems to have cast on others as well, despite—or perhaps because of—his difficult personality. Scholem acknowledges in his memoirs that Benjamin was the only person to whom he was invariably polite, again evidence that he was under a kind of spell. And then there was Benjamin's extraordinary originality, which Scholem found more stimulating than the ideas of any other interlocutor. With Benjamin, he felt that he was in the presence of genius, even though he admitted that he often found Benjamin's ideas opaque.

But with the deterioration in his relations with Walter and Dora, Scholem seems to have experienced a bout of desperate depression. To Aharon Heller, he wrote:

> Never before have I been in such desperate shape. . . . I see no one other than Walter Benjamin and his wife. I sit completely withdrawn in my attic room above the fields—like Agnon's Torah Scribe, minus his peace of mind. For weeks I have feared the worst and I feel crushed by a tormenting uncertainty about whether my recovery, obtained through Herculean efforts and at the most exacting price, will prove permanent. Here, of course, I can do what I want: I can work, think, take walks, or cry. . . . I also know quite well that I would be defenseless if my genius (I cannot use a lesser word for it) were to let me down. I now live as I did last sum-

mer, which is all the more terrifying since I must now fend
off real, not feigned madness.[31]

This is an extraordinary letter: it alludes to the illness that he
feigned in the military hospital but which has now asserted itself as a real illness, whatever it was before. And it also contains
an allusion to his sense of himself as a genius whose intellectual
gifts will be the antidote to his depression. The cause of this
depression must have been a combination of the disastrous affair with Grete Brauer, his disillusionment with the Benjamins
and their marriage, and the lack of the companionship that was
so essential to his life in Germany, as much as he wished to
leave that country. As important—indeed crucial—as Scholem's
Swiss period was in his intellectual evolution, the year in Switzerland was full of crises and repeated thoughts of suicide.

Despite these mood swings, he was not yet ready to declare
defeat in the search for love. A few weeks after his arrival in
Switzerland, he wrote to Meta Jahr, a member of Jung Juda
with whom he been carrying on a bit of a flirtation for some
time. Now that his relationship with Grete Brauer was defini-
tively over, he could indulge in other possibilities. Addressing
her as "liebes Kind," he says that he writes to almost no one in
Germany except a couple of young women. But he adjures her
not to think too much about him: "In earnest, you should live
entirely 'anti-Scholemisch.' But you do so also already."[32] In the
subsequent months, he exchanged a number of touching letters
with Jahr, who like many of the Jung Juda members immigrated to Palestine in the early 1920s and was one of the founding members of Kibbutz Bet Zera. In fact, it was Jahr to whom
Scholem sent that sonnet originally written for Grete Brauer.

Whatever Scholem's feelings may have been for Meta Jahr,
a new woman had appeared on the horizon. While in Heidelberg
the previous January, he had met Elsa (Escha) Burchhardt, the
daughter of an Orthodox family who was studying medicine

but found philosophy much more attractive. As was Scholem's style, he immediately engaged her in philosophical and Zionist conversation. Burchhardt wrote to him in the middle of March, but, consumed by his tumultuous feelings for Grete Brauer, he failed to answer. After the breakup with Brauer, though, he responded to Burchhardt, calling his visit to Berlin, as we have seen, an abysmal explosion.

In July 1918, he wrote to Burchhardt from Bern, upbraiding her for not dating her letters, perhaps already cognizant of their later importance for his historical persona. In the middle of a serious discussion of intellectual matters, he suddenly noted that her last letter "in the deepest sense" didn't have a stamp, which "cost me significant expense." Given Scholem's notorious stinginess and impish sense of humor, it is hard to know whether he meant this seriously or as a joke. But he then went on to say that he was writing to elicit her "wordless silence" which was "to be encompassed in your love." The theme of silence had recurred in Scholem's adolescent writing as a highly prized virtue (albeit one to which he devoted many words). Here he deployed it in the service of romance. The letter is surprising because no indication of such feelings had appeared in earlier correspondence or even in his diaries. And it is also noteworthy that he is still using the formal *Sie*. Only in October did she write him in the familiar *Du*, which left him as ecstatic, he says, as after a first kiss. In November, he reports rereading her letters: "One is more mysterious than the other and yet there is no mystery. If she loves me, she could not write in any other way."[33]

The next month, though, everything turned topsy-turvy. Grete Brauer came to visit her brother Erich in Bern, throwing Scholem into a state of extreme agitation. In his diary he refers cryptically to "the problem of Heller," which suggests that the course that would lead to Grete's future marriage had already been set (he also says of Heller, "Naturally I do not say his name").[34] In a feverish set of diary entries, he compares Grete to Escha and both of them to Dora! He now thinks that it is the role of women to renew Zionism, and he even speculates about their place in the messianic realm. He was clearly in a highly volatile state in which he could scarcely decide toward whom to direct his romantic emotions. A week later, though, the turmoil began to resolve itself: he now realized that his three-year infatuation with Walter and Dora was over, and while his feelings for Grete remained strong (throughout the spring of 1919, he continued to contrast her "purity" to the ethical failings of the Benjamins), his return to Germany, which he now saw as necessary, depended on Escha.

In a diary entry from this period, he reveals that for six weeks he has not written any poetry. This is an indication that he was in a healthy state of mind: "When I feel well, I don't write poetry. When I'm in [a state] of pure enthusiasm, I write prose, when I'm unhappy, a poem, when angry, a letter, and when I'm in [a state] of my *tikkun* [perfection, wholeness], I am silent."[35] Although his fluctuating moods found reflection in the genre in which he wrote, and although he would never stop writing either poetry or letters, from this point on more and more of his energies would find expression in prose.

In February 1919, Escha Burchhardt came to Bern, and this visit cemented the relationship. In June he wrote a diary entry in memory of the time they spent together during the winter: "When she came to me, she didn't love me yet, but this took only a few days. Now she wants everything she can get: to be my lover, my wife, but all she really wants is to have children. Escha is the type of mother God intended. Is it necessary for this eternal picture of motherhood to languish without children? . . . But I told her I couldn't have a lover. It's certain that one should love her deeply; she has such a feminine movement to her."[36] Even in this outburst of enthusiasm, he conveys confusion about his role in their relationship. In later years the question of children would loom large.

In September, Scholem returned to Germany, enrolling in a doctoral program in Munich. Letters from his father make plain that Arthur could no longer afford to continue supporting him in Switzerland, given the deterioration in the German mark. But Gerhard was ready to leave Switzerland in any case. Although his choice of university was certainly dictated by the strong program in Semitic languages and the trove of Kabbalistic manuscripts and books to be found there, it was perhaps no coincidence that Munich was where Escha Burchhardt resided. Soon they were living in facing rooms on the Türkenstrasse.

The year before this momentous move, which marked his turn to professional training and also preparation for immigration to Palestine, Scholem resolved to write a farewell to the German Zionist youth movement, echoing the two earlier essays I discussed in the previous chapter. He completed the essay, "Abschied" (Farewell), in Switzerland in June 1918 and published it in Siegfried Bernfeld's *Jerubbaal*, a youth movement journal. The essay, truth be told, is a bewildering onslaught of ideas, many of them hard to decipher. Scholem characterized the culture of the youth movement as "chatter" (*Geschwätz*), "confusion" (*Verwirrung*), and "chimeras," all favorite pejoratives in the young Scholem's vocabulary. Hebrew must be the core of Zionism, but for the youth movement, "Hebrew has been robbed of its meaning, for the Hebrew of the chatterers could never become the revelation of a community that proves its reality by the possibility of being silent in Hebrew." The only appropriate response to all this verbiage was silence: "Community demands solitude: not the possibility of together desiring the same [thing], but only that of common solitude establishes community."[37] This is surely a strange, even paradoxical, definition of community, and it suggests that Scholem was far from endorsing the kind of collectivism that led some of his comrades to found a kibbutz. He wanted community, but, above all, he also wanted solitude. The tension between the two may explain why he found it so hard to fulfill his Zionist dreams.

As a denunciation of garrulous chatter, the essay certainly falls short, for it suffers from the very sin it claims to expose (we recall Julie Schächter's telling criticism of Scholem's earlier writing). A religious tone underlies the essay, even if its writer was no longer religious. Zionism was linked in his mind to a revival of Judaism based on an immersion in the sources of Judaism. This immersion was possible only if its adherents learned Hebrew, which was at the core of Scholem's ideology. But they then had to learn to be silent in Hebrew and to create a community of solitary individuals, a condition that perhaps reflects Scholem's own sense of loneliness after he came to Switzerland. Exactly how this philosophy might be put into practice remained unexplained, but there was a clear tension here and elsewhere in Scholem's early writings between the solitary intellectual and the highly social student and activist whose life we have been tracing. Both personas remained true for him not only in these early years but throughout his life.

4

The Book of Brightness

BETWEEN THE FALL of 1919 and the spring of 1923, Scholem transformed himself from a brilliant autodidact with broad, eclectic interests into a highly disciplined scholar of Kabbalah. He mastered an astonishing range of sources as well as languages, all in an extraordinarily short time. Where he had earlier suffered from swings of mood, he now came to focus like a laser on his subject. No doubt his relationship with Escha Burchhardt played a major role in calming the storms that had raged inside him throughout his adolescence and early adulthood. We find confirmation of his greater emotional stability in the fact that he virtually stopped writing in his diary after he moved to Munich, although he did continue to write fragmentary essays that he never published. If, as we saw in the previous chapter, writing prose signified for him a state of "enthusiasm" and poetry, depression, the Munich period was one of pure enthusiasm and the prose increasingly academic. Since he only wrote in his diary episodically, from this period on we must rely more on letters and Scholem's other writings to reconstruct his biography.

Scholem stood out in his generation for mastering classical and modern Hebrew, as well as a full range of Jewish sources from the Bible to the twentieth century. What distinguished him, even before he undertook academic studies in Judaism, was an almost fanatical insistence on historical accuracy. Where a writer like Martin Buber might adapt Hasidic texts for his own purposes, Scholem demanded we read these texts on their own terms, located within history. In order to do so, he came increasingly to believe that the critical tool he had to learn was philology. To the contemporary reader, this discipline might appear arcane, and, in fact, one rarely encounters it in today's universities. But in Scholem's time the glory of the humanistic sciences in Germany was precisely this careful tracing of terms and texts to demonstrate their inner relationships, authorship, authenticity, and transmission of ideas. Philology combined literary criticism with history and linguistics. Scholem's genius lay in harnessing this seemingly dry academic discipline to an urgent philosophical agenda.

As early as July 1918, shortly after he arrived in Switzerland, he meditated in his diary on the relations among philology, tradition, and silence. As we have seen, the last two terms were among the most frequent in his early vocabulary. For instance, he mobilized the concept of tradition—the whole Jewish library—against Buber's mysticism of experience: the first was historical, the second fallaciously contemporary. Where Buber's philosophy degenerated into idle chatter and gibberish, the true Jewish philosophy had to privilege silence. And the key to these two was philology, by which he meant a kind of speech governed by strict rules of evidence.

But it was not a foregone conclusion that he would do a doctorate in Judaism. Well into his Swiss period, he was still considering a career in mathematics, even though he had earlier concluded that he lacked true genius in that discipline. The University of Göttingen seemed the best place to pursue such studies, but he learned from a friend that the town was deadly dull. On May 15, 1919, he seems to have arrived at a final decision: "My passion is now for philosophy and Judaism. And I have an urgent necessity for philology."[1] Oddly, in the lines before this declaration, he confesses to extreme tiredness and inability to work. The decision for Jewish Studies seems therefore not to have been made without inner turmoil. After all, there were no positions in the field in Germany and certainly not in Palestine, which had no universities. From a career point of view, mathematics was a better bet, and, in fact, when he set sail for Palestine, even though he had a doctorate in Semitics, he expected to teach mathematics in a high school.

Exactly when he decided to make the study of Kabbalah his primary subject is not entirely clear. His keen interest in that esoteric discipline had been awakened years before as he filled notebooks with thoughts on the subject. In July 1919, he indicated that he wanted to write on Jewish theories of language and that this work would require studying the *Zohar.* The philosophical question seemingly preceded the disciplinary one. As intrigued as Scholem was with the subject, however, he ended up deferring his essay on the Kabbalah's philosophy of language for fifty years.

Scholem's interest in this theme may reflect the influence of Walter Benjamin, whose 1916 essay on divine and human language had struck a dominant chord. The Kabbalistic ideas in Benjamin's essay came from his study of the German Christian Kabbalist Johann Georg Hamann rather than from Jewish sources. It is striking that not only Benjamin but also Scholem derived his early ideas about Jewish mysticism from Christian sources. Scholem had been greatly excited by his reading of Franz Josef Molitor, a nineteenth-century Christian Kabbalist whose philosophical treatment of Kabbalistic ideas appealed to his own ruminations. In essays throughout his career, he returned again and again to Molitor, even as he disparaged his own Jewish predecessors. Molitor's idea that Kabbalah represented a true subterranean tradition (the meaning of the word in Hebrew) clearly appealed to Scholem, as did the philosophical approach that Molitor took to this esoteric subject.

Although Scholem's letters and diaries do not provide a conclusive contemporary answer for why and when he decided to study the Kabbalah, there is retrospective evidence for how he understood his decision. In 1937 he sent a birthday letter to the department store magnate and patron of Jewish publishing Salman Schocken. Schocken had heard about Scholem in 1918 when he was a student at Jena and after meeting him supported Scholem's translation work and later both his research and publications. Schocken clearly appreciated Scholem's genius, but, as might be expected, Scholem at times chafed under their patronage relationship, which had its ups and downs.

Scholem titled his birthday letter "A Candid Word About the True Motives of My Kabbalistic Studies." He claimed that his decision was not arbitrary, only that he thought his task would be much easier: "Three years, 1916–1918, which were decisive for my entire life, lay behind me: many exciting thoughts had led me as much to the most rationalistic skepticism about my fields of study as to intuitive affirmation of mystical theses that walked the fine line between religion and nihilism." When he discovered the writer Frank Kafka, he found in him a secular expression of this Kabbalistic spirit.

> So I arrived at the intention of writing not the history but the metaphysics of the Kabbalah. I was struck by the impoverishment of what some like to call the Philosophy of Judaism. I was particularly incensed by three authors whom I knew, Saadiah [Gaon], Maimonides and Hermann Cohen,

who conceived as their main task to construct antitheses to myth and pantheism, although they should have concerned themselves with raising them to a high level. . . .

I sensed such a higher level in the Kabbalah. . . . It seemed to me that here, beyond the perceptions of my generation, existed a realm of associations, which had to touch our own most human experiences.

To be sure, the key to the understanding of these things seemed to have been lost. . . . And perhaps it wasn't so much the key that was missing, but courage: courage to venture out into the abyss, which one day could end up in us ourselves.[2]

There are many themes here that would resonate for Scholem throughout his life, and I shall have occasion to return to this pregnant letter, especially when I come to discussing the context in which he wrote it in 1937. Even if he largely abandoned a philosophical approach to the Kabbalah, at least for the first decades of his career, his decision to study this esoteric subject had to do with a philosophical question: What is the status of myth and of pantheism in the world's oldest monotheistic religion? Whereas Jewish philosophers like Saadiah Gaon and Moses Maimonides in the Middle Ages and Hermann Cohen in the twentieth century asserted that they had no place, Scholem—following Buber—believed that they were essential to understanding Judaism. (At the time of Cohen's death in 1918, however, Scholem treated the philosopher as a kind of intellectual hero, an opinion he seems to have repressed.) If pantheism was heretical then perhaps heresy—and with it, even modern secularism—was a part of Judaism and not outside it. There was something in these recondite, even bizarre books and manuscripts that might still speak urgently to modern people.

The key was lost and yet might still be recovered if one had the courage to venture into this abyss (a favorite word in Scholem's vocabulary, as we have seen). But why an abyss? Because the Kabbalistic library was like a maze in which one could become a nihilist or even go mad. In the concluding paragraphs of the letter, Scholem speaks of the "misty wall of history" that hangs around the mountain (Mount Sinai?), noting that in trying to penetrate this mist, he risks suffering a "professorial death." However, if the mountain represents metaphysical truth, there is no alternative to trying to hear a genuine communication from it than using the tools of philological criticism. Whereas Cohen, Buber, and other philosophers thought that they could acquire this truth either by divine revelation or by means of reason, Scholem believed only in the painstaking spadework of deciphering historical texts. His initial intention to write the metaphysics of the Kabbalah could not be done without first writing its history.

A shorter manuscript found in Scholem's papers dated 1921 contains strikingly similar ideas about the ironic necessity of discovering a mystical truth with the tools of philology (note that in Scholem's vocabulary, historical study and philology were often synonymous). Nearly forty years later, he would return to these philosophical meditations (he called them then "unhistorical theses") about the relationship between the critical historian and the Kabbalah. What all these texts demonstrate is that he never abandoned the philosophical questions that animated him from the first. Or, as he wrote to his mother in a humorous poem dated November 23, 1919:

> What will become of Gerhard Scholem?
> First he will become Gershom Scholem
> Then he will (hopefully) become Dr. Phil.,
> Then a Jewish philosopher
> Then an angel in the Seventh Heaven.[3]

Once he had taken up residence in Munich, he threw himself into a wide range of studies, as he reported in a letter to his parents: philosophy, psychology, Arabic, Hebrew, Syriac, Greek, and even a final course in mathematics. As heavy a load as this might have been, he still spent the majority of his time in the Bavarian State Library consuming Kabbalistic texts and manuscripts. He needed to teach himself medieval Hebrew paleography in order to decipher the difficult handwriting in the manuscripts. And he continued his obsession with mastering the tools of philology by tracing terms and ideas from one text to another.

After abandoning the idea of writing on the Kabbalah's philosophy of language, perhaps because the subject was insufficiently philological, he turned to one of the more idiosyncratic medieval Spanish mystics, Abraham Abulafia. Abulafia had developed a prophetic form of Kabbalism that emphasized mystical experience, something less common among other Spanish Kabbalists. In the Hebrew edition of his memoir, Scholem confesses that he even attempted some of Abulafia's mystical practices and apparently succeeded in experiencing alterations of consciousness. This is the only time he admitted to practicing Kabbalah. In a hilarious letter to his parents in June 1920, he reports rumors that as a result of his Kabbalistic studies he has learned how to employ black magic to conjure up mice and elephants. Unfortunately, he says, at the present time, all he can really conjure are texts free of errors (the goal of philology). But by the time of his examinations, he hopes to be able to produce camels and similar animals. For reasons he never elucidated, he abandoned Abulafia for nearly two decades and instead zeroed in on one of the most difficult early Kabbalistic texts from the twelfth century, the *Sefer ha-Bahir*, or "Book of Brightness."

As focused as he was on his dissertation, he still found time for many other activities. He took long walks with S. Y. Agnon, who spent part of the same years in Munich. Together with Escha Burchhardt, he studied Talmud under the instruction of a rabbi, Heinrich Ehrentreu. He also continued his translation work from Hebrew to German, translating a story by Agnon, Hayim Nahman Bialik's "Halakhah and Aggada," a lamentation poem composed after a medieval pogrom, and a poem by the Spanish writer Judah Halevi. Another translation, about which he felt more ambivalent, was a memorial book for Zionist watchmen in Palestine who had been killed by Arabs. Here he felt that a cult of martyrdom created too nationalistic and militaristic a form of Zionism. As a result, he signed a pseudonym to the translation.

He also wrote a number of essays of fierce criticism, now applying his polemical pen to scholarship rather than Zionist youth movement politics. He attacked a translation of selections from the *Zohar* by Jankew Seidman and an anthology, *Lyrik der Kabbala*, by Meir Wiener. In both these cases he argued that the authors had translated Kabbalistic texts in the style of German expressionism under the influence of Buber's highly romantic reworkings of the *Tales of Rabbi Nahman*. Wiener's book, in particular, explicitly gestured to Buber's Erlebnis mysticism, which, of course, could only arouse Scholem's ire. He utterly rejected the idea that mystical writing read as poetry might inspire a metaphysical awakening. This was a thorough misunderstanding of Kabbalah, a technical corpus of literature that required not the enthusiasm of the poet but the painstaking investigations of the philologist.

During the spring of 1920, Scholem was not exclusively holed up in the library. Munich had been the site of the short-lived Bavarian Socialist Republic in 1919, and its suppression a few months later led to the murder of the anarchist Gustav Landauer (among many others), who had inspired Scholem several years earlier. Scholem arrived not long afterward, to find that a great deal of political turmoil remained. Shortly after his arrival, his eldest brother, Reinhold, whose politics were the most conservative of the four brothers, sent him a birthday greeting: "I hope that your stay in Munich will show you that the German idea is still alive and kicking and has not been drowned out by the resonant phrases of coffeehouse socialists. . . . I would be very interested if you wrote me about the political happenings among students. There, too, the Russian and Bavarian Jews have given us a bad name. Has anti-Semitism flared up at the university?"[4] Reinhold signed the letter, tongue in cheek, Reserve Lieutenant and Member of the German Volkspartei (a party of the center-right). The signature aroused Gerhard's irony when he wrote to his parents: "By the way, I want to thank M.d.V.L.d.R.X.Y.Z. [a parody of Reinhold's signature] for his pompous letter, which just goes to show how 'the reaction rears its head.'"[5] The brothers appeared able to rib each other for their very different politics.

Gerhard also wrote that there was a great deal of anti-Semitism afoot at the university, although he steered clear of student politics, which he labeled a farce. But in March 1920, he could no longer remain aloof. The Kapp Putsch, which broke out that month, was an attempt by army officers and members of the Freikorps (militia units aligned with the far right) to overthrow the Weimar Republic. The government called a general strike, which was an overwhelming success (indeed, it was the biggest such strike in Germany's history). The putsch was put down, but it is generally thought to have severely undermined the republic. Gerhard found himself on the streets, and he reported back to his parents rather laconically that he had engaged in a fistfight with an anti-Semite.

Another shadow fell over the Munich period in the summer of 1920. Scholem wrote home complaining of chronic fatigue and reporting that a doctor had diagnosed childhood scrofula (a form of tuberculosis of the lymphatic system). Perhaps his earlier bouts of neurasthenia were in fact the result of this disease. Subsequent letters from that summer suggest that he continued to feel ill. It is remarkable, given his condition, that he was able to be so productive (the condition seems to have cleared up on its own since no medical treatment for it was then available, except perhaps Kabbalistic magic!).

It was during his Munich period that Scholem came into contact with one of the most important Jewish thinkers of the Weimar Republic, Franz Rosenzweig. A decade older than Scholem, Rosenzweig followed a path back to Judaism that partly resembled Scholem's. He came from an assimilated background and was on the verge of conversion to Christianity when a religious epiphany turned him back to Judaism. He served in the First World War and began writing his magnum opus, *The Star of Redemption*, on postcards from the front (the book was published in 1921). Like Scholem, he learned Hebrew and undertook translations of traditional texts into German. It was, in fact, over a translation that the two first came into contact, although Rosenzweig had known of Scholem earlier through his polemics against the youth movement.

Rosenzweig had translated the blessing after meals into German and had heard that Scholem had attempted to do the same. In the spring of 1921, he sent his translation to Scholem and received a complicated reply. Scholem found the translation significant and believed that Rosenzweig had solved a problem of translating religious hymns that he himself had failed to solve: "The almost blessed richness of your translation . . . along with the nonmetaphorical uniformity of your stance . . . something which I regard without hesitation as the legitimate seal over the abyss of the religious agitation of our wretched people . . . prove that such a realm exists in the German language."[6] In this somewhat puzzling statement, he invoked the "abyss" to characterize contemporary German Jewish life and lauded Rosenzweig for covering over this abyss with the purity of his translation. But then he pivoted to attack Rosenzweig's adoption of Christian language in order to accomplish his translation. Rosenzweig answered reasonably that one couldn't translate a religious text into German without invoking the language of Luther.

This debate had deeper ramifications. In *The Star of Re-*

71

demption, which Scholem read around the time of this first exchange of letters, Rosenzweig linked Judaism and Christianity: each had a different path to redemption, the first outside history and the second within it. The two religions were, in a sense, fraternal twins. Although Scholem regarded this book as the most significant product of German Jewish thought in the twentieth century, he rejected Rosenzweig's basic premise. For Scholem, the history of the Jews was radically independent of the history of the Christians. And far from celebrating the fact that Jews in the Diaspora were outside history, as a Zionist he believed that the renewal of Judaism could come about only when they reentered history in the Land of Israel. Whereas Rosenzweig, a non-Zionist, believed in the potential for a "German Judaism" (that is, a place for a renewed Judaism in Germany), Scholem rejected the very possibility of a German–Jewish symbiosis. Yet, perhaps paradoxically, to study the Kabbalah, most of which was written outside the Land of Israel, required recognizing that much Jewish creativity took place in the Diaspora.

Two months after this first exchange, in May 1921, Scholem came to the Frankfurt area to meet with Agnon and Buber (he still kept Buber abreast of his scholarly adventures). He used the opportunity to meet with Rosenzweig, a meeting that lasted a day and a half. Rosenzweig was deeply impressed by his guest, but his description of the meeting in a letter to a friend was highly ambiguous:

> It was a great day and a half, but not as you think. You *fight* with him [but] I immediately laid down my weapons and learned from and with him. . . . For him, his Judaism is *only* a monastery. There he holds his spiritual exercises and, despite all his side remarks, he fundamentally doesn't care about [other] human beings. As a result, he has become *speechless*. He has only gestures of admiration or opposition. . . . He is *really* "without any dogmas." One cannot define him by

principles of faith. I have not yet found such a thing among
West European Jews. He is perhaps the only one who has
really already come home. But he has come home *alone*.[7]

This was a remarkably perceptive analysis of the young Scholem: his extreme statements, his pugnaciousness, and his intense inner drive to master Judaism. Rosenzweig's observation
that Scholem held to no dogmas captures Scholem's willingness to consider even heresy as part of Judaism. In fact, Rosenzweig in another letter labeled him a nihilist who reveled in
nothingness. But Rosenzweig was only partially correct in his
assessment: even if Scholem's ideas at that age were often confused, he believed in his own version of Zionism and in a return
to Jewish sources, hardly the views of a nihilist. And he was not
a solitary monk of Judaism but, as we have seen, a highly social
animal who believed in utopian Zionism as a collective project.

In March 1922, Scholem was back in Frankfurt for an even
longer meeting with Rosenzweig. He had not been not aware
that the amyotrophic lateral sclerosis (Lou Gehrig's disease)
that would eventually kill Rosenzweig in 1929 had begun to
manifest itself in December 1921. This time, the debate turned
bitter as Scholem violently took issue with the older man's rejection of Zionism. Scholem disagreed with Rosenzweig's spiritual-
ized approach to Judaism: Rosenzweig had embraced Orthodoxy. Just as he had been unable to stomach Buber's spirituality,
so Rosenzweig's religiosity now left him cold. Scholem came
away from the meeting with the feeling that Rosenzweig was
dictatorial and unable to tolerate differences of opinion; considering Scholem's own personality, this suggests that the two
shared too many personality traits to ever achieve a modus vivendi. It was only after this stormy meeting that Scholem learned
of Rosenzweig's illness, a discovery that left him uncharacteris-
tically feeling guilty. This guilt would affect his later feelings
about Rosenzweig and his philosophy.

Scholem also harbored doubts about Rosenzweig's Lehr-haus, an adult education school in Frankfurt that played a major role in the Jewish renaissance in Weimar Germany. It was virtually impossible to study Jewish subjects in German universities at that time; Scholem was offered a lectureship in Munich after completing his Ph.D., which would have made him one of the only academics in the field in Germany. The Lehrhaus provided an inspiring alternative to the nonexistent academic Jewish Studies, attracting intellectuals such as Erich Fromm and Leo Löwenthal, who would go on to have distinguished scholarly careers in the United States. But it also attracted a wider public of young German Jews thirsty for the kind of Jewish knowledge whose sources had been cut off when the older generation assimilated. Whatever Scholem's hesitations might have been about this enterprise, and regardless of his break with Rosenzweig in the spring of 1922, he nevertheless taught twice at the Lehrhaus, offering a wide range of courses (Kabbalah, the works of Agnon, the book of Daniel). In the summer of 1923, just before his emigration for Palestine, he was once again in Frankfurt, leading Rosenzweig to comment: "Scholem is here for the summer and he is, as always, unspeakably ill-behaved, but likewise, as always, brilliant."[8]

Franz Rosenzweig was probably the most intellectually impressive of all the people Scholem met during his Munich studies. In *From Berlin to Jerusalem*, Scholem describes other, more dubious characters with whom he came into contact at the time, many of them charlatans and imposters who claimed fraudulently to have knowledge of Kabbalah or other forms of esotericism. They were drawn to Scholem as his reputation spread, but he seems to have been equally drawn to them. Of course, he was only too pleased to demonstrate his monopoly on Kabbalistic knowledge, but he also seems to have found genuine amusement in the absurdity of such frauds. Here is another side of Scholem that is perhaps too easily forgotten: his ironic sense of humor, which more and more came to replace the fanaticism of his youth.

One group of such charlatans he did not find amusing was the circle around Oskar Goldberg. Goldberg, who came from an Orthodox background, developed a bizarre theology focused on the five books of Moses interpreted in terms of numerological magic. Following the Kabbalah, Goldberg held that the Pentateuch was based on the letters of the Tetragrammaton. Since all the laws and rituals of the Torah are, in effect, the name of God, the Hebrews had activated the "metaphysical reality" at their "center" by means of these rituals. By virtue of this magical procedure, the Hebrews became the most metaphysical of all peoples. All subsequent biblical and Jewish history represented a fall from this "reality of the Hebrews" (the title of Goldberg's 1925 book). Goldberg's goal was to recapture this magical essence in the modern world, which, in his view, had become mired in polytheistic materialism. Surprisingly, Thomas Mann based the metaphysical ideas in the first part of his *Joseph and His Brothers* on Goldberg's, but he later satirized Goldberg as "Dr. Chaim Breisacher," the purveyor of a Nazi-like magical racial theory, in his *Doktor Faustus*.

In the 1920s, the members of the Goldberg circle tried to entice Scholem to join their ranks since the Kabbalah fascinated them but they had little access to its texts. Scholem rebuffed their advances, in part in reaction to Goldberg's hostility to Zionism but also because he rejected Goldberg's ahistorical metaphysics, which sought to re-create the primordial "reality" of the Hebrews. Goldberg's odd synthesis of magical metaphysics with a biological (even racial) definition of the Jews was utterly repugnant to him. When Goldberg's *Reality of the Hebrews* appeared, Scholem attacked it as *"the classical work of Jewish Satanism."*[9] Although the Goldberg circle was never large, references to Goldberg and his book occur repeatedly in Scholem's essays and letters, to the extent that Goldberg almost appears to have become an obsession, which continued for decades: Scholem even wrote the entry on Goldberg for the 1971 *Encyclopedia Judaica*. It was as if Goldberg's magical and mystical ideas required a thoroughgoing debunking, rather than being allowed to vanish into obscurity. For Scholem, such ideas had no place in the modern world. Despite his fascination with magic and mysticism, Scholem was neither a magician nor a mystic.

A figure whom Scholem regarded far more positively, although he also considered him a bit of a charlatan, was Robert Eisler. Martin Buber first suggested to Scholem that he contact Eisler, who had founded the Johann Albert Widmanstetter Society for Kabbalah Research. Eisler was an academically gifted Viennese Jew who came from a wealthy family and had converted to Christianity for the love of a woman (he nevertheless still considered himself fully Jewish). He had received two Ph.D.s from the University of Vienna, in philosophy and art history, a feat that was theoretically impossible, but he pulled it off because no one believed the same person could be doing both. Eisler had published a book on comparative religion titled *Cosmic Cloak and Heavenly Canopy*, which Scholem dubbed "hypothesis-happy." Scholem found it so hilarious that he wrote to Walter Benjamin to propose a course by Robert Eisler in their fictitious University of Muri to be called "Ladies Coats and Beach Cabanas in the Light of the History of Religion."

Eisler received Scholem as "the heaven-sent angel who would breathe Kabbalistic life into his paper society." Scholem was both charmed and amused by Eisler's ideas: "The substance of [his] research was so frivolous that it only drew a skeptical shudder from me, since I was now subjecting myself to serious philological discipline. Eisler's eloquence was as fantastic as his education. . . . I, at any rate, had never before seen such a brilliant, captivating yet suspiciously glittering scholarly phenomenon."[10] Scholem was astounded by Eisler's flood of ideas, which were usually ungrounded in factual reality. But Eisler took no offense when Scholem challenged his premises and his knowledge of Hebrew.

The upshot of their encounter was not the fierce polemical rejection one might have expected from Scholem but rather surprising indulgence. And when Scholem came to publish his first two books (his dissertation and his 1927 bibliography of Kabbalistic books), they appeared as the first—and only—publications in Eisler's series "Sources of Kabbalah," under the aegis of Eisler's phony society. After the Second World War, Eisler sent Scholem a bizarre plan for solving the Palestine question by shipping all nonreligious Jews back to their countries of origin or, if they still wanted to live in a Jewish state, by creating autonomous Jewish enclaves in Vienna and Frankfurt. Scholem finally lost patience with Eisler and returned the manuscript to him with a one-word comment: "Genug!" (Enough!).[11]

At the end of December 1921, Scholem completed his dissertation. Given the ambitious questions he had been asking before he took up his studies over two years earlier, the result might appear to be quite modest. He had produced a German translation of the *Sefer ha-Bahir* with copious notes. But the initial appearance is deceptive. The *Bahir* was the earliest work of medieval Kabbalah, stemming from the twelfth century, probably in Provence. It introduced the symbolism of the *sefirot*, the emanations of God, which would be central to all subsequent Kabbalah. One of Scholem's lifelong preoccupations was to be the question of how and why the Kabbalah arose in southern France and Spain when it did. The *Bahir* held the key to this question, although the answer would emerge only in his later studies.

When we examine Scholem's dissertation notes, his achievement becomes even more remarkable. Immediately after each passage in the text, he appends citations for where later writers quoted the *Bahir*. The notes, which are much longer than the text itself, explore the *Bahir*'s own Talmudic and midrash sources, as well as discuss the interpretations of earlier scholars. The implication of these notes was that the *Bahir* served as the bridge between ancient Jewish mysticism and the Middle Ages: the book thus confirmed the meaning of *Kabbalah* as "tradition"—namely, something passed down from antiquity. In order to provide his scholarly apparatus, Scholem had to work through seventy-one Kabbalistic texts and manuscripts, as well as various manuscripts of the *Bahir* in Hebrew and Latin. This was in addition to three German-language compilations of Kabbalistic sources. (The existence of these earlier German books demonstrates that contrary to the impression he sometimes tried to give, Scholem was not the first to plow this field.) As a result of his herculean efforts, he now had a sufficient library of sources under his belt to launch a scholarly career.

Just as he was finishing his dissertation, Gerhard received a birthday greeting from his father, which is in many ways so astonishing that it is worth quoting at length:

> I have not heard much from you, and I would like very much to know if your doctoral dissertation is in process. I hope that it will be more readable than the critique of Kabbalistic lyric [Scholem's review of Wiener's *Lyrik der Kabbala*], whose virtue seems to lie in the long period it dealt with. In any case, the mass of knowledge contained in this critique stands in inverse relationship to the clarity of its expression—and, I'm sorry to say, that it cost me a mighty intellectual effort and many tries in order to overcome those lengthy periods of time. In fact, it pains me to confess that I was unable to grasp what was described to me as the beauty of the matter. But maybe that's only me. And, in my view, it would be inappropriate to claim that the many recipients of the first number of *Der Jude*, who got your essay as an inducement to subscribe, were won over by it.
>
> So, when I ask myself how I would write this critique from the standpoint of the, unfortunately not yet defined,

"man on the street," I would say: a pity for all this empty scholarship and a double pity for all these productive powers and intellectual labors to have been expended so uselessly. . . .

And so I come again to your birthday with this quiet wish and strong hope: that you may grasp in this year of your life that it is necessary in this difficult period to stand with both feet on the ground, in order not to be blown away by every wind in the air [*Luft*] of ideas. Three cheers for Hebraica and Judaica, but not as a career! You will suffer a bad shipwreck and who knows if it will prove too difficult for you to reach safe shores, since you are all-too lacking in strong arms.

So, my son, these are my good and right wishes for you![12]

This was not the first time that Arthur had expressed strong reservations about his youngest son's vocation or about his physical condition. (Arthur's one involvement with a Jewish organization was as a board member of the Jewish gymnastics club, whose cult of physical fitness positioned him closer to the Zionists than to his Zionist son.) For many of the hardheaded businessmen of Arthur's generation, the intellectual pursuits of their sons made the sons look like the luftmenschen (literally, "men who live from the air") of the eastern European shtetl. This anxiety over Gerhard's livelihood was surely sharpened by the inflation of the early 1920s, which was just beginning to accelerate.

Yet we should not be too hasty in assuming an irreparable rift between father and son. Arthur's letter was unquestionably harsh, but it was also funny. Its tongue-in-cheek humor reminds us of nothing as much as Gerhard's own epistolary style: hilarious, biting, ironic—even, at times, self-mocking. The apple, it seems, had not fallen far from the tree. How much Gerhard was aware of his similarity to his father, both in temperament and in style, is unknown. And since Arthur succumbed to his heart condition in 1925 (he had a serious attack in March 1922, the day after Scholem defended his dissertation), he did not live to see his prophecy of his son's "shipwreck" disproven. Indeed, of the four Scholem brothers, it was Gerhard who was to have the greatest success. But it may be that Arthur's view of his son was not as negative as the letter implies. In 1920, when Walter Benjamin met Arthur, he reported to Gerhard: "Your father succinctly pronounced you a genius—he should know. But may God preserve every father from having such a genius."[13] If we turn over the title page of Gerhard's published dissertation, we find in small letters a statement of paternal pride: "Printed in the shop of A. Scholem." And in October 1925, after Arthur had died, Betty wrote to Gerhard of how proud he would have been at his son's faculty appointment at the Hebrew University. True, he valued success in business, but like most German Jews, including those lacking even a gymnasium degree, Arthur also placed high value on intellectual achievement.

Scholem defended his dissertation in March 1922 and since none of the members of his committee knew anything about Kabbalah, he was examined on completely unrelated subjects. He not only passed with flying colors, he was told that if he wrote a *Habilitation* (the second dissertation required in German universities for an academic position), he would be offered a teaching post. Already committed to emigrating, he declined the honor but made sure that his father knew of his teachers' assessment.

In the next year and a half, he returned to Berlin, took the State Examination in mathematics to prepare for teaching the subject in Palestine, and also prepared his dissertation for publication. He and Escha Burchhardt were now in different cities, but saw each other a number of times. They resolved to marry once they had arrived in Palestine (she left before him in the spring of 1923). But as busy as he was with his scholarship and teaching at a number of venues, he still had time for Zionist politics. He wrote several manifestos and took part in a fiery meeting at which the Blau-Weiss debated whether to merge with the Association of Jewish University Students, at whose meeting, as we saw, the philosopher Hans Jonas witnessed him disrupting the speakers.

Possibly in response to this meeting, he organized a final open letter to the *Jüdische Rundschau* in December 1922. The letter was a reaction to a development in the Blau-Weiss that Scholem viewed with great alarm. The movement, which Scholem had earlier attacked for insufficient Zionism, now turned toward a commitment to immigrate to Palestine. But it had organized itself along military lines and elevated its leader Walter Moses to a position of total authority, a disturbing change in light of the rise of fascist movements in Italy and Germany. Scholem saw the reliance on the leader's decrees as a product of the movement's earlier lack of ideology. He labeled the new ideology "unscrupulous mysticism." Echoing his earlier polemics, he claimed that the Blau-Weiss's lack of commitment to Hebrew and to the cultural heritage of the Jewish people was responsible for its political bankruptcy. A great abyss therefore separated the sterile Blau-Weiss from the figure of the *halutz*, or pioneer, in Palestine.

The letter, Scholem's final volley against the German Zionist youth movement, laid out some themes that we shall encounter again. Mysticism was a dangerous doctrine that in the wrong hands could fuel the militaristic and authoritarian nationalism that had so infuriated him during the Great War. The antidote to such an ideology was the Hebrew language and the renaissance of Jewish tradition. The letter was signed by fourteen others, some of them the dramatis personae we have encountered from Scholem's early years: Erich Brauer, Grete Brauer, Aharon Heller, Meta Jahr, and Elsa Burchhardt. All these would fulfill their Zionist commitment in Palestine.

In the summer months of 1923, Scholem prepared his own journey to the land of his utopian dreams. He packed up his library of 1,709 books for shipment. The customs required him to provide a list of the books, a copy of which he kept and which gives us today an excellent window into the range of his reading. In Frankfurt, he met and befriended Fritz (Shelomo Dov) Goitein, a young Jewish scholar who was also on his way to Palestine, and they resolved to travel together. Goitein was to become the greatest historian of the Jews in the Muslim world and especially of the famed Cairo Geniza.

In order to enter Palestine, then under the British Mandate, it was necessary to have a "certificate," or visa. These were limited, and the Zionist Executive reserved them for pioneers. If an immigrant had no capital, which could also be used for admission, he or she had to show either marriage or engagement to someone in Palestine or the promise of employment with the necessary skills. Escha Burchhardt had proclaimed a fictitious engagement to a resident, Abu Hushi, who would later become the longtime mayor of Haifa. When she arrived, she was invited to live at the home of Hugo Bergman, whom she and Scholem had met in Bern. Bergman, a classmate of Franz Kafka and a member of the Prague Zionist Bar Kokhba circle, had immigrated to Palestine in 1920 and was the director of the new Jewish National Library. In order to get a visa for Scholem, Escha arranged to have Bergman offer him a fictitious position as head of the Hebrew section of the National Library. This fiction would open the door to his entire future.

Scholem left Berlin on September 9, 1923, and traveled to Munich, where he celebrated Rosh Hashanah. From there, he proceeded to Trieste, where he met Goitein, and on September 14 they took a steamer to Alexandria. At Alexandria, they boarded a small coastal ship that brought them to Jaffa on September 20. Burchhardt was waiting for him, and they traveled to Jerusalem, where they were domiciled in the Bergman household. And so began the almost sixty-year saga of Gershom Scholem in the Land of Israel.

5

A University in Jerusalem

JERUSALEM, 1923. A very different place from the booming city of Berlin that Scholem had left. Although it was the largest city in Palestine at the time, Jerusalem remained a dusty backwater. When Scholem arrived, it was still not electrified, and sewage flowed through the streets. But the British authorities, who had recently received a mandate over Palestine from the League of Nations, had begun the process of modernizing the city, paving roads and establishing a modern postal system (the latter of great importance to Scholem as an inveterate correspondent). Jerusalem had grown slowly over the preceding quarter-century. In 1896, it had forty-five thousand residents, but the number had risen to sixty-two thousand the year before Scholem's arrival. Of these, thirty-four thousand were Jews, thirteen thousand Muslims, and nearly fifteen thousand Christians (the latter a mixture of Arabs and foreigners). The increasing number of Jews owed much to the wave of immigration—referred to in Zionist history as the Third Aliya—that resulted from the Balfour Declaration in 1917, the British conquest of Palestine in early 1918, and the civil war in Russia from 1918 to 1921. Most of the forty thousand immigrants who arrived between 1919 and 1923 were from eastern Europe, and only small numbers, like Gerhard Scholem and Escha Burchhardt, who came at the tail end of the Third Aliya, hailed from German-speaking lands.

Within a few weeks of his arrival, Gerhard announced his engagement to Escha and married her on a Jerusalem rooftop on his birthday, December 5, 1923. Even Arthur was delighted with the news of the engagement, responding on November 1 in his customary ironic fashion:

> I have read your letter with its somewhat timid announce-ment of your engagement to Fräulein Burchhardt. I am not nearly as surprised as you, in your naiveté, seemed to think I would be. . . . So I wish you every happiness in your marriage. You seem to think I have something against Fräulein Burch-hardt. This isn't true. She comes from a good home, which I consider so important that I can't raise the least objection to your marriage. . . . How you'll run a household on such a small salary is your business. You cannot count on financial help from either set of parents—at least, not from me.[1]

Arthur's warning that he was not about to support his youngest son's Zionist adventure was, for once, not merely the result of his reflexive stinginess. The inflation in Germany had reached record heights. Betty reported to Gerhard two weeks earlier that her letter to him would cost 15 million marks in postage and probably 30 million two days hence. Bread cost 900 million, then 2.5 billion, then 5.5 billion. Although Arthur, with his two eldest sons, kept the business afloat by printing money for the government, the one thing for which there was an insatiable demand, he had good reason to fear for his financial future. But around the time of Gerhard's marriage, the mark was stabilized with the issuance of a new currency, and Germany entered into a period of relative stability.

The financial travails of his family seemed to have had little effect on Gerhard, who made it a practice to order both necessities and luxuries—chocolates, marzipan, sausages—from his mother. Some four years later, when he had a secure academic appointment, Betty wrote to him in annoyance, probably both real and feigned:

> It's really dreadful to get a list of everything we *should* send you, followed by a hue and cry because we sent the wrong thing. . . . You can buy your own filing cabinet, instead of constantly nagging me for one. I bought two *sausages* for you today with my last penny. They'll be off to you tomorrow. Leave me in peace for a while! . . . There's no cure for an irritable temperament.
>
> Two ties, two books, a towel, and new sausages are on their way. I haven't even managed to say a thing about the family or myself; I've done nothing but respond to your screams, to the point that it brings tears to my eyes. Oh, son![2]

Scholem had expected to make a living in Palestine by teaching mathematics, and he quickly received an offer of a position in a teachers college in Jerusalem. But unexpectedly his host, Hugo Bergman, turned the fictitious job offer created for his visa into a real position at the National Library. The library had its origins in the Midrash Abravanel Public Library, established in 1892. In 1905, a group of cultural Zionists laid the plans for the National Library, and in 1920 the World Zionist Organization took over the Abravanel Library and renamed it, placing Bergman at its head. The position that Bergman created for his houseguest was as head of the Hebrew Division. Although the salary was lower than the one offered by the teachers college, Scholem eagerly accepted it, since nothing could have been closer to his heart than Hebrew books.

For the better part of the next two years he spent his days working in the library and devoted his nights to his scholarship. But then, in another stroke of luck, the long-planned Hebrew University was inaugurated, on April 1, 1925, and, with his Ph.D. from the University of Munich, he was ideally positioned for an appointment. The idea of a Jewish university, like that for the National Library, predated Zionism and was motivated in part by anti-Semitic quotas on Jewish university students and professors in Europe. But Zionist intellectuals like Ahad Ha'am and Hayim Nahman Bialik saw a university in Jerusalem not just as an answer to anti-Semitism but as the embodiment of the new Hebrew culture that would emanate from Zion. The enterprise was not without contention since the dominant Zionist labor movement in Palestine regarded intellectual projects as less pressing than agricultural settlement, and some even thought a university belonged better in the Galut. Nevertheless, with the energetic efforts of an unusual American rabbi, Judah L. Magnes, who would become the university's first chancellor, sufficient resources were mobilized from donors to permit three initial institutes to be opened: Microbiology, Chemistry, and Jewish Studies. The Institute for Jewish Studies was initially tiny, and the department of philosophy consisted of one faculty member: Gershom Scholem (whose field of studies was, of course, not exactly philosophical).

On November 1, 1925, a half-year after the university's opening ceremony on Mount Scopus, several of the newly appointed faculty gave inaugural lectures. Scholem was preceded by Joseph Klausner, who had been appointed to the chair in modern Hebrew literature. Klausner was a passionate nationalist who supported Vladimir Jabotinsky's militant, antisocialist Revisionist Party. Although he saw himself primarily as a historian of the Second Temple Period (his book on Jesus of Nazareth was a widely hailed, if controversial, effort to reclaim the founder of Christianity for Jewish history), a sharp conflict among the founders of the university blocked his appointment in that field.

Scholem had heard a speech by Klausner in Petah Tikva shortly after his arrival in Palestine. He found Klausner's nationalist views repellant and his scholarship superficial. To his friend Ernst Simon, he wrote of Klausner's inaugural lecture in 1925: "I consider the appointment of Klausner in an ostensibly 'non-dangerous' post like the history of literature as a highly questionable mistake of pure cowardice (or, in the long run, fear). . . . You can believe me, it's obscene to let [someone better suited to teach] in a girls' school hold a position in the Jerusalem University. . . . I had the terribly painful task of speaking after Klausner's unbelievably stupid and self-important lecture. In short, God makes his sun shine on all sorts of beasts."[3] Klausner would continue to be Scholem's bête noire, representing both a politics and a kind of popularized scholarship he abhorred; in 1927, Scholem would clash with Klausner over the appointment of a lecturer in Yiddish, which Klausner opposed on the grounds of extremist Hebraism.

Scholem's lecture took up a subject that had a long history: whether Moses de León, a thirteenth-century Kabbalist, had written the *Zohar*, the greatest work of Jewish mysticism. The *Zohar* purports to have been written by its main protagonist, the second-century rabbi Shimon bar Yohai, but persistent rumors held that the real author was León, who had promoted the book in writings under his own name. Several modern Jewish historians, notably Heinrich Graetz, elevated these rumors to historical fact. Scholem's lecture was a refutation of Graetz, claiming that important sections of the *Zohar* dated back to antiquity, if not to Shimon bar Yohai. He was no doubt motivated by Graetz's contemptuous dismissal of the *Zohar* as a forgery, and he had an interest in showing that the Kabbalah, of which the *Zohar* was the most important book, had ancient roots. But the lecture, later published, was based on a strong philological foundation, arguing that León's early writings quote from the *Zohar*, which must have come earlier. I shall return to this question in a later chapter, because it was one of the few subjects about which Scholem—so definite in his opinions—changed his mind.

The next few years witnessed a veritable explosion of publications. Many of these were reviews in the new bibliographical journal of the National Library, *Kiryat Sefer*. But Scholem also published substantive articles on alchemy and Kabbalah, a translation of a Hebrew version of a work of Arabic esotericism, an article on the Sabbatian theologian Abraham Cardozo, essays on eighteenth-century Hasidism, and a series of articles on unknown texts of Kabbalistic literature. Some of these were written in German and some, particularly those in *Kiryat Sefer*, in Hebrew. (For much of the period before World War II, Scholem signed his German writings "Gerhard Scholem"; in Hebrew, he went under "Gershom Scholem," the Hebrew name he began to use with his Zionist comrades during World War I. However, most of his close German-speaking friends as well as family continued to call him Gerhard, the name I shall use when treating his most personal relations.)

Perhaps the most important of his publications during the 1920s were an annotated bibliography of books and articles dealing with Kabbalah (*Bibliographia Kabbalistica*, 1927, published, like his dissertation, in Robert Eisler's bogus series) and a long essay titled "On the Question of the Emergence of the Kabbalah" (1928). The first, 230 pages long, represents a synthesis of all prior scholarship and lays the groundwork for Scholem's own enterprise. It is divided into sections: "Gnosis," "Kabbalah," "Sabbatianism," "Frankism," and "Hasidism." This organization of the history of Jewish mysticism shows that Scholem already had a clear sense of the range of his field—from late antiquity to the Middle Ages and culminating in the seventeenth and eighteenth centuries. This periodization would dictate the table of contents of his *Major Trends in Jewish Mysticism* a decade later, as well as for the subsequent field as a whole.

"The Emergence of the Kabbalah" was a companion piece to Scholem's dissertation of six years earlier. Whereas there the argument was buried in the footnotes, here Scholem undertook more directly to analyze how and why medieval Kabbalah emerged when it did. (He would return to this subject in full-length books in Hebrew in 1947 and, more extensively, in German in 1962.) He clearly distinguished Kabbalah from Jewish philosophy and insisted that it be understood as part of the history of religion. Naturally, *Sefer ha-Bahir* appears as a bridge between the mysticism of the late rabbinic and Geonic periods of the sixth to the eleventh century and the Kabbalah of the thirteenth century. The *Bahir*, he says, is not a systematic treatise; rather it is a collection of myths and symbols from different sources whose author (or authors) are unknown to us. From what the *Bahir* took the symbolism of the sefirot (divine emanations) also remained unclear. Thus, the emergence of the Kabbalah, in terms of how it arose from earlier mysticism, remained a mystery, although a mystery that Scholem believed had its origins in the Orient and in the Judaization of ancient Gnostic myths.

In addition to scholarship, Lecturer Scholem was expected to devote 50 percent of his time to teaching. The Institute for Jewish Studies was originally intended to be a pure research institute, but the public's demand for courses proved too great. Scholem was not an immediate success as a teacher, at least by his own account: "[My] attempt to create a philosophical discussion about the fundamentals of Kabbalah among my students failed as a result of their absolute lack of talent for thinking."[4] His legacy as a teacher would rest more on his doctoral students.

In later years, Scholem would become perhaps the most powerful faculty member at the Hebrew University, often passing judgments on appointments in fields far removed from his own. In these early years, his influence was considerably more modest, but he did try to exercise it on a matter of deep personal concern: bringing Walter Benjamin to Jerusalem as a professor of literature. In 1927, while on a six-month sabbatical devoted to examining manuscripts in France and England, he spent time with Benjamin twice in Paris, first in April and then again in August and September (on August 23, the two took part in a massive demonstration against the execution of Sacco and Vanzetti and barely escaped a beating by the police). During their second meeting, Scholem introduced Benjamin to Judah L. Magnes. Although Magnes was American-born, he had been educated in Germany and was able to converse with Benjamin in German. He was much impressed by Benjamin's desire to learn Hebrew and undertake studies of Jewish literature from a metaphysical point of view. Magnes arranged a stipend for Benjamin's Hebrew instruction, for which Scholem's wife, Escha, agreed to serve as instructor. But Benjamin had by then met the Latvian Communist Asja Lacis, with whom he had fallen love, and although he repeatedly promised to come to Jerusalem, he also repeatedly put it off. In October 1928, Magnes sent the stipend in one lump sum for Benjamin to study Hebrew in Berlin, and he finally spent a couple of months doing so in the spring of 1929. Scholem was opposed to this method of paying Benjamin, and he turned out to be prescient. The whole project of Benjamin's learning Hebrew came to naught, the result of his entangled personal life, his indecisiveness, and his duplicity. Although Scholem's deep connection to his friend continued, this episode left a permanent scar.

Scholem's unexpected academic appointment as well as his marriage to Escha Burchhardt would suggest that his integration into his new home was as successful as it was quick. But these personal and professional achievements do not tell the whole story. On the contrary, he experienced profound disillusionment with both the political and cultural climate of the Zionist Yishuv (settlement) in Palestine. At the end of December

1924, after he had been in the country only a little over a year, he described to his friend Werner Kraft the absurd mix of people one might encounter there: would-be messiahs and other strange characters. Of his own attitude toward this menagerie, he wrote: "I belong in the most decisive sense to the sect of those who attach apocalyptic views to what will be the fate of the Zionist movement here." This enigmatic statement did not mean that Scholem thought that Zionism should be apocalyptic, but, on the contrary that the movement was threatened by those who held such views. And he added: "I personally suffer in the most catastrophic way from linguistic conditions which one cannot write about rationally. If I should write a treatise about this one day, I won't keep it hidden from you." Here, too, Scholem was hinting at some ideas that recurred in a number of his writings from those first years in the land.[5]

Around the end of 1924, he wrote in an unpublished text that "the dessication of the language has dried out our hearts. . . . Metaphysically, the battle that Zionism has won in the world, we have lost in the land." Exactly what he meant by *dessication* is unclear. Perhaps, to judge from a later writing, he meant that spoken Hebrew had lost its connection to the literary language with its deep historical resonance. Nevertheless, he held that Zionism would "survive its catastrophe."[6]

A year later, he wrote to Ernst Simon: "You know that I came to Palestine without many illusions. After two years, I can assure you that unfortunately I have no more. We are in God's hands on this boat—and we surely have no other—since we can no longer place our hopes in history. No one should foster the illusion that what happens here and will occur in the future (after the open retreat from everything to do with human *tikkun*) has the slightest thing of substance in common with Zionism, in whose name your faithful servant is here." The problem was "the conniving sharks and the seven floods out of hell which have washed over us . . . out of Lodz."[7] This was a frankly prejudiced response to the so-called Fourth Aliya from Poland that began in 1924. These urbanized and middle-class Polish immigrants had no interest in becoming *halutzim* (agricultural pioneers), and even though Scholem himself never got his hands dirty in the fields, he evidently thought that they were corrupting the Zionist ethos by engaging in petty commerce. In the same letter, he also distanced himself from socialism, although not the socialism he associated with Hasidism, a distinction that made his critique largely incoherent. The utopian tikkun that had motivated his Zionism could not be found in the fields of the kibbutzim or in the shops of Tel Aviv. And it was certainly too soon to say that it could be found on the streets of Jerusalem.

Scholem's expressions of disillusionment reached a crescendo in 1926, in a letter in honor of Franz Rosenzweig's fortieth birthday (Rosenzweig's friends had organized a collection of such contributions since he was now quite ill). The letter, which was published only after Scholem's death, has been widely referenced, but in order to understand it properly, we need to look at a number of Scholem's other unpublished manuscripts from the same time.

On April 12, 1926, he titled a two-page rumination "The Despair of Victory." Zionism had achieved its victory "too early," he thought. Zionism and the building of Palestine were not the same and, indeed, an "abyss" had opened up between "victory and reality, Zionism and existence. . . . But we have no language and therefore our sacrifice is in vain."[8] "Zionism" here seems to signify not Scholem's own Zionism but rather the official movement from which he continued to feel alienated, as he had in Germany. On Yom Kippur, 1926, he noted that he had arrived in Palestine exactly three years earlier. The Zionism that had lured him there was not what he found. Instead, it had become a farce, and he could find no bridge between his "secret hopes" and the "hypocritical petty bourgeois nationalist phrases" of the Yishuv. At least, though, he had succeeded in finding one thing: silence, that is, a personal realm of quiet in which he could work.[9]

In an undated text, also evidently from 1926, he raised the question for his generation of German Zionists: "Can we learn Hebrew?" The problem that had aroused his polemics in Germany had not found a solution in the Land of Israel. In the Yishuv, one confronted the clash between Hebrew as a literary language and Hebrew as a vernacular, a spoken language. Modern literary Hebrew was the product and culmination of a long tradition, and it preserved the echoes of revelation. This language is the "fullness and silence of true life . . . [and] is the only genuine sign of the certainty of rebirth." Not so spoken Hebrew, which still lacked any real connection to the literary language and served as a kind of "perfected Volapük" for the Jews who didn't embrace Esperanto (Volapük was an invented nineteenth-century universal language; it preceded Esperanto). But it was not a language that could "live in the world." He concluded: "The possibility of a language like [the one] in Bialik's novella 'Arye Ba'al Guf' would be a [kind of] redemption for us."[10] The Hebrew that had so captivated Scholem in Berlin was the literary language, and it was wrapped up in his utopian hopes for Zionism. Instead, he found himself alienated from the day-to-day spoken Hebrew of the Jerusalem streets.

It was in this frame of mind that he wrote his "confession about our language" for Rosenzweig on December 12, 1926.[11] The Land of Israel was like a volcano, but the eruption that everyone feared—the conflict with the Arabs—masked a more sinister threat: the "actualization of Hebrew." People thought that secularizing Hebrew would "remove the apocalyptic sting" from the language. But that was an illusion. The "ghostly Volapük" that people spoke on the streets still possessed the religious power of the words that might, any day, break through and cause us to fall into the abyss. Now, as opposed to his argument in the earlier essay on Hebrew, the problem was not that written and spoken Hebrew were two divorced languages, but that the degraded spoken language was dangerous because it concealed old religious meaning.

Referring to the Kabbalistic doctrine that the hidden Torah consists only of divine names, he wrote: "In the names the power of the language is decided, its abyss is sealed. . . . God will not remain silent in the language in which he affirmed our lives a thousand times and more. This unavoidable revolution in the language is the only subject that is not spoken about today in this country. Those who have called the language back to life do not believe in the trial that they have inflicted on us. May this recklessness, which leads us on the way to apocalypse, not bring us to ruin."[12] Scholem feared that even secular Zionism might fall victim to religious radicalism—the "abyss" of "apocalypse"—because it had revived the Hebrew language. Zionists took a gigantic risk in creating a nationalist movement based on Hebrew: they walked the fine line between a pragmatic return to history and the apocalyptic drive to end history. But since Scholem's own Zionism was wrapped up in the revival of Hebrew, it would seem that he himself could not escape the danger he pointed out for Zionism generally.

It is fascinating that Scholem should send these pessimistic reflections to Franz Rosenzweig, whose opposition to Zionism had aroused such fervor in him when the two met in 1922. While not a Zionist, Rosenzweig was deeply committed to the Hebrew language as the medium through which the literary tradition of Judaism was transmitted. Perhaps now that he had lived in Palestine for three years, Scholem had come somewhat closer to Rosenzweig's position, even though he still rejected the idea that the Jews were a people outside of history. Or perhaps he felt twinges of guilt over having so fiercely attacked Rosenzweig at a time when he was suffering the first phase of his fatal illness. Indeed, the following year, on a trip to Germany, he was told that Rosenzweig, who was now almost totally paralyzed,

wanted to see him, and he paid him a visit that evidently profoundly affected him.

If Scholem thought that the main problem facing Zionism
was the apocalyptic potential of the Hebrew language, the problem of the Arabs nevertheless asserted itself as equally pressing
and ultimately linked to the dangers of apocalypticism. In 1925,
Arthur Ruppin, who headed the Zionist land settlement office
in Palestine, organized a study group called Brit Shalom (Peace
Covenant), dedicated to rapprochement between Jews and Arabs.
Although initially not intended to act independently of official
Zionist institutions, it soon took on a distinctly political color-
ation. The founding charter of Brit Shalom, published in 1927,
called for creating "a common life between Hebrews and Arabs
in the Land of Israel on the foundation of fully equal political
rights for the two nations with broad autonomy [for each]."[13]
At times Brit Shalom called for limiting Jewish immigration and
land purchases, as well as for founding a binational state of Jews
and Arabs with a united parliament. The group's position challenged the Zionist consensus for a Jewish majority in Palestine.

Brit Shalom had members throughout Palestine and abroad.
Martin Buber joined from Germany, while Albert Einstein and
Judah Magnes voiced their support without formally joining.
In fact, the total membership of Brit Shalom never exceeded
one hundred (a membership list from 1930 that Scholem kept
listed only thirty-eight names); the extensive library of books
and articles about its history is thus in inverse proportion to its
size and influence. Nevertheless, the group offered a fascinating window into the thinking of its mainly central European
members, most of them intellectuals.

A number of the leading members of Brit Shalom, such as
Samuel Hugo Bergman, Hans Kohn, and Felix Weltsch were
products of the Bar Kokhba Zionist group in Prague. They
brought with them to Palestine an acute awareness of the problem of balancing competing ethnic claims, as was the case in

the Bohemian province of the Austro-Hungarian Empire. They were not liberals but rather cultural, even mystical, nationalists who rejected "integral" nationalism—that is, nationalism based solely on one ethnic group. The new Hebrew University was a focal point for Brit Shalom, although many of its members were not connected to the university and certainly not all the faculty were members (Joseph Klausner was a particularly vociferous opponent). Hugo Bergman was perhaps the most prominent faculty member in Brit Shalom; he held an appointment to teach philosophy.

One of the most junior members was Gershom Scholem, but he quickly took a leadership role. Escha Burchhardt also played an active, if unacknowledged, role, and the Scholem Archive contains extensive reflections that she wrote on the political situation. An early proclamation by Brit Shalom members that appeared in both Hebrew and German denounced the call by Jabotinsky's Revisionist Zionists for a Jewish legion that would liberate Palestine for the Jews. Arguing that social justice rather than military force was the correct instrument for promoting Arab-Jewish harmony, the letter lauded the Mandatory government for withdrawing units of the British Army from Palestine and for relying on its police force instead; both the British and the Jews would come to regret this move three years later. But the six signatories deplored the failure of the British to enlist equal numbers of Jews and Arabs in the police auxiliary. Although his name appears last among the signers, Scholem was the letter's author.

A series of events at the end of the 1920s dashed Brit Shalom's hopes for rapprochement between Jews and Arabs. The casus belli was a dispute over the Wailing (Western) Wall, a flashpoint not only then but since. In September 1928, the Jews set up a partition between male and female worshippers, an act that violated a 1925 ruling. When they failed to take the partition down at the end of the prayers, the British, egged on by Arab protestors, sent in armed police, who removed it with a great deal of force.

In response to the ensuing controversy, Scholem published an article in the *Jüdische Rundschau* ("Has an Understanding with the Arabs Failed?"), stating Brit Shalom's position on the Wailing Wall. He tried to strike a balanced tone, criticizing the "ill will of the Arab side, which Brit Shalom has never denied, but rather seeks to explain," and the "tactlessness of the British authorities." But he also laid a significant portion of the blame on a "man who plays an outstanding role in Zionism" and who had excited the fanatical response of the Arabs by claiming that the Jews wished to possess the whole Temple Mount (not just the Wailing Wall).[14] Without naming this man, Scholem was pointing his finger at Menachem Ussishkin, the chairman of the Zionist movement's Jewish National Fund, who had made a speech several months earlier demanding a Jewish state in all of Mandatory Palestine, including Transjordan. Ussishkin also made a specific point of demanding that the Temple Mount be given to the Jews. For Scholem, such dangerous talk had consequences in the increasing Arab enmity.

But worse was yet to come. On August 15, 1929, a group of Jewish nationalists from Joseph Klausner's Committee for the Western Wall, together with members of the Betar youth group of the Revisionist movement, staged a march to the Wall and raised the Zionist flag there. Convinced, evidently, that the Zionists planned to take over the Temple Mount, or what Muslims call Haram al-Sharif ("Noble Sanctuary," the plateau where the ancient temples had stood and where two important mosques now took their place), Arabs began disturbances in Jerusalem. On August 23, the rioting escalated as thousands of villagers streamed into the city. The rioting spread throughout the country, but the worst outbreak occurred in Hebron, where, on August 24, 65–68 Jews, most of them ultra-Orthodox non-Zionists who had lived in the city for generations, were slaughtered. By the time the rioting ended, on August 29, 133 Jews and 116 Arabs lay dead, and 198 Jews and 232 Arabs were injured.

Scholem had some firsthand involvement in these traumatic events, and his reactions to them are very revealing about his conflicted state of mind. He resided until 1932 at 139 Abyssinian Road on the border of Me'ah She'arim, an ultra-Orthodox neighborhood. Although the area was mostly Jewish, it also had Arab residents. On the first day of severe rioting in Jerusalem, Friday, August 23, Scholem left his house to pick up his lunch from his cook, who lived in Me'ah She'arim. He saw a wounded Arab on the street. When he returned home, his housekeeper related with great agitation that she had seen Jews attacking the Arab. He tried to phone either a Jewish doctor or the British authorities to come to the man's aid, but to no avail. After eating his lunch, he decided to go on foot to the Me'ah She'arim police station. His later testimony continues: "When I reached the corner where the Arab lay, I saw a truck driven by a Jew, [with] Dr. Shammas [a Christian Arab doctor], along with several Jews standing by the Arab's body. I, along with several other Jews, helped Dr. Shammas lift the body of the Arab onto the truck. I did not go on to the police station. At least an hour had gone by between my first noticing the Arab and when he was evacuated to the hospital."[15] Why Scholem waited an hour before going to the police remains unclear. He was sufficiently shaken by this and the broader series of events that when he wrote to his mother to describe what had happened, he noted that it was only in areas where the Jews were not armed that the Arab attackers were successful. He failed to note the irony that in his first political declaration, three years earlier, he had argued against the Jews arming themselves.

The Zionist authorities charged the attorney Bernard Joseph with assembling Jewish testimony for the Shaw Commission, which the British government sent to investigate the riots. Joseph approached Scholem about whether his Arab neighbors had had advance warning of the attacks on Jews. Scholem failed to respond, which prompted Joseph to write a curt note urging him to do so. At the bottom of the note, Scholem wrote that he was reluctant to answer because he thought that Arabs might have evacuated not because of advance warnings but because of fear of the Jews. This was a position consonant with Brit Shalom's view that all sides bore responsibility for the events, and one that was certainly supported by Scholem's belief that the Arab he found on the street had been assaulted by Jews. Nevertheless, he did compose an affidavit in English stating that his neighbor, Hassan Boudiri, had left his house with his whole family on August 21. After the "disturbances," Scholem met Boudiri's nephew, who told him that the family left not for political but for medical reasons. Scholem was obviously skeptical that such was the case. He also noted that Bedouins who lived in the area had similarly evacuated two or three days before the riots. This may not have proved that the attacks were premeditated, but it certainly suggests some advance planning.[16]

Scholem's public involvement with the 1929 riots had an afterlife. In 1931, the Vaad Leumi (the National Council governing body of the Yishuv during the British Mandate period) appointed a committee, led by the venerable Zionist David Yellin, which undertook to bring a lawsuit to establish Jewish control over the Western Wall. An article in the Revisionist daily *Do'ar ha-Yom* accused Scholem of refusing in his professional capacity to make Kabbalistic books on the Jewish attachment to the Wall available to the committee. He responded angrily by stating that he was no longer an official in the National Library and that he had never been asked for such books in any official capacity. The committee was free to take out whatever books that it might want without his assistance. However, Yellin, whom he had encountered by chance, had asked him privately for books from his own library. But since he rejected the idea of settling the dispute over the Wall in court—a position, he noted, that was the same as that held by the chief rabbinate—rather than by political negotiation, he refused to assist the committee.

In the two years after the Wailing Wall riots, Scholem published prolifically in Brit Shalom's journal as well as in the general press on political matters. He argued for a binational parliament in which the rights of both communities would be spelled out in advance. He defended Brit Shalom against the charge that it was no more than a "junior partner" of the ultra-Orthodox and anti-Zionist Agudat Yisrael. And he wrote strongly in favor of the nonpolitical, cultural Zionism—the legacy of Ahad Ha'am—to which he had pledged allegiance in Germany. The following, from 1931, gives a good sense of his point of view in terms that remain relevant today: "If the dream of Zionism is numbers and borders, and if we can't exist without them, then Zionism will fail, or, more precisely, has already failed. . . . The Zionist movement still has not freed itself from the reactionary and imperialistic image that not only the Revisionists have given it but also all those who refuse to take into account the reality of our movement in the awakening East."[17]

Above all, his fears that the secularization of Hebrew might unleash apocalyptic politics took increasingly concrete form in the highly charged atmosphere of this period. An exchange with the novelist Yehuda Burla sharpened the issue for Scholem. Burla, writing in the trade-union newspaper *Davar,* accused Brit Shalom of trying to sever the national ties between the Jews in the Yishuv and those in the Diaspora by calling for limits on immigration and the formation of a binational entity with the Arabs. He concluded that Brit Shalom "profaned the nation's holy of holies—its hope for complete redemption." Scholem responded by denying that redemption—the religious doctrine of messianism—had any place in Zionism: "I absolutely deny that Zionism is a messianic movement and that it has the right to employ religious terminology for political goals. The redemption of the Jewish people, which as a Zionist I desire, is in no way identical to the religious redemption I hope for in the future. . . . The Zionist ideal is one thing and the messianic ideal another, and the two do not meet except in the pompous phraseology of mass rallies, which often infuse our youth with a spirit of new Sabbatianism, which must inevitably fail. The Zionist movement has nothing in common with Sabbatianism."[18] This is an extraordinarily significant statement of Scholem's views of Zionism and messianism. It surely flowed out of his resistance to the militaristic nationalism of World War I Germany, an ideology that he believed reflected the dangers of applying messianic language and aspirations to politics. The "mass rallies" which promoted a new Sabbatianism clearly referred to Revisionist Zionism, the party of Vladimir Jabotinsky and its militaristic youth movement.

Scholem's invocation of the seventeenth-century Sabbatians also reflected the new turn his research had taken two years earlier. When he was in Oxford reading Kabbalistic manuscripts, he came across a text by Abraham Cardozo, one of the leading disciples of Shabbatai Zvi. Cardozo had justified Shabbatai's conversion to Islam with a doctrine of the "holiness of sin": the Messiah had to descend into the realm of evil in order to effect redemption. Scholem found this heretical doctrine within the heart of premodern Judaism both fascinating and frightening. In 1928 he published an essay on Carodozo's theology, his first foray into the study of Sabbatianism. He concluded the essay with a contemporary warning:

> Thus it was that before the powers of world history uprooted Judaism in the nineteenth century, its reality was threatened from within. Already at that time [i.e., the time of Sabbatianism] the "reality of the Hebrews," the sphere of Judaism, threatened to become an illusion. . . . The messianic phraseology of Zionism . . . is not the least of those Sabbatian temptations which could bring to disaster the renewal of Judaism. . . . As transient in time as all the theological con-

structions, including those of Cardozo and Jacob Frank [the leader of an eighteenth-century Sabbatian offshoot in Poland], may be, the deepest and most destructive impulse of Sabbatianism, the hubris of the Jews, remains.[19]

Jabotinsky's Revisionist movement might have been totally secular, but by making maximalist demands, it awakened the same messianic fervor that brought seventeenth-century Sabbatianism to grief. (Shabbatai Zvi and some of his followers converted to Islam, while Jacob Frank and his followers converted to Catholicism.) Note also that Scholem invoked the title of Oskar Goldberg's *Reality of the Hebrews*, which he detested, even though Goldberg had no connection to right-wing Zionism. For Scholem, the "renewal of Judaism"—and not borders, numbers, and nationalist slogans—was the real goal of Zionism. Or, as he put it in a letter to Walter Benjamin on August 1, 1931: "The development of the last two years . . . made evident the radical split between my conception of Zionism, which I heard characterized as a religious-mystical quest for a regeneration of Judaism . . . , and empirical Zionism, whose point of departure is an impossible and provocative distortion of an alleged 'solution to the Jewish question.' . . . I do not believe that there is such a thing as a 'solution to the Jewish question' in the sense of a normalization of the Jews. . . . Between London and Moscow we strayed into the desert of Araby on our way to Zion, and our own hubris blocked the path that leads to our people."[20]

Scholem's despondency was in reaction to the Seventeenth Zionist Congress, which took place in Basel, Switzerland, where the first congress had taken place in 1897. During a fiery debate over the Passfield Commission's White Paper, which restricted immigration, Vladimir Jabotinsky demanded that the Zionist movement embrace an "end goal" of statehood on both sides of the Jordan River. When the congress rejected his demand, he tore up his delegate card and denounced the congress as not

Zionist. For Scholem, Jabotinsky's position was an ominous threat: if his definition of Zionism should prevail, Scholem and his comrades in Brit Shalom would be drummed out of the movement and declared heretics. Echoing his earlier statement that "Zionism succeeded too early," he wrote to Benjamin: "When Zionism prevailed in Berlin, which means in a vacuum from the point of view of our task—it no longer could be victorious in Jerusalem."[21]

It was in this cast of mind that Scholem responded to the death of Franz Rosenzweig, which occurred on December 10, 1929. Thirty days later, he spoke at length at a commemorative gathering at the Hebrew University and also published a separate review of a new edition of Rosenzweig's *Star of Redemption* in a Jewish community newspaper in Frankfurt. Rosenzweig's death clearly upset him and seemed to call forth the need to define his relationship to the older philosopher. The eulogy demonstrated Scholem's profound grasp of the history of philosophy and Rosenzweig's place in it refuting the abstract doctrines of German idealism. Rosenzweig had returned philosophy to the questions of everyday existence and especially death, a stance that he himself exemplified in his illness and untimely demise. But in addition to an appreciation of Rosenzweig's thought, Scholem used the occasion to articulate his own philosophical position, with which he had struggled since his youth.

Theology, he believed, had gone into eclipse in the modern world, and the efforts of various rationalists to revive it largely added up to a failure: "The divinity, banished from man by psychology and from the world by sociology, no longer wanting to reside in the heavens, has handed over the throne of justice to dialectical materialism and the seat of mercy to psychoanalysis and has withdrawn to some hidden place and does not disclose Himself. Is He truly undisclosed? Perhaps this last withdrawal is His revelation."[22] Modern man had removed God from the world by substituting scientific disciplines for the divine attributes of justice and mercy. But paradoxically, Scholem thought, God's disappearance from the world might be a kind of revelation. Rosenzweig, for his part, believed that the vehicle for restoring humans' relationship to the banished God was the "star of redemption," configured for Jews as the Star of David, a symbol that created a connection through Jewish rituals between God, humans, and the world.

Scholem clearly found in Rosenzweig's star a mystical response to rational Jewish philosophies, but he also believed that Rosenzweig missed the core of such a theology: Kabbalah. Rosenzweig had disdained Kabbalah, but, not surprisingly, for Scholem the Kabbalah provided the key to the star of redemption: "The Kabbalah in its last dialectical form is the last theological domain in which the questions of the Jew's life found a living reply."[23] To be sure, modern Jews, from rationalist philosophers like Hermann Cohen to secular Zionists, ignored or denigrated the Kabbalah: paradoxically, just when it was most needed, it was most overlooked. Although Rosenzweig was unaware of it, he had provided the question for which Scholem had the answer: the star of redemption was nothing less than an invitation to the Kabbalah. In other words, Scholem used his eulogy not just to celebrate Rosenzweig's contribution to modern Jewish thought but more particularly as a springboard for Scholem's own theology.

In his review of the tenth anniversary edition of the *Star of Redemption* the same year, Scholem added another dimension to his simultaneous appreciation and critique of Rosenzweig. He pointed out that Rosenzweig had rejected apocalypticism: his version of redemption lacked catastrophe or rupture in history. Scholem saw the question of messianism differently: "Apocalypticism, as a doubtlessly anarchic element, provided some air in the house of Judaism; it provided a recognition of the catastrophic potential of all historical order in an unredeemed world. . . . Redemption possesses not only a liberating but also a destructive force. . . . Rosenzweig sought at least to neutralize it in a higher order of truth. . . . [I]n Rosenzweig's work the life of the Jew must be seen as the lightning rod whose task it is to render harmless its destructive power."[24] This 1930 text contained almost identical language to what Scholem would use nearly three decades later in an essay on the messianic idea in Judaism. Apocalyptic and the anarchic forces gave new vitality to the "well-ordered house" of Judaism, but they did so at a high price. These forces needed to be "neutralized" if they were not to destroy Judaism and the Jews. It was this neutralization that Rosenzweig provided in his philosophy. Scholem clearly endorsed the move, but he also regretted that Rosenzweig had made it without acknowledging the historical power of Jewish apocalypticism. So sensitive was Scholem about his interpretation of Rosenzweig, however, that when Rosenzweig's widow, Edith, wrote in October 1931 to congratulate him for coming around to a positive view of *Star of Redemption*, he responded with an essay-length letter making his position even more complicated.

As his political statements from the same time reveal, Scholem viewed the Revisionist Zionists as conjuring up the same dangerous forces of apocalypticism in the realm of politics. He, too, wanted to neutralize these forces but not at the expense of eradicating them entirely. In his historical work—and especially in the great essay "Redemption Through Sin"—Scholem remained at once fascinated but also horrified by the anarchic forces that Rosenzweig had ignored but that continued to animate even the modern history of the Jews.

And so it was that Scholem's first eight years in the Land of Israel were marked at once by professional success and political despair. His own secret yearnings for Zion, which had brought him into conflict with the German Zionist youth movement, were now replicated in a new form in Zion itself. His utopian vision for Zionism had little to do with a return to the East ("the desert of Araby") and certainly not with the trappings of a state. The more Zionism strove for such a state, the farther it seemed from his goal, as unclear as that goal often seemed. And the more Zionism embraced nationalism, the more it seemed to him to summon the demons of apocalypse, as his study of Jewish history made plain. It was that study, the discovery of old Jewish texts, writing about them, and teaching about them to a growing circle of students, that Scholem now came to see as his contribution to the renewal of Judaism.

6

———◆❖◆———

Redemption Through Sin

In March 1932, Gershom Scholem received a research leave from the Hebrew University and departed to spend more than half a year in Italy and Germany. Traveling, it seems, without Escha, he disembarked at Naples and hurried on to Rome, eliciting an admonishment from his mother for failing to visit the sights. She wrote, quoting ironically from Goethe's *Faust:* "Parchment—is that the sacred fount/from which you drink, to still your thirst forever?"[1] But parchment was his sacred fount, so he immersed himself in the Vatican Library, imbibing Kabbalistic manuscripts at a furious pace. He did not, however, entirely isolate himself in scholarship. In response to Betty Scholem's inquiry about conditions in fascist Italy, he noted that while Mussolini's regime had little interest in anti-Semitism, it otherwise trumpeted extreme nationalism.

Fascism in Italy certainly had relevance for Germany. Although neither Scholem nor his mother could have known what was coming, they both harbored serious anxieties as the Weimar Republic came apart. Indeed, over the previous year, Betty's letters to her son had been filled with frantic accounts of the hardships facing the family in the deepening economic depression. Gerhard's response was characteristically self-interested. His father's will had tied up his share of the inheritance in the print shop, which was now in danger of failing. He complained to his mother that he could not live as a scholar in Jerusalem without the additional income provided by the business. But the family would soon have more ominous problems.

From Rome, he traveled to Berlin. There he missed seeing Walter Benjamin, who was in France. But he met for the first time Hannah Arendt, a young philosopher who would become a close friend and important interpreter of his work. Arendt had written a doctoral dissertation with Karl Jaspers after having studied with the philosopher Martin Heidegger. She had become a convert to the Zionist cause and would soon flee to Paris, where she befriended Benjamin and worked for the Zionist organization evacuating Jewish children to Palestine.

While Arendt was very much to his liking, he had an allergic reaction to another German Jewish intellectual, Hans-Joachim Schoeps. Only twenty-three years old in 1932, Schoeps was already making political and theological waves among the German Jews. Although most Jews were politically liberal, or even farther to the left, Schoeps favored a far-right politics, including a hankering for the Prussian monarchy, and he had formed a youth group, the Vortrupp, to advance his goals. He vehemently rejected Zionism for its secularism and failure to embrace German identity. After the Nazis came to power, he attempted without a shred of success to negotiate a modus vivendi with them. Scholem was unable to stomach either his views or his actions.

In addition to his bizarre politics, Schoeps had completed a doctoral dissertation, which he published as a book, *Jewish Belief in This Epoch*. Scholem acquired a copy of the work and wrote a savage denunciation of it in the Bavarian Jewish community newspaper. His article has received little attention, perhaps because of the obscure publication in which it appeared and because it was a review of an equally obscure book, one that is, by now, long forgotten. But the review was of signal importance for Scholem since he used the occasion to develop his own theology beyond his earlier reflections on Franz Rosenzweig. When he sent the article to Benjamin, his friend immediately understood its significance and congratulated Scholem on his achievement.

Schoeps had fallen under the influence of the Swiss German Protestant theologian Karl Barth, and he aspired to write a Jewish version of Barth's theology. He rejected the Oral Law and wanted to resurrect a biblical theology based on a "dialectical theology" of revelation. For Scholem, such pandering to Barth's theology was no better than the nineteenth-century German Jewish rationalist aping of liberal Christianity. Schoeps's theology was virtually devoid of Jewish sources, which, predictably, also enraged Scholem, for whom mastery of the whole Jewish canon was essential.

It would have been easy to dismiss Schoeps, but Scholem offered his own alternative to his opponent's theology. In terms that we can recognize from his youthful writings, he asserted that the truth of Judaism lay in *tradition*, the vast and variegated literary sources of the previous three thousand years. This tradition was grounded in revelation, but revelation was "the absolute, meaning bestowing that becomes explicable only through ... tradition. ... Nothing in historical time requires concretization more than the 'absolute concreteness' of the word of revelation." The "concrete word of God" (the phrase was one that Schoeps lifted from Barth) had no meaning in itself but became meaningful only as human beings responded to it and gave it meaning in the literary tradition.[2]

Scholem's theology had its roots in the Kabbalists' idea of

a hidden God and of a secret tradition, but it also sounds similar to the negative theology of Moses Maimonides, the great medieval Jewish rationalist, about whom Scholem was teaching at the time at the Hebrew University. (Since there was not yet a scholar of Jewish philosophy at the Hebrew University, Scholem had to teach philosophy in addition to Kabbalah.) Both Maimonides and the Kabbalists, though approaching the problem from different angles, imagined God as inaccessible and unknowable to human beings directly. (On this point, they were not so distant from Barth.) The Kabbalists tried to solve this problem by portraying emanations of God, called sefirot, as knowable dimensions of God, but, like Maimonides, they believed that beyond these emanations lay the unknowable Infinite, or *ain sof*. These ideas from the historical sources of Judaism resonated deeply with Scholem since they seemed to provide the key to how to think about God in the modern world. As he concluded from reading Rosenzweig, perhaps God's revelation in the modern world could only be his absence.

The ideas that Scholem developed in the Schoeps review would reappear over the next several years in an intensive correspondence with Walter Benjamin about Franz Kafka. For both Benjamin and Scholem, Kafka had become an essential figure, although they differed on how to understand him (we saw how Scholem deployed Kafka as a secular Kabbalist in his 1937 letter to Salman Schocken). Benjamin spent a number of years writing a long essay on Kafka, a shortened version of which Scholem arranged to have published in 1934 in the *Jüdische Rundschau*. For his part, Scholem introduced Kafka to a generation of students at the Hebrew University by teaching seminars on his work. He told Benjamin that Kafka considered himself a Zionist, although whether Kafka, who did devote himself to studying Hebrew toward the end of his life, considered himself a Zionist is debatable.

Benjamin argued that God and revelation were utterly absent from Kafka's work; his writing was instead all about exile and the desire for redemption. For Scholem, on the other hand, God was a nihilistic force in Kafka's writings, and the main problem was the question of revelation and the Law rather than redemption. Kafka expressed from a secular point of view the Kabbalistic idea that the true meaning of the Law, and thus revelation, is hidden and esoteric: "Kafka's world is the world of revelation, but of revelation seen of course from that perspective in which it is returned to its own nothingness."[3] But where the Kabbalists believed they had the key to unlock this hidden wisdom, Kafka's "Kabbalah" was modern: the key to the esoteric truth was forever lost. The Law, Scholem wrote, can never be fulfilled, a formulation that echoes his statements about Zionism. Indeed, in 1934, combining his despair about God's revelation with his despair about Zion, he wrote a poem about Kafka's *Trial* which begins:

> Are we totally separated from you?
> Is there not meant for us, God, in such a night,
> Any breath of your peace
> Or of your message?
>
> Can the sound of your word
> Have so faded in Zion's emptiness
> Or has it not even entered
> This magical realm of appearance?[4]

Scholem returned to Jerusalem in early November 1932 for the opening of the academic year. By now, the drumbeat heralding Germany's descent into Nazism was loud and furious. On November 20, Betty wrote to her son, "I read in *Voss* [the *Vossische Zeitung*, a liberal Berlin newspaper favored by many Jews] that Hitler will become chancellor after all. But he won't be any different from the others."[5] It is hard to think of a less accurate prophecy. Hitler was appointed chancellor on January 30, 1933. A month later, a deranged Dutchman set fire to the

Reichstag, providing the Nazis with the pretext to smash their enemies on the left. One of the first people they picked up was Werner Scholem, although they released him after five days.

Werner had reason to feel that he might not be harmed further. He had been expelled from the German Communist Party in 1926 for Trotskyist leanings and had soon afterward abandoned politics completely for a career as a lawyer. He was hardly a threat to the Nazis. But his prominence in the early 1920s as one of the most vociferous members of the Reichstag and his easily caricatured Jewish physiognomy were not forgotten, especially by Joseph Goebbels, who mentioned him by name in a number of his speeches before and after the Nazis seized power. On April 23, 1933, Werner and his wife, Emmy, were both arrested. It appears that Emmy was the regime's initial target; she was accused of involvement in a conspiracy to infiltrate the army. However, she was released five months later while Werner continued to languish in prison (Emmy soon escaped to London with their two daughters). Two years later, he was put on trial for treason and acquitted, but immediately thereafter taken into "protective custody": imprisonment in a concentration camp. Goebbels was not about to forgive the Jew Scholem for his barbed taunts of the Nazis ten years earlier.

Betty Scholem was frantic to help her son, spending untold hours at Gestapo headquarters and making arduous trips to concentration camps. Her efforts proved futile and took an enormous toll on her health. Her letters to Gerhard offer a remarkable account of what life was like for Jews in Nazi Germany, especially when a family member fell afoul of the regime. Gerhard himself was equally concerned about his brother, although, like Betty, he could not understand why Werner, who had had an exit visa and a letter of recommendation to a university in Switzerland, had not decamped before he could be rearrested. Later, in 1935, he tried to get Werner a certificate to immigrate to Palestine, but without success. Walter Benjamin's brother

Georg also fell into the hands of the Gestapo, and Walter and Gerhard exchanged anxious information about the fate of their respective siblings.

Scholem immediately understood the historical import of what was happening in Germany. On several occasions, starting in 1933, he compared the situation of Jews in Germany to the expulsion of the Jews from Spain in 1492, one of the greatest traumas in Jewish history and one that would play a major role in his own later reflections. But the main difference between Spain in 1492 and Germany in 1933, he believed, was that there were no "national Spanish Jews"—that is, Jews whose primary identification was with their country rather than their religion. (He might have been thinking of his brother Reinhold, who identified first and foremost as a "national German.") The German Jews, because they had assimilated and viewed themselves as German, were less able to resist the new regime. Of course, for the Spanish Jews, conversion to Christianity had offered an escape from expulsion, something that was not true for the German Jews. Writing to Benjamin after the April 1, 1933, boycott of Jewish shops, Scholem wondered whether an active pogrom in Germany, as opposed to the "cold pogrom" of the boycott, might benefit the Jews since it "represent[ed] almost the only chance of bringing about something positive from such an eruption."[6] Such an eruption, of course, did occur five and half years later on Kristallnacht and, as Scholem intuited, it caused a new torrent of refugees to flee Germany, many of them to Palestine.

In Palestine, the effect of the Nazis' seizure of power was felt almost immediately as terrified German Jews flooded the country. By July 1933, over six thousand Jews had immigrated, a number that would rise to ten thousand by year's end. Many of these immigrants were professionals. Employment could be found for doctors and engineers, but for academics, especially in the humanities, the prospects were dismal. Scholem exerted himself on behalf of some of these scholars. In August 1933, at a time when many Jewish professors were being thrown out of their positions in Germany, Scholem received his promotion to full professor.

Scholem helped secure employment for Hans Jonas, a scholar of ancient Gnosticism whom he had met during his student years. And he made a major effort to bring Martin Buber to Jerusalem by chairing a task force charged with creating a chair in comparative religion. In a letter to the university authorities, he wrote that there was no one better in the world to teach the subject than Buber. And in a letter to Buber, he reported on his efforts with extravagant praise for the man with whom he had clashed so ferociously during the First World War. Scholem must now have been aware that he was secure in his professorship whereas Buber, who had lost his position at the University of Frankfurt, was a supplicant. Buber would elect to remain in Germany to support educational efforts among the besieged German Jews, finally coming to Jerusalem in 1938, when he took up a chair at the Hebrew University.

Other friends were not so fortunate. The literary critic Werner Kraft, who had been working as a librarian in Hannover, had no real hope of employment, as Scholem wrote to Benjamin. Kraft came to Palestine in 1934, but, like many German Jews, he failed to learn Hebrew and had to eke out a marginal existence working for foreign institutions in Jerusalem. Another of Scholem's friends, Gustav Steinschneider, had a more surprising career in exile. We recall that Scholem and Steinschneider met in the German army before Scholem was hospitalized in the psychiatric ward. Steinschneider never acquired either an academic degree or a profession. Although he was not a Zionist, he came to Palestine after Hitler's rise, with no hopes of employment. Scholem intervened with his old boardinghouse friend Zalman Rubashov, who in turn contacted Meir Dizengoff, the mayor of Tel Aviv, and a solution was found: Steinschneider became a street sweeper, a "profession" that allowed him the free time during the day to inhabit Tel Aviv's literary cafés. Later on, he married Toni Halle, Scholem's friend from his university days.

Steinschneider's younger brother Karl also came to Palestine, though not from Germany; he had been in California for the previous six years working in the citrus industry. Scholem had met Karl in the German Zionist youth movement in 1916. Karl spent several years in Palestine in the early 1920s, working in agriculture; he would become a teacher in agricultural training schools. On the side, Karl developed into S. Y. Agnon's main translator into German, and, as Scholem would write after Agnon received the Nobel Prize in 1966, it was Karl who made it possible for the Swedish committee to read Agnon's work. For both literary and ideological reasons, Scholem felt a deep kinship with Karl, whom he referred to in a letter to Benjamin as "one of the people in Palestine closest to my heart."[7]

Perhaps most important among the new arrivals was Kitty Marx, the niece of Agnon's wife, Esther, who was to marry Karl Steinschneider in April 1933, a month after leaving Germany, with Scholem serving as a witness at the wedding. Scholem had evidently met Marx while still in Germany, possibly through Karl, although he was also friendly with the Judaica scholar Moses Marx, her uncle. The two met again in Oxford in 1927 when Marx was working on her Ph.D. in English literature, which she received from Freiburg University. During that visit, Scholem introduced her to his mother. After Marx arrived in Palestine, Scholem reminded his mother of that meeting, referring to her as "the enchanting Kitty Marx."[8] Marx, a highly intelligent and strikingly beautiful woman, would work in Mandatory Palestine and the young State of Israel in senior positions in the government bureaucracy. She attracted many suitors, and Scholem, reporting to Benjamin on her wedding, wrote that Marx was "the undisputed world record holder for rejected marriage proposals."[9] Her uncle S. Y. Agnon even wrote a (probably fictional) story in which Marx rejects a Gentile suitor as a result of a prayer book that Agnon gives her.

Before immigrating to Palestine, Marx, on Scholem's recommendation, visited Benjamin, bringing with her Scholem's polemic against Hans-Joachim Schoeps. The two evidently hit it off and immediately developed a strong intellectual affinity. Marx brought several of Benjamin's manuscripts to Palestine for safekeeping with Scholem. Shortly after her arrival, she and Scholem talked far into the night about Benjamin, since Scholem was thirsty for news about his friend. In the subsequent weeks and months, Kitty Steinschneider's name appears with great frequency in the Scholem-Benjamin correspondence as they sent greetings to and from her, while Benjamin complained flirtatiously that she owed him a letter. She also served as a kind of secretary, copying Benjamin's important essay on language so Scholem could send his copy to Benjamin (Benjamin, now in France, had fled without most of his papers). Kitty also offered to pay for Benjamin to come to Palestine, but that project continued to flounder.

The arrival of so many German-speaking intellectuals changed the social makeup of the Jerusalem community. Many of them settled in Rehavia, where in 1932 the Scholems and the Bergmans had built a house with two apartments. From 1935 to 1946, a group of these intellectuals met to socialize and exchange ideas. Initially composed of the Egyptologist Ya'akov Polotsky, the classicist Yohanan (Hans) Levy, and Hans Jonas, the group called itself "Pil" (Hebrew for "elephant") after the first letters of each of their last names. They were soon joined by Shmuel Sambursky, the first physicist at the Hebrew University and later a historian of science; George Lichtheim, a historian of Marxism; and, inevitably, Gershom Scholem. Scholem immediately grasped the joke in the group's name and proposed a modification based on the names of the new members:

"Pilegesh" (Hebrew for "concubine"). The Pilegesh Society met on a weekly basis, and the conversation took place in German. Although Scholem had repudiated the German language while still in Germany, in fact, he never abandoned his mother tongue, writing scholarly articles in both German and Hebrew. Even his daily life was bilingual, and this at a time when Hebrew purists were demanding monolingualism.

The Pilegesh Society debated theology, history, and politics. Members also enjoyed writing poems in German about each other. Shmuel Sambursky was particularly talented, and one of his favorite subjects was Scholem. This witticism captures, tongue in cheek, Scholem's domineering personality:

> When he speaks masterfully, in a voice
> That brooks no contradiction and boldly scales
> The mountain, determined that no other's choice
> To follow him shall succeed, no matter how he rails,
>
> He'll seize the dwarf and bat him to and fro
> Till all audacity gone, the fellow says "enough!"
> While others, looking on, enjoy each throw,
> When suddenly a thoughtless word and rough
>
> Short-circuit-like renders him mute.
> He moves his mouth like an insentient beast
> Speaking with muscles that utter not a toot,
> As if life had no value in the least.[10]

Scholem's tempestuous character had evidently not changed much since his youth, although his position as a respected professor and the admiration of his friends had tamed its more destructive tendencies.

This was not, however, the case in the most intimate sphere, his marriage. Precisely when his relationship with Escha began to disintegrate is not entirely clear. In January and again in May 1929, she wrote two letters to Scholem, in the first of which, titled "On the Characteristics of a Boy (*Bube*)," she lamented

Gerhard's lack of appreciation for her as both an intellectual and as an intimate partner (she complains that he is more attracted to actresses in the cinema). As we might expect, he made high demands in terms of food. The picture she draws is of someone who is not really prepared for a companionate marriage based on love and mutual respect.[11] What she does not say, but what became clear later, was that Scholem was not willing—or perhaps unable—to have children. (Scholem's childlessness with both of his wives is a subject he has left no trace of in his diaries or letters, so we don't know whether it was a deliberate choice.)

By 1932 or 1933, it seems, he had become sufficiently detached from his marriage to contemplate alternatives. In 1932, a young Polish woman who had recently arrived in Palestine enrolled in his seminar on Kabbalah. Fania Freud, a distant cousin of Sigmund, was, according to Hans Jonas, not particularly attractive, but she possessed a highly desirable skill in Jerusalem at that time: excellent knowledge of modern Hebrew, acquired during her gymnasium education in Poland. As a result, a number of German Jewish intellectuals vied for her attention. In addition, she was intelligent, well-educated, and blunt in her opinions. When the relationship started between Freud and Scholem is unclear, but something was certainly afoot by 1934.

After a silence of over eleven years, Scholem suddenly began to write again in his diary. The often-feverish tone recalls an earlier period in his life when inner turmoil also produced the need to put his thoughts down on paper. In the first new entry, dated July 13, 1934, he attributed his desire to write to the death of the poet Hayim Nahman Bialik, an important figure in Scholem's intellectual life, whom he met through Agnon in Germany. (Recall that one of Scholem's earliest publications was a translation of Bialik's "Halakhah and Aggada" into German.) He also wrote a four-page essay on Kafka and Kabbalah, recapitulating themes that were appearing in his letters to Benjamin during this same period. In this diary entry, he struggled with the questions of whether there is divine justice and whether it is possible to be both a sinner and a just person.

Did he mean this last question in a personal sense, perhaps related to his marriage? Perhaps so; he was not only involved in a relationship with Freud (we do not know whether it was platonic), but he had also now fallen in love with his friend Kitty Steinschneider. Kitty and Karl had moved to Rehovot shortly after their marriage, and Scholem, who had corresponded with her on occasion before she came to Palestine, now began to write much more frequently. The two met a number of times during this period. One such get-together had to be aborted due to an unexpected meeting of the humanities faculty at the university, causing Scholem to write humorously—and perhaps flirtatiously—that he hoped they would find an occasion when "a man might meet his [female] friend (not his wife)." The words for "female friend" and "wife" are almost identical in Hebrew, giving him the opportunity for the coy wordplay. Kitty may have also functioned as a kind of muse: the poem he sent to Benjamin about Kafka was dedicated to her and written "for her theological education."[12] And his archive contains two other poems evidently inspired by her.

In the summer and fall of 1934, his feelings for Kitty intensified. Since she did not reciprocate, he told himself to pack away his emotions. He petulantly wrote in his diary that he had to do all the work to keep the relationship—whatever it might have been—alive. On September 12, 1934, he wrote to her complaining of an "infinite and unexplained alienation that exists between us" and of her failure to inform him when she came to Jerusalem. He confessed rather obliquely that the previous half-year had been especially depressing for him. Since Yom Kippur was approaching, he allowed that perhaps he was at fault for their breach and he asked her forgiveness.[13]

This inner turmoil continued at least until November. He confessed then to his diary that what he had experienced was "the truest feeling. Much truer than Grete. But it is dead and love has nothing here that can transform into friendship." He also wrote that Fania Freud, who was visiting her family in Poland, was about to return, and he had therefore decided to lock away his correspondence with Steinschneider, along with "a beautiful picture unworthy of belief that she has sent me."[14] This was the only time after 1920, it seems, that he spoke of his buried feelings about Grete Brauer, whose place in his affections was now taken by Steinschneider.

It is little wonder that Kitty Steinschneider failed to respond to his advances. She had married Karl only a year and a half earlier and in July 1934 gave birth to their son, Assaf. Moreover, it is not at all clear what Scholem wanted from her: perhaps a platonic ménage à trois. The situation bears an uncanny resemblance to Scholem's relationship with Walter and Dora Benjamin in Switzerland shortly after the birth of their son. He seems here to suggest that Kitty did write back, but what her response was remains mysterious since the Scholem Archive contains only a few letters from her to him, while preserving well over seventy letters written over some fifty years from him to her, donated by her son after her death. These later letters suggest no special passion but are rather filled with reports of his activities. Since Scholem saved every letter he ever got, two possibilities exist: Kitty never answered him, which might have been the case in 1934 but cannot have been for all the other years of their friendship, or someone—Scholem himself? Fania Freud?—destroyed her letters. In any event, despite the tensions that arose between them in 1934, Kitty and Gerhard remained close the rest of their lives.

In 1935, his marriage to Escha took a disastrous turn: he learned that she was having an affair with Hugo Bergman, the Scholems' next-door neighbor, for whom Escha worked at the National Library as private secretary. In the incestuous world of Jerusalem intellectuals, this was one of the most incestuous of affairs, given the intertwining of Bergman's and Scholem's careers, first at the National Library and then at the university (Bergman became rector of the university in 1935), not to mention their shared house. Some evidence exists that the affair started in the 1920s, perhaps as early as when Escha came to Jerusalem in 1923, a half-year before Scholem arrival, and stayed in Bergman's house.

Bergman's diary from the time contains painful evidence of the breakdown of the Scholems' marriage. Escha was in a fragile state. Several times during this period, she left Jerusalem for long stays at the hot springs in Tiberias. Gerhard reported these trips to Benjamin as cures for sciatica, but it seems as likely that she felt herself unable to be in his presence. It seems also possible that she suffered bouts of depression. As we might expect, Gerhard could not contain his anger and treated her very badly, frequently shouting at her. Escha came crying to Bergman proclaiming: "Either a radical solution or death."[15] On another occasion, she told Bergman how desperately she wanted children; she did not want to be left alone in the world.

By June 1935, a separation seemed increasingly inevitable. In light of the chaos this prospect produced in Scholem's life, he wrote to Benjamin that a visit to Jerusalem was impossible— although Benjamin was not really ready to set sail. Gerhard remained conflicted for at least a half a year about whether he should divorce Escha, but he finally did so on March 26, 1936, writing a few weeks later to Benjamin that these events had "caused very great inward and external difficulties in my personal life." A few days after the divorce, Fania Freud broke off their relationship. In his diary, he speaks about a crisis in his work and notes that this crisis was one of the reasons for his divorce (the opposite seems more likely). To Benjamin he wrote, perhaps more accurately, "My ability to work has been quite paralyzed."[16]

Working through mutual friends, he was able to convince Freud to change her mind. By the fall, they were engaged, and they married on December 4, 1936, the day before his birthday. The same day, he wrote to his mother: "I'm afraid that I have some news that will disappoint you. I must inform you that I decided to marry Fania Freud, a woman whom you know but who has been unjustly and unfortunately cast in a bad light." Signed: "Your newly married but regrettably disobedient (thank God disobedient) son."[17] Betty had visited Jerusalem in 1935 and must have met Fania then, and evidently she blamed her for ruining Gerhard's marriage to Escha. She clearly held Escha in high regard and as late as the 1940s corresponded with her from her exile in Australia.

Escha married Hugo Bergman as soon as Bergman was able to obtain a divorce from his own wife. She fulfilled her wish to have children with Bergman, bearing two daughters. And it appears that Scholem made his peace with the new arrangement: the correspondence over the divorce suggests that it was surprisingly amicable. In fact, his relations with both Hugo and Escha remained friendly, and he corresponded warmly with them when they were abroad.

Gerhard and Fania moved to 28 Abarbanel Street in Rehavia, no small operation given the size of his library. He would remain there for the rest of his life, but as a renter, since, as Fania reported after his death, he believed quixotically that a Jew should not own property in the Land of Israel. At a later date, he purchased two cemetery plots, one for himself and one for Fania, and told her with impish humor that now he had become a property owner. His sole real property was his library, which lined every wall, leaving only a space on which was later hung Paul Klee's *Angelus Novus*, the painting that inspired Walter Benjamin's meditations on the philosophy of history. In 1937, Scholem published a small, tongue-in-cheek booklet, "Kabbalistic Books Missing from the Library of Gershom Scholem."

To his chagrin, the appearance of the booklet immediately drove up the prices of the missing books.

In the spring of 1936, an uprising of the Palestinian Arabs swept the country, surpassing the riots of 1929. The violence also reached Jerusalem. Scholem reported to Benjamin: "Life goes on as usual on the surface, but in reality everything has changed. Almost every younger person, which, above all, includes students at the university, has been conscripted . . . even if privately, to defend against open raids which may occur at any time (and are often attempted). If this keeps up much longer, I will also be obliged to spend several hours at night surveying the landscape from the rooftop."[18] Later, Fania also stood watch on the roof.

Scholem's claim to have been paralyzed by inner turmoil in the period before his divorce is belied by his bibliography. He may have felt paralyzed, but he continued to publish, often at a furious pace. Of particular note are books and articles that appeared in German from the Schocken Publishing House in Germany. Salman Schocken had undertaken to publish translations of important Jewish sources as well as scholarly articles aimed at a wide public. When the Nazis came to power, Schocken became an important force in the cultural resistance to persecution. In addition to books, he published an almanac (pocketbook-size collections of essays and translations), which came out annually between 1933 and 1939, when the Nazis shut down Schocken's operation and he moved it to Jerusalem (the Schocken Library in Jerusalem became an important research institution). Scholem published a series of works in the 1930s through Schocken, including a reissue of his doctoral dissertation and a small volume of translations from the *Zohar*, "The Secrets of Creation," as well as studies on Sabbatianism and Ashkenazi Hasidism. He had proposed to Schocken a comprehensive program for studying Kabbalistic literature, and these publications were down payments on that project. Although his relations

with Schocken were at times rocky, the department store magnate remained an ongoing and important source of cultural and
financial support.

Scholem's first publication in the Schocken Almanac in
1933–1934 was an essay on the Kabbalah after the 1492 expulsion of Jews from Spain. In light of the comparisons he made in
his letters between 1492 and the flight of Jews from Germany
in 1933, the essay must be read not only as historical explication
but also as a meditation on contemporary events. The Lurianic
Kabbalah, named for Isaac Luria of Safed in the sixteenth century, taught that the cosmos started with the self-expulsion of
God; the world could only be created in the empty space from
which God was absent. Luria's myth of creation thus involved
a catastrophe of divine exile. God not only reveals himself; he
also hides himself. This paradoxical theology could not have
arisen, in Scholem's view, without the catastrophe of 1492. If
read together with the theological views Scholem expressed in
his review of Schoeps, it might now appear that the Jews needed
a new Kabbalah to address the catastrophe of 1933. This new
Kabbalah Scholem seems to have found in the fiction of Franz
Kafka, since the modern age required a kind of secular Kabbalah from which God is absent.

What do these publications in German tell us about Scholem? He had, of course, bid good-bye to Germany and to the
German Jews when he emigrated in 1923, but, as we have seen,
he continued to publish in German, not only in scholarly jour-
nals but also in more popular venues like the *Jüdische Rundschau*
and Jewish community newspapers. And as the Pilegesh Society also demonstrates, he continued to enjoy intellectual banter
in his mother tongue. More important, by publishing in German for German Jews during the Nazi period, Scholem showed
that he never turned his back on the community of his birth, no
matter how much he disdained its desire to assimilate.

It was, however, in Hebrew that his most important work of this period appeared, a long essay that, possibly more than any other of his writings, secured his reputation in the eyes of both his colleagues and a wider public as the most provocative Jewish scholar of his generation. The essay appeared in 1937 in the journal *Knesset* of Mosad Bialik, the publishing house established after the great poet's death in 1934. The title of the essay was "The Commandment Fulfilled by Its Transgression" (*Mitzvah ha-Ba'ah be-Averah*) or, as it would appear in a later English translation, "Redemption Through Sin." Scholem appears to have launched research on this essay as early as 1934, when he referred to it in a letter to Walter Benjamin dated June 20. There he reported ironically that he had purchased a seat in a Jerusalem synagogue as "atonement" for writing an essay on religious nihilism. He noted several times that he wrote the essay in Hebrew because "this essay . . . can only be written in Hebrew, anyway, at least if the author is to remain free from apologetic inhibitions."[19] Zionism had made it possible for Jews to explore the most heretical moments in Jewish history since it freed them from the need to justify themselves in the eyes of the non-Jewish world. In later years, Scholem would emphasize repeatedly that Zionism should not dictate a particular view of Jewish history but rather make possible the fullest exploration of all facets of the Jewish experience.

The subject of "Redemption Through Sin" is the theology of the Sabbatian movement, especially after Shabbatai Zvi's apostasy to Islam in 1666. While Shabbatai had performed various "strange acts" before his conversion, such as turning the fast of the Ninth of Av (the date when the two Temples in Jerusalem were destroyed, also supposedly the date of the Messiah's birth) into a feast day, recent historians had tended to view the messianic movement he led with some sympathy. But this attitude did not extend to the period after he converted and the movement descended into religious nihilism and wholesale vi- olation of Jewish law. Insofar as historians had paid attention to these later Sabbatians—and Scholem thought that no one had fully appreciated how widespread their movement was—they treated them with criticism and contempt. It was this picture that Scholem proposed to correct.

Many of the faithful eventually returned to normal Jewish practice, but others, probably the minority, continued to believe that Shabbatai Zvi was the Messiah. These believers split into two groups: the "moderates" who thought that only Shabbatai Zvi needed to descend into the deepest realms of evil (namely, to convert to Islam) to accomplish his mission and that they there- fore remained halakhic Jews, and the "radicals" who thought that they should emulate him. The latter group evolved into the Dön- meh sect in the Ottoman Empire (these *ma'aminim*, or believ- ers, converted to Islam but had their own Sabbatian rituals) and the Frankists in eighteenth-century Poland, followers of Jacob Frank, who converted to Catholicism. In the case of the Frankists, even before their conversion they performed antinomian acts (deliberate violations of the Law), including sexual orgies. With Frank, Sabbatianism descended decisively into nihilism.

Scholem starts his essay by pointing out that both Ortho- dox and modern rationalist scholars were blinded by their own apologetic positions from giving this movement of religious nihilism its due. For Scholem—and this was his most explosive claim—Sabbatianism was the central event in Jewish history on the eve of modernity. He describes how the Sabbatians' hereti- cal theology grew out of earlier Jewish mysticism, a key pillar of medieval Jewish religion, which, while not heretical, neverthe- less contained the seeds of heresy. By shaking the foundations of traditional faith, Sabbatianism paved the way for modern movements, such as the Jewish Enlightenment (Haskalah), Re- form Judaism, and even secularism.

Sabbatianism therefore had a paradoxical career: it was a

movement within Jewish mysticism, but it produced the secular rejection of traditional religion:

> Even while still "believers"—in fact, precisely because they were "believers"—they [the Sabbatians] had long been drawing closer to the spirit of Haskalah all along, so that when the flame of their faith finally flickered out they soon reappeared as leaders of Reform Judaism, secular intellectuals, or simply complete and indifferent skeptics. . . . Those who survived the ruin were now open to any alternative or wind of change; and so, their "mad visions" behind them, they turned their energies and hidden desires for a more positive life to assimilation and the Haskalah, two forces that accomplished without paradoxes, indeed without religion at all, what they, the members of "the accursed sect," had earnestly striven for in a stormy contention with truth, carried on in the half-light of a faith pregnant with paradoxes.[20]

No reader can ignore the passionate rhetoric in which Scholem tells his story; this is anything but dry history. Phrases like "ruin," "wind of change," "pregnant with paradoxes," "catastrophe," and "rupture" fill the essay and give it a sense of existential urgency. There can be little doubt that Scholem had come to inhabit the minds of his subjects, experiencing the crisis of their faith in a very personal way.

Nowhere did Scholem's tense relationship to his subject become more fraught than in in the last section of the essay, devoted to Jacob Frank (Fania had translated Frank's Polish writings for him). He begins:

> Jacob Frank (1726–91) will always be remembered as one of the most frightening phenomena in the whole of Jewish history; a religious leader who, whether for purely self-interested motives or otherwise, was in all his actions a truly corrupt and degenerate individual. Indeed it might be plausibly argued that in order to completely exhaust its seemingly endless potential for the contradictory and the unexpected the

Sabbatian movement was in need of just such a tyrant, a man
who could snuff out its last inner lights and pervert whatever
will to truth and goodness was still to be found in the maze-
like ruins of the "believers'" souls. . . . [H]e remains a figure
with something hidden, tremendous if satanic power.[21]

There is something shockingly vitriolic about Scholem's language here. It was as if, when it came to Frank, he had abandoned the objectivity he preached at the beginning of the essay,
as if he felt it necessary to construct him as a demonic or satanic
figure, to make Frank so repulsive that he, the historian, would
not fall for his seductive charms.

Shmuel Sambursky intuited as much in a poem he wrote
about Scholem three or four years after the publication of "Redemption Through Sin:"

O, fisher in the quagmire of murky waters,
You interpret distant stammering as form
Transform a whirling, whipping wave of words
Into sense-filled sentences well-structured and long,
Expending thus the intellect's precious hoard
On matters of a lower order, true.
You should rise up from Zohar's swirling bleak and blackish fog
Into the realm of true and healthful light
Before the Frankists' rotting, poisonous fruits
Accomplish their dark deed and do you in.[22]

Did Scholem escape the "Frankists' rotting, poisonous fruits"?
The years 1934–1936 were a period of profound personal turmoil, as his marriage collapsed and he found himself buffeted
by powerful romantic emotions. He clearly struggled with issues
of good and evil, as his ruminations on Kafka show, and perhaps he felt deep guilt about his behavior in his personal relationships. We have seen that in the birthday letter to Salman
Schocken of 1937 (thus written just after the publication of "Redemption Through Sin") he confessed to his attraction to the

"fine line between religion and nihilism." Could he have seen in the Sabbatians—and perhaps most of all in Jacob Frank—a frightening example of what happens when there is no law and no morality? In fact, beneath his damning words about Frank lies an inescapable fascination, as if Frank personified his own demons. This simultaneous attraction and repulsion hints that, even though Scholem never says so explicitly, the remarkable rhetoric of the essay might be a projection onto history of its author's own innermost struggles.

At the same time, "Redemption Through Sin" can also be read against the backdrop of the political catastrophe of the 1930s. It is hard to escape the feeling that the way Scholem described Jacob Frank, the demonic "tyrant," pointed toward a much more demonic figure on the contemporary stage. If Scholem had earlier worried about right-wing Zionists resurrecting the "hubris" of the Sabbatians, the world now faced a much greater evil, which had already seized one member of his family. The historical catastrophe of the expulsion from Spain now seemed to foreshadow a world in which God was hidden and nihilism unleashed.

7

—◆◄◆►◆—

Kabbalah and Catastrophe

BY 1937, Scholem's personal life had regained stability, his marriage to Fania providing him with an intellectual and domestic helpmeet. But the situation in Germany continued to deteriorate. While his two older brothers began to organize their immigration to Australia, Werner remained in the hands of the Gestapo. During her 1935 visit, Betty had opened an account in Palestine with three hundred pounds sterling in case of emergencies. In July 1937, she protested what she called Gerhard's blocking of withdrawals from the account as well as his chutzpah in using the money in the account—her own money—to buy her a jacket as a seventieth birthday present. The money would become essential the following year to buy an exit visit for Erich.

In Palestine, the most hotly debated political news was the report of the Peel Commission, which the British had dispatched to propose a solution to the Arab uprising. The commission's

White Paper, issued in July 1937, for the first time suggested partitioning the country between Jews and Arabs. Scholem's stance was ambivalent: "I am in principle against partition because I consider an Arab-Jewish federation for the entire area of Palestine to be the ideal solution," he wrote on July 10.[1] However, he recognized that conditions for such a federation, which Brit Shalom had advocated in the 1920s, no longer existed and that there was no possibility of achieving anything better than partition. He also lamented the Peel Commission's rejection of the Balfour Declaration and of Hebrew as an official language, as well as what seemed to be the abolition of Jewish rights in Jerusalem. He had now become a political pragmatist, even though he had not forgotten the utopian ideals of his youth. In the end, the Arabs rejected the Peel Commission's recommendations, and it would take more than a decade—and much bloodshed— for partition to become a reality.

In the same month, Scholem received an invitation from the American Reform rabbi and Zionist leader Stephen S. Wise to serve as a visiting professor at the Jewish Institute of Religion in New York and to present the Hilda Stroock Lectures. Here was a golden opportunity to summarize and synthesize his studies of Kabbalah for a general audience. The shape of these lectures, to be titled "Major Trends in Jewish Mysticism," was already apparent in the article he published in 1932 in the German *Encyclopedia Judaica*, whose table of contents closely mirrors that of the later lectures. It was also apparent in the detailed proposals he made to Salman Schocken for a comprehensive account of Kabbalistic literature and its content. But while the Schocken program never came to fruition, the Stroock Lectures provided the occasion for a partial fulfillment of his more ambitious agenda.

Remarkably, Scholem wrote the lectures (there were seven, with two more added later) before he left Jerusalem, in less than two months, from the middle of November 1937 to early January 1938. His English was not yet adequate for writing lectures, so he decided to have them translated. He feared that translating from Hebrew to English would present too steep a challenge, so he wrote the lectures in German, and George Lichtheim, the scholar of Marxism in the Pilegesh Society who had spent part of his youth in England, rapidly rendered them into fluent English. It is also likely that given the time constraints, Scholem felt he could write the lectures faster in his native tongue. In later years, a mythology surrounded the lectures, since they never appeared in Hebrew during his lifetime, although they were translated into many other languages. Some said that Scholem wanted to force his students to read them in English. Closer to the truth was Scholem's stated view that, if he had allowed a Hebrew translation, he would have felt compelled to drastically revise and expand the lectures. A Hebrew version of the book did not appear until 2016.

In February 1938, Scholem stopped off in Paris on his way to New York where he met up with Hannah Arendt and her husband, Heinrich Blücher. As the head of the Paris office of Youth Aliya, Arendt had several times accompanied groups of children to Palestine, and the friendship between her and Scholem deepened there. Walter Benjamin had also become friends with Arendt, who would later play a significant role in bringing his work to the attention of the English-reading public. The four friends met several times during Scholem's Paris stay.

Scholem had not seen Benjamin now for eleven years. The two engaged in extended debates, mostly over Marxism, which had long claimed Benjamin's allegiance. Although Scholem had previously indicated his reservations about Benjamin's politics in letters as well as in restrained conversation during their last meeting, the discussion in Paris was much more bitter and vociferous. Benjamin now presented his views on language from a Marxist perspective, which clashed dramatically with the earlier theological approach that had so enamored Scholem.

Benjamin had become connected with the neo-Marxist Institute for Social Research, later known as the Frankfurt School,
which had transferred its operations from Germany to New
York. He feared in particular that conflicts with Max Horkheimer, the institute's director, over ideology—Horkheimer saw
Benjamin as more of a mystic than a Marxist—could jeopardize
his stipend, virtually his only source of financial support. This
was also the rather implausible reason he gave in the late 1930s
for not visiting Palestine. Although neither man knew it, this was
to be their last meeting, since Benjamin canceled their planned
meeting in Paris for August 1938, when Scholem was to return
to Palestine via France. How his final meeting with Benjamin
might have affected Scholem's feelings about him remains unclear. As exasperating as he had found Benjamin over the years—
in their difficult personal relations in Switzerland, Benjamin's
scandalous misuse of the Hebrew University stipend, their political differences—his deep feelings for his friend seemed to
overcome any obstacles.

From Paris, Gerhard, accompanied by Fania, set sail for
America. He was obviously greatly excited by the adventure. He
had requested his mother to find him American guidebooks in
Berlin; she had trouble finding any, and no doubt preoccupied
with more pressing concerns in 1938 Nazi Germany, asked him
acerbically why he couldn't get some in Jerusalem. On the boat,
he met the theologian Paul Tillich and his wife (Tillich had
fled Germany for America in 1933), who immediately befriended
him. He was just as warmly received in New York and quickly
made friends with a number of important intellectuals, notably
Shalom Spiegel of the Jewish Theological Seminary and the
neo-Marxist philosopher Theodor Wiesengrund Adorno, whom
he met at the Tillichs' apartment and who had himself just arrived in the United States from England (he had fled Germany
in 1934).

On the face of it, he and Adorno, who was a leading figure

in the Frankfurt School, had little in common, especially politically. But they immediately hit it off, and the correspondence between them, which lasted from 1938 until Adorno's death thirty-one years later, testifies to deep intellectual affinities as well as personal affection and a shared sense of humor. In the 1960s, Adorno sent Scholem his book *Negative Dialectics*, and Scholem confessed that he had nearly broken his head trying to comprehend it. But he made a valiant effort to do so and treated Adorno's very different sensibility with great sympathy. Adorno, for his part, was more open to theological reflections than one would expect of a philosopher steeped in dialectical materialism. He was astonished when Scholem showed him how the Kabbalists wedded Gnostic myth to Neoplatonic philosophy, thus making it comprehensible to a philosopher like himself. Their correspondence does not contain exclusively weighty intellectual matters. At one point, Scholem wittily sends Adorno a recipe for *cholent* (the traditional eastern European Sabbath casserole) for his Christmas dinner; Adorno was Christian on his mother's side and Jewish on his father's.

It appears that Adorno, who himself possessed an overbearing intellect, remained in awe of Scholem, at least in part because Scholem had access to esoteric knowledge beyond Adorno's ken. Here was an excellent example of how Scholem's grounding in the German philosophical tradition had made him an intellectual who could hold his own with others outside the Jewish tradition, even as he made the Kabbalah accessible to them. Adorno immediately recognized in him not a parochial scholar but a world-class intellect whose field of study happened to be Judaism.

During his stay in America, Scholem paid a visit to the Frankfurt Institute's New York office and found much to applaud, including the presence of Leo Löwenthal, the sociologist whom he knew from Rosenzweig's Lehrhaus, and Herbert Marcuse, the Hegelian philosopher and later guru of the New

Left, whom Scholem had met in Berlin. On the other hand, he had a distinctly negative reaction to Max Horkheimer, whose personality and Marxist views he could not abide.

Scholem's lectures took place between the end of February and March 25 and were a great success. Over the next three years, he worked to expand them significantly for publication by Schocken's new American branch (the actual printing was done in Tel Aviv, leading Scholem to complain bitterly about delays in proofreading the English text). Since the book that ensued, *Major Trends in Jewish Mysticism*, still counts as Scholem's most influential publication, it is worth taking stock of some of the key arguments he presented there. Before doing so, however, we should note what was not included in the lectures. Most notably absent was the subject of Scholem's dissertation, the origins of the Kabbalah in Provence and Spain in the twelfth and early thirteenth centuries. This would be the theme of a book in Hebrew published in 1948 and later translated into German and English. He probably decided to leave out this central question because he had amassed so much material on it that he could not imagine confining it to one lecture or chapter.

In the preface to *Major Trends*, he also confesses that the last chapter, on Hasidism, was only a preliminary and tentative survey of that eighteenth-century movement. To delve more deeply would also require an entire book, one that Scholem never wrote. He did write a series of lectures on the subject, which were delivered in English in 1949, but he never published them as a book. Only long after his death did a group of Israeli scholars assemble his various articles on Hasidism into a Hebrew volume titled *The Latest Phase*, while the manuscript of the English lectures remained buried in the archives.

The preface to *Major Trends* is a colorfully written reflection on the twenty years of Scholem's career as a scholar of Jewish mysticism. He presents himself as an archaeologist confronting "a field strewn with ruins" that required painstaking spadework in order uncover the riches that lay beneath the surface. All others who had approached this task had contributed little more than obfuscation and unfounded conclusions. He was therefore a pioneer in virgin territory, "constrained by circumstance and by inclination to perform the modest but necessary task of clearing the ground of much scattered debris and laying bare the outlines of a great and significant chapter in the history of Jewish religion."[2] Note that Scholem's language here mimics the rhetoric of Labor Zionism: he, too, was redeeming the land with his scholarly labor.

While it was certainly the case that no one had undertaken the philological and historical studies to which he had devoted himself since 1919, this self-presentation obscures the fact that both Jewish and Christian scholars had laid the groundwork for Scholem's achievement. A cursory perusal of Scholem's *Bibliographia Kabbalistica* of 1928 makes this plain. He may have thought himself a giant standing on the shoulders of pygmies, but without those "pygmies" it is doubtful if he could have seen as far.

The first chapter of *Major Trends* is a general introduction that takes on the questions What is mysticism? and What distinguishes Jewish mysticism from others? Scholem lays out his general theory of mysticism. Religions start with an immediate experience of God, which they then formulate with laws and other social institutions that distance human beings from the divine. Mysticism represents a "romantic" return to the religion's revelation, an attempt to recapture the immediacy that the laws and institutions have obscured. But of course this third stage can never recover the primitive religion of revelation. Instead, it represents something new, since it recognizes the "abyss" between man and God. This theory was hardly original. In the sphere of Judaism, thinkers such as the liberal German Jewish rabbi Leo Baeck and Martin Buber had already suggested similar ideas, although not focused on Kabbalah as the core of "romantic religion," a term used by Baeck. With this theory, Scholem was taking his place among those who wanted a return to Judaism that did not involve adopting Jewish Law.

Jewish mysticism had certain unique characteristics. As opposed to other mystical traditions which tended to privilege ineffable experiences of God, Kabbalah had a positive attitude toward language, for it saw revelation as a linguistic event (a favorite theme of Scholem's since his student days). It represented the resurgence of myth within a monotheistic religion; the Kabbalists did not consider myth and monotheism opposites. And its focus was not on mystical experience, but on esoteric knowledge of God. The Jewish mystics did not write autobiographies in which they related their experience of union with the divine, but effaced their own lives by writing "theosophy," speculations on God's inner workings. (Scholem described an exception to this rule, the thirteenth-century "prophetic Kabbalist" Abraham Abulafia, in the fourth lecture, which is devoted solely to this remarkable figure.)

An especially troubling distinction between Jewish and other mysticisms—Scholem was thinking primarily of Christian mysticism—appeared at the end of this introductory chapter. Kabbalah, he says, is a masculine doctrine: "It lacks the element of feminine emotion . . . but it also remains comparatively free from the dangers entailed by the tendency towards hysterical extravagance. This exclusive masculinity[,] for which Kabbalism has paid a high price, appears rather to be connected with an inherent tendency to lay stress on the demonic nature of woman and the feminine element of the cosmos."[3] Women represent God's attribute of "stern judgment" (the female "side" of the divine sefirot), and the demonic is the offspring of this feminine sphere. The Kabbalah's failure to include personal mystical experience was also connected to the masculine since women in other traditions were outstanding writers of mystical autobiography.

Scholem here veered away from pure description—there were no female Kabbalists—into a much more subjective judgment when he equated "feminine emotion" with "hysterical extravagance." Of course, as a man of his time, he was not free of prejudice against women (we recall that when he was in Jung Juda in Germany, he declared himself not a feminist, but he also argued for the inclusion of women). What makes this statement more complicated is that Scholem believed strongly that the "demonic" was an integral part of Judaism and that only he was willing and able to ferret it out. In thirteenth-century Kabbalah, the demonic was seen as originating with God, as a result of the masculine failing to properly counterbalance the feminine. Is this why he says that Kabbalah paid a "high price" for its "exclusive" masculinity? What would Kabbalah have been if it were not exclusively masculine? Although Scholem never answered these questions, it would seem that his understanding of gender in the Kabbalah was more complicated than a simplistic dismissal of the feminine as hysteria. In fact, in his chapter on the theology of the *Zohar* (chapter 6), he emphasized with evident fascination the highly erotic nature of the Kabbalah's depiction of God, consisting of male and female elements in a state of constant sexual coupling.

Indeed, Scholem's fascination with the demonic generally underlies much of his writing, especially about Sabbatianism, as we saw in the previous chapter. If the demonic originated out of God in Kabbalah, it also had a highly ambivalent meaning in German literature. Goethe's *Faust* plays upon the demonic as both positive and negative, so when Scholem came to study the Kabbalah, he already possessed such a contradictory sense of the demonic from German culture. The centrality of this word in his vocabulary can be understood only against this German background.

The fifth chapter of *Major Trends* was the only one to present the kind of philological arguments found in his more technical articles, and he delivered it in Hebrew to an audience consisting largely of American Hebraists such as Shalom Spiegel. He did so because he assumed, as he wrote in the book's preface, that most of his English-speaking audience would not be interested in his subject, the authorship of the *Zohar*. He advised his readers to skip the chapter unless they were specialists.

But this modesty was misplaced. In both the lecture and the chapter, Scholem unleashed a bombshell: the author of the *Zohar* was Moses de Léon, the thirteenth-century Kabbalist whom traditional enemies of Kabbalah in the seventeenth and eighteenth centuries had charged with fabricating the work and attributing it falsely to a rabbinic sage. As noted earlier, in his inaugural lecture at the Hebrew University, Scholem had argued that the *Zohar* was based on an ancient text that Moses de Léon had found and quoted from in writings under his own name.

But now, in a rare reversal for someone usually so sure of himself, he came around to Heinrich Graetz's view that Moses de Léon was the author of the *Zohar*. Noting the appearance of Spanish words and place-names in the text's oddly artificial Aramaic and pointing out how Moses de Léon had cleverly quoted from the *Zohar* in order to promote the book he had allegedly found, Scholem came to the conclusion that the *Zohar* was in reality a forgery. Yet where those hostile to the Kabbalah (such as Graetz) used the charge to besmirch its cardinal text, Scholem made this conclusion support his general theory of mysticism and employed a less judgmental term: "pseudepigraphy" (false writing), that is, attributing one's own authorship to a venerable ancient figure. If the third stage of religion was meant to recover the ancient immediacy of God's revelation, what better way to do so than by writing a mystical text in the name of an ancient authority? For the medieval mystics the teachings of Kabbalah were anything but new; they were handed down in secret for centuries and only made visible at a late stage of history. Given Scholem's own belief in the centrality of tradition as the realm in which revelation is interpreted and transmitted, Moses de Léon's brilliant forgery was precisely what made it such a powerful text.

After solving the problem of the *Zohar*'s authorship, Scholem turned to a discussion of its major ideas. He followed this with the history of the Kabbalah after the Jews' expulsion from Spain, enlarging on the article he had published in German on the subject that was also a response to the Nazis' assault on the German Jews. Although he never mentioned contemporary events in the Stroock Lectures (nor had he in the German article), there can be little doubt that he continued to see the watershed event in 1492 as a historical precedent for what was happening before his eyes in Germany. The sixteenth-century Lurianic Kabbalah offered a myth of divine exile and catastrophe that paralleled the historical exile of the Jews from Spain. And it also offered a myth of tikkun, the restoration of God's original harmony, that paralleled the Jews' hope for messianic redemption.

The Lurianic myth provided the theological springboard for the chapter "Sabbatianism and Mystical Heresy." Building on his "Redemption Through Sin" essay, Scholem explained the development of Sabbatianism's heretical theology out of the writings of Nathan of Gaza, the leading prophet of the movement. Sabbatianism was not, as Graetz and others had argued, a response to persecution in the seventeenth century, such as the pogroms against the Polish Jews in 1648–1649, but instead a direct product of the ideas of Lurianic Kabbalah. Insofar as any historical event had caused this mass messianic outbreak, it was the expulsion from Spain. Since Scholem believed, as he first argued in "Redemption Through Sin," that Sabbatianism destroyed rabbinic authority and prepared the way for Jews to enter the modern age, a direct line could be drawn between the expulsion from Spain, Lurianic Kabbalah, Sabbatianism, and modernity.

Whether or not this theory was historically valid, what Scholem accomplished in his book was to fashion a grand myth of his own to explain the great turning points in Jewish history of the previous five hundred years. This was a secular myth that joined the history of national trauma to mystical ideas. And even though the expulsion from Spain was the catalyst, Scholem's myth argued for the development of Jewish history largely through *internal* forces rather than as a result of external causes. At the heart of his sweeping picture were esoteric ideas, the secret doctrines of the Kabbalists. Scholem's area of study, far from being on the margins of Jewish history, he now turned into its core.

The Sabbatianism chapter also contained a surprising argument about why Shabbatai Zvi was seen as the Messiah: he suffered from manic depression. Nathan of Gaza had interpreted the Messiah's alternating states of euphoria and passivity in Kabbalistic terms, which explained Shabbatai's "strange actions" as having meaning beyond the psychological. His depressive states were the result of "demonic and erotic" temptations, while his "states of exaltation" produced his charismatic influence over his followers.

This is the only instance in all Scholem's voluminous writings where he resorted to a psychiatric diagnosis (including learned footnotes!) of one of his subjects. His argument strikingly employs terms that might have applied to his own mental states twenty years earlier. Did he see some resemblance between the Messiah of Izmir and his own youthful messianic fervor? It is noteworthy that he emphasized in this context that manic-depressive illness "does not lead to decomposition and destruction of the human personality and in particular does not affect intelligence." He then notes of Shabbatai Zvi that "as a Kabbalist and a scholar he does not appear to have raised himself above mediocrity."[4] Why follow the first statement with the second? If Scholem saw a similarity between himself and

Shabbatai, he also hastened to distinguish himself from his less intellectually gifted subject. We cannot do more than speculate on Scholem's motivation for offering this diagnosis, but it is noteworthy that he never entirely liberated himself from the conflicting states of ecstatic enthusiasm and paralyzing melancholy that he had experienced in his youth.

The final chapter of *Major Trends* concerned eighteenth-century Hasidism, the movement of charismatic rabbis and their circles of followers, which Scholem argued was the "latest phase" of the history of the Kabbalah. He held, along with other students of Hasidism such as Martin Buber and Simon Dubnow, that the creative period in this movement was limited to the eighteenth century. And since eighteenth-century Hasidism was the latest creative phase, the history of Kabbalah effectively ended then. (After Scholem's death, this conclusion would come under attack.) Based on his belief in the centrality of Sabbatianism to all subsequent Jewish history, he tried to show that Hasidism, too, arose out of the vestiges of Sabbatianism in Poland. But instead of aligning itself with the acute messianism of the Sabbatians, such as Jacob Frank, Hasidism "neutralized" messianism by channeling it into the relationship between the *Tsaddik* (the spiritual leader) and his Hasidim (the term literally means "pious," but in the context of Hasidism it means "followers").

Scholem ended *Major Trends in Jewish Mysticism* with a highly provocative story initially told by the nineteenth-century Hasidic leader Israel of Rishin and transmitted to him by S. Y. Agnon:

> When the Baal Shem had a difficult task before him, he would go to a certain place in the woods, light a fire and meditate in prayer—and what he had set out to perform was done. When a generation later the "Maggid" of Meseritz was faced with the same task he would go to the same place in the woods and say: We can no longer light the fire, but we can still speak the prayers—and what he wanted done be-

came reality. Again a generation later Rabbi Moshe Leib of Sassov had to perform this task. And he too went into the woods and said: We can no longer light a fire, nor do we know the secret meditations belonging to the prayer, but we do know the place in the woods to which it all belongs—and that should be sufficient; and sufficient it was. But when another generation had passed and Rabbi Israel of Rishin was called up to perform the task, he sat down on his golden chair in his castle and said: We cannot light the fire, we cannot speak the prayers, we do not know the place, but we can tell the story of how it was done. And, the storyteller adds, the story, which he told, had the same effect as the actions of the other three.[5]

Does this story indicate the decay of a religious movement transformed from a mystery into a tale? Not at all: the tale itself contains the same miraculous power as the place in the forest and the lighting of the fire. In our time, Scholem implied, the historian is the one who tells the tale and connects his audience to the sacred tradition, even if he himself is not a believer.

For all that, Scholem held out the possibility that the story might not be over: "The story is not ended, it has not yet become history, and the secret life it holds can break out tomorrow in you or in me. . . . To speak of the mystical course which, in the great cataclysm now stirring the Jewish people more deeply than in the entire history of Exile, destiny may still have in store for us . . . is the task of prophets, not of professors."[6] The last sentence of the lectures clearly alluded to the expulsion of the German Jews—and possibly also the looming assault on European Jews generally—which Scholem now saw as an even greater catastrophe than the expulsion from Spain.

Following the completion of his lectures, Scholem spent time in the library of the Jewish Theological Seminary examining Kabbalistic manuscripts that had been unavailable in Europe. He next took a road trip to Cincinnati in order to visit

Hebrew Union College for the same purpose. The trip gave him a chance to experience America outside New York City. As he wrote to Benjamin, although he found America a "strange world," he was clearly fascinated by everything he found.[7] European to his core, he would return eagerly to America in the future as a visiting professor at Brown and Boston Universities in addition to lecturing elsewhere.

He returned to Palestine at the end of the summer, greatly satisfied with his U.S. expedition. But his high spirits were not to last. In November came the news of Kristallnacht in Germany, and Betty, who had resisted emigration on account of Werner's imprisonment, now realized that she had to leave as soon as possible. He also developed a problem with his eyes and had to undergo an operation that left him temporarily unable to work. As he wrote to Shalom Spiegel on January 1, 1939, he was completely exhausted. Moreover, the partition plan proposed by the Peel Commission had gone up in smoke and the Mandatory government had stopped issuing certificates, a disaster only mitigated by officials turning a blind eye to illegal immigration (four thousand Viennese Jews had just arrived in that fashion, fleeing the Nazi terror which had overtaken their country the previous March).

As winter turned to spring and summer, matters did not improve. His eye problems continued at least into March. On May 23, the British Parliament, anticipating war and wanting to ensure that the Arabs would remain quiescent in the coming conflict, approved a new White Paper that severely limited Jewish immigration and land purchases. At the end of June, Scholem wrote to Benjamin of the "unmitigated despondency and paralysis, which have gripped me for months in the face of the state of things here. . . . In this darkness I only know how to be silent." He believed that the capitulation of the English to the Arabs' violence would only encourage Jewish violence. And he was particularly concerned that "the future of Judaism is totally cloaked in darkness." As he had long thought, Palestine was necessary for the revival of Judaism, but it appeared now that Palestine itself was endangered: "We are living in terror." As a result, he was unable to undertake new research, but instead worked on turning his New York lectures into a book, a task he completed in the summer of 1940, and preparing lectures on Shabbatai Zvi.[8]

At the same time, he reported some positive accomplishments. He was lecturing on Sabbatianism for the first time to a class of sixty or seventy students, an enormous number for the Hebrew University at the time. And Salman Schocken had decided to fund a Center for Kabbalistic Research in his library in Jerusalem, to be headed by Scholem, who tongue in cheek referred to it as the "Scholem School."

In the spring of 1939, Hannah Arendt sent him the manuscript of her book on Rahel Varnhagen, the German Jew who had run an Enlightenment-era salon in Berlin and had ultimately converted to Christianity. Arendt had been working on this project for around a decade since finishing her doctoral dissertation and had described it to Scholem during their Paris meeting in 1938. The book was a case study in the failure of Jewish integration in Germany and, as such, could only have won Scholem's admiration, albeit with an interpretation that reflected somewhat more his ideas than Arendt's: "It's a superb analysis . . . and shows that a relationship built on fraud, such as the German Jews' relationship to 'Germanness' could not end without misfortune. By fraud, I mean the assumption that everything always had to come from one side, and that the other side was only ever allowed to deny itself. . . . Pity, I don't see how the book will ever find a publisher."[9] In fact, Scholem would play a significant role in the book's ultimate publication in 1957. When in 1940 Arendt had to flee the Nazis in France, Scholem's copy of the manuscript was the only one that survived, and it became the basis for Arendt's book. Moreover,

Scholem's understanding of its thesis would lead to his own later essay "Against the Myth of the German-Jewish Dialogue." He and Arendt, both committed, even if idiosyncratic Zionists, shared a deep affinity concerning the failure of German Jewish assimilation.

The onset of the Second World War found all the Scholem family except Werner out of harm's way: Betty, Reinhold, and Erich, with their families, in Australia, and Werner's wife, Emmy, and their two children in London. During the period of the Phoney War (September 1, 1939, until the invasion of the Low Countries and France in May 1940), Scholem was able to continue his correspondence with Benjamin, although in schoolboy French, since German was now verboten. As an "enemy alien," Benjamin was interned by the French government, but he was released after three months (Arendt went through the same experience).

But the summer and early fall of 1940 brought disaster. On July 17, an S.S. guard in Buchenwald murdered Werner. The circumstances of his death are not clear. It is possible that Communist prisoners, who ruled the camp internally, might have betrayed Werner to the S.S. since he was a Trotskyist—Trotsky was murdered by an agent of Stalin in Mexico the following month. Word of Werner's death did not reach Gerhard until October, in a letter from Betty written on September 27 (he noted it in an undated diary entry). His reaction to his brother's death is hard to gauge since he did not mention it in any of his writings during the war. It was only in 1977, when he published his memoir *From Berlin to Jerusalem*, that he acknowledged it in print, dedicating the book to his murdered sibling.

This terrible news was soon followed by an even greater shock. After the Germans conquered France, both Benjamin and Arendt fled to the south. On September 25, 1940, Benjamin was turned back while trying to cross the Spanish border. He had in his possession a visa to the United States, obtained for him by Adorno and Horkheimer, but he lacked a transit visa from Spain to Portugal. Sometime that night, he poisoned himself with morphine and was found dead the next day. Arendt, in Marseille, heard the story of Benjamin's suicide and passed on the dreadful news to Scholem. It quickly became the main subject in his correspondence with Adorno.

There is something curious about Scholem's reaction to this tragic turn of events. Adorno was deeply upset and kept asking why Benjamin had done it—after all, the rest of his party was eventually allowed into Spain. Scholem's response was surprisingly restrained, even cold; like the bibliophile he was, he quickly turned to a plan to save Benjamin's writings: he and Adorno later collaborated on publishing Benjamin's correspondence and collected writings, a project that launched the recovery of Benjamin's reputation. He also dedicated *Major Trends* to Benjamin, something he had planned to do even before Benjamin's suicide. But the only explicit expression of Scholem's feelings on hearing this news came in a letter to Shalom Spiegel nearly a year later: "I'll never recover from this terrible blow."[10]

Could it be that Scholem was incapable of expressing an emotional response to the deaths of these two important figures in his life? This seems unlikely. More probable is the opposite: he was so profoundly shaken that he could not bring himself to respond, as if he had to harshly suppress his feelings in order to carry on. The two deaths, coming almost simultaneously, may have provoked an extended period of melancholy and even occasional paralysis that lasted for most of the war, emotions that merged with his response to the larger catastrophe of the Holocaust.

A diary entry from January 9, 1943, conveys the depths of his despair. The entry seems to have been occasioned by the death on January 1 of Arthur Ruppin, the venerable German Zionist activist who was also the founder of Brit Shalom: "The death of Ruppin is reflected for me from only one perspective:

it arouses envy. As such, I am not able to distance myself from my travails and from my innermost desires. . . . In the past two weeks, I have not exchanged a word with anyone in which I have not had to fight against yawning. I now realize for the first time in a decisive and truthful way that my youth, in which I believed in such a paradoxical way, is over. This is what is so difficult to grasp. My youth is over, but I can't grasp a different life. Things have reached such a state that I am no longer able to read in a focused way. This is the worst sign for me."[11] In the same lengthy entry, he moved from his sense of personal despair to equally dismal reflections on Zionism. Of the five hundred thousand Jews in Palestine, only fifty thousand were there for the same reason he was, to revive Judaism. The others were building the land, of course, but, reacting to the recent news of the Holocaust, he believed that they were doing so for a nation that no longer existed. Alienated from the political and social projects of the official Zionist movement, Scholem staked out a lonely, elitist position.

Several months later, he took issue with a declaration put out by a group of intellectuals in response to news of the Holocaust. The Yishuv had become aware of the dimensions of the Holocaust in late 1942 when sixty-nine Palestinian citizens held by the Nazis were freed in an exchange and brought the information with them. The intellectuals, who ranged from Joseph Klausner on the right to Hugo Bergman on the left, issued a declaration calling for a vigorous campaign to rescue the European Jews. Scholem refused to sign the declaration, claiming that no adequate historical perspective existed to help Jews know how to respond to the terrible news from Europe. More important, he denied that Zionism had prophesied the Holocaust, as the declaration stated. This was a retrospective distortion of the meaning of Zionism, which, in his view, was not a movement to save Jews but a movement to save Judaism. In fact, it is striking how little Scholem wrote about the Holocaust in later years, and he repeatedly refused to use the European catastrophe as the primary justification for Zionism.

Other diary entries from the period of the war reflect similar despondency. The day after his birthday in 1944, he penned an even darker meditation: "Is it true that God is revealed in the isolation of a broken life? Why, then, is everything in my life so dark, without any way out, and jarring? . . . Sometimes I still struggle desperately with the remnants of the great dreams that once inspired me, as if I could still write them on some piece of paper or another—and I've lost faith in the strength needed for that. Everything is so much in vain, so hopeless." And on May 7, 1945, reflecting on the imminent end of the European war, he was consumed by a sense that all the sacrifices of the Jewish people had been in vain. In addition to the national tragedy he felt personal despair: "I am alone. How alone I am is hard to say. I went through this war alone. Friends in the true sense are no longer."[12] In an interview after his death, Fania revealed that she had had no idea of how alone Scholem had felt during his life and deeply regretted that he could not share this feeling even with her. She may have been referring especially to the war years.

There were other deaths during the war besides those of Benjamin and Werner Scholem. In 1942, his childhood friend Erich Brauer passed away. Brauer had suffered since childhood from a crippling disability (he had a deformed spine), which may have shortened his life: he was only forty-five at the time of his death. Scholem memorialized him in a short but moving article in the Hebrew labor daily *Davar*. Even more consequential was the death of Berl Katznelson on August 12, 1944, at the age of fifty-seven. Katznelson was one of the founding fathers of the labor movement in Palestine, and as the editor of *Davar* and the founder of the Am Oved publishing house, its cultural leader. Scholem had become a close friend of Berl (as he was familiarly known). The labor leader would frequently drop by the Scholem household and was visiting the night before his death, a coincidence that shook Scholem to his core. A year later, he wrote a powerful reminiscence of that night, "The Last Night of Berl Katznelson."

Perhaps as a result of the deaths of so many who were close to him, on July 14, 1943, at age forty-five, Scholem composed his will in handwritten Hebrew, leaving all his possessions, which amounted primarily to his library, to Fania. He specified that she could choose to sell or donate his books to the Hebrew University, but he also requested that she arrange for the publication of his collected writings "in three or four volumes"[13] in his memory. While there is nothing out of the ordinary about a middle-aged man making his will, in Scholem's case, it may well have reflected his morbid frame of mind.

Although his private ruminations suggest that he suffered from paralysis, Scholem continued to be active in his scholarship and at the university. At the end of May 1941, he campaigned for the position of dean of humanities against his old nemesis, Joseph Klausner, defeating Klausner by a vote of 16 to 11. This result was followed by right-wing student protests in favor of Klausner. There can be little doubt that Scholem's victory was seen as having political overtones, even though he was no longer active in any political organization such as Brit Shalom. He closely followed the activities of Brit Shalom's successor, the Ichud, led by Judah Magnes and Martin Buber, but he did not join the group.

He was becoming increasingly uncomfortable with the politicization of the university and in July 1943 resigned from the Friends of the Hebrew University when they imposed a political litmus test on faculty members. It would appear that this litmus test was directed against left-wing professors, and it may have been a by-product of the Biltmore Program of the previous year, a Zionist resolution demanding Jewish statehood (or "confederation," as it was called) in Palestine. For those like Scholem who had never favored statehood as the "end goal" of Zionism, the new political orthodoxy was hard to stomach. His resignation letter argued passionately for academic freedom: the Hebrew University ought to be equally tolerant of a Martin Buber, who favored a binational Jewish-Arab state, as of a Joseph Klausner, the militant nationalist.

These personal and political contexts are essential to an understanding of Scholem's most important and even shocking publication of the war years. In 1944 he unleashed an extraordinary fusillade against the field of Jewish Studies, both historical and contemporary. "Meditations on Jewish Studies" purported to be "a preamble to a Jubilee Lecture that will never be given,"[14] for the twentieth anniversary of the Institute for Jewish Studies of the Hebrew University. Instead of delivering the address to his colleagues, he published it in *Luah Ha'aretz*, the annual booklet of the daily newspaper *Ha'aretz*, which Salman Schocken had purchased in 1937. Scholem intended a broad, general audience for his remarks.

He wrote in a rich, acerbic Hebrew similar to the language of "Redemption Through Sin." On one level, it was a devastating condemnation of the German Jewish founders of the Science of Judaism. They had wanted to use scholarship to support their assimilationist goals: Moritz Steinschneider (one of the movement's founders, as well as the grandfather of Karl and Gustav) was reputed—perhaps apocryphally—to have said that he regarded it as his task to give Judaism a decent burial. These bourgeois rationalists wanted "to remove the irrational stinger and banish the demonic enthusiasm from Jewish history. . . . This was the decisive original sin. This terrifying giant, our history, is called to task . . . and this enormous creature, full of destructive power, made up of vitality, evil, and perfection, must contract itself, stunt its growth, and declare that it has no substance. The demonic giant is nothing but a simple fool who fulfills the duties of a solid citizen, and every decent Jewish bourgeois could unashamedly bid him good-day in the streets of the city, the immaculate city of the nineteenth century."[15]

However, the nineteenth-century historians were not entirely blameworthy. About Leopold Zunz and Steinschneider, two of the most important representatives of this school, he wrote: "The optimism famous in their opinions is a lie and a mask—there is something of the *sitra ahra* [the "other side," the Kabbalistic name for evil]. . . . I must confess that the figures of Zunz and Steinschneider have attracted me [for a long time]. . . . [T]hey are truly demonic figures."[16] By calling these scholars "demonic," Scholem was expressing grudging admiration. If historical Judaism itself contained elements of the demonic, then these historians were not so far, after all, from the true content of their subject. The very destructive side of their scholarship had a positive role to play since history was an eternal dialectic between destruction and construction.

How did this work? The elements of Jewish history that the rationalist scholars condemned might become the building blocks of a new world: "It is possible that what was termed degeneracy will be thought of as a revelation and light and what seemed to them impotent hallucinations will be revealed as a great myth . . . not the washing and mummification of the dead, but the discovery of hidden life by removal of the obfuscating masks."[17] This grand reversal, in which irrational myth might claim pride of place over rationalism, was only possible because of Zionism, which removed the need for Jews to pretend to be consistently respectable and rational.

But here Scholem turned to his real target: his colleagues at the Hebrew University. In place of assimilationist sermons and rationalist apologetics, they substituted nationalist rhetoric and apologetics: "We came to rebel but we ended up continuing. . . . All these plagues have now disguised themselves in nationalism. From the frying pan into the fire: after the emptiness of assimilation comes another, that of nationalist excess. We have cultivated nationalist 'sermons' and 'rhetoric' in science to take the place of religious sermons and rhetoric. In both cases, the real forces operating in our world, the genuine demonic, remains outside the picture we have created."[18]

Why did Scholem train his rhetorical artillery on the university that was his intellectual home? The sense of alienation he experienced during the war years surely played a role. The increasing nationalism of the period also provided the context for his attack on the harnessing of scholarship for political ends. But there may be more to it than that. The word *demonic* appears primarily in Scholem's vocabulary in his discussion of Sabbatianism, especially Jacob Frank, in "Redemption Through Sin." Jewish history required the demonic, even if the demons might threaten to destroy it. When Scholem spoke of the failure to give the demonic its due in Jewish Studies, could he have been thinking not only about his colleagues but also about himself? Could it be that he, too, felt himself to blame for the failure he attributed to the other historians of his day?

During the early 1940s, Scholem had planned to write a book-length version of the ideas that he proposed in "Redemption Through Sin" and in the Sabbatianism chapter of *Major Trends*. The book was intended to encompass the Kabbalistic ideas that preceded Sabbatianism, the Sabbatian movement during Shabbatai Zvi's lifetime, and the afterlife of Sabbatianism until the early nineteenth century. The idea came originally from Berl Katznelson, who had heard Scholem lecture on Jewish messianism, including Sabbatianism, at a "month of learning" for workers in Rehovot in August 1941. Katznelson proposed to Scholem a three-volume work that would be published by Am Oved. But the book failed to materialize on schedule. In letters from the war years, Scholem repeatedly referred to it as forthcoming while he produced instead a series of focused studies on Sabbatianism.

According to Fania, reporting after Gerhard's death, he

stopped working on the book when he misplaced the extensive introduction he wrote between 1942 and 1945. This introduction resurfaced shortly before his death, and it was published in a posthumous edition of his biography of Shabbatai Zvi. There is something unconvincing in this story, however. In the first place, Scholem kept meticulous records and saved much less important writing. In addition, it would have been an easy matter for him to reconstruct the introduction from memory, since most of it repeated his earlier arguments about the failure of Orthodox and Enlightenment scholars to give Sabbatianism its due. In fact, Scholem did write a manuscript on Shabbatai Zvi during the war, as was revealed by a recent discovery in the Schocken Library. It turns out that he promised it to two publishers: Berl Katznelson and Salman Schocken, who was his patron. Schocken, for his part, expressed great irritation with Scholem for behaving duplicitously about this manuscript, which was never published in the form he wrote it during the war. Whether due to the conflict between publishers, the additional discoveries he continued to make about the subject, or his depressed state of mind—or all of these together—Scholem felt compelled to postpone his promise to restore the demonic to Jewish history.

The "lost" introduction reveals a great deal about his mental state during those years. The first few pages are an extended rumination on truth in history. He declares that there is "no greater error than a simple truth." Truths bandied about like slogans may excite people, but they serve only appearances. The real truth of history is concealed, full of complications and paradoxes. History works by a dialectical process in which ideas go underground and are then transmuted into their opposites. We recognize this as the process Scholem described in "Redemption Through Sin," where the religious nihilism of the Sabbatians resurfaced in the form of secular Enlightenment. Historians who only paid attention to the nihilism of the movement missed the more complicated truth: Sabbatianism represented a powerful drive for a new world of freedom and for the renewal of Judaism from within. This drive came to a tragic end because the times were not ripe for its fulfillment.

This introduction contains Scholem's strongest affirmation of Sabbatianism as a movement of liberation whose failure was a tragedy. It is hard to avoid the conclusion that the "simple truth" he excoriated was nationalist propaganda, by which he meant not only nationalism generally but Zionism specifically. The inward renewal of Judaism, the ideal that attracted him to Zionism in his youth, had never been realized, and instead of embracing the dialectic of creation and destruction necessary for such a renewal, the Zionists had become like all other nationalists throughout the world. The failure of Sabbatianism, its collapse into nihilism, presaged the failure of Zionism as Scholem understood it.

By reading this lost introduction together with "Meditations on Jewish Studies" from 1944, we can arrive at a complicated picture of Gershom Scholem during the war. Shocked by the deaths of two of his closest companions from his youth and in despair over the fate of the European Jews, he questioned whether he could tell the "demonic" story of Sabbatianism in such a way as to contribute to the contemporary renewal of Judaism. If the Holocaust he witnessed was a catastrophe even greater than the Jews' expulsion from Spain, where was the revolutionary movement of renewal that might succeed where Sabbatianism had failed?

8

The Zionist Return to History

IN 1945, Hannah Arendt published an article titled "Zionism Reconsidered" in the *Menorah Journal*. It marked the culmination of a number of earlier articles that Arendt had written in New York during the war years in which, despite her earlier work with the Zionist Youth Aliya, she voiced increasing criticisms of the official Zionist movement. The essay, written in 1944, was a response to the World Zionist Organization's meeting in Atlantic City, New Jersey, that year. The organization reaffirmed and strengthened the Biltmore Program of two years earlier, which had made some form of a Jewish state Zionism's goal after the war. For Arendt, the demand for a Jewish state marked the victory of the right-wing Revisionists over the Labor Zionists, who had earlier refused to foreclose other solutions to the problem of Palestine. Arendt herself would soon become active in the Ichud group of Martin Buber and Judah Magnes, serving as their American spokesperson as they advocated for a

binational state. But the essay took an even more extreme position, attacking the kibbutz movement for political passivity and
praising the Soviet Union's nationalities policy as a model for
Zionism.

Scholem reacted vehemently when Arendt sent him the article: "I read the elaboration of your argument while vigorously
shaking my head."[1] While he shared her distaste for the politics
of David Ben-Gurion (although why, he does not say), he took
great exception to her tone and her bewildering embrace of
Marxist arguments. He accused her of assembling an array of
accusations against Zionism that amounted to anti-Zionism.
For Scholem, whose utopian Zionism had repeatedly foundered
when faced with reality, Arendt's own utopianism was divorced
from the reality of Palestine and, he implied, lacked the most
elementary sympathy for the challenges that the Jews faced there.
He, too, had favored a binational solution but he had come to
the bitter realization that it was no longer possible. And while
the exchange over Zionism included no reference to the Holocaust, there can be little doubt that Scholem's impatience with
Arendt's ethereal criticisms reflected his horror at the events in
Europe. The exchange of letters between the two over this essay
is highly revealing. Although they agreed to disagree and not
let their dispute ruin their friendship, a line had been drawn over
Zionism that would lead to all-out warfare over similar issues
nearly two decades later.

After the defeat of Nazi Germany, Scholem would come
face to face with the catastrophe in a way not yet possible in
Palestine. It became clear even before the Nazis surrendered
that they had pillaged vast quantities of books, manuscripts, and
archives from Jewish institutions throughout Occupied Europe. The American occupation forces in Germany gathered
together much of this material in warehouses, eventually con-
centrating them in Offenbach, outside Frankfurt. A committee
that included Scholem was formed at the Hebrew University

on May 6, 1945 (two days before the German surrender), to consider how to repatriate this literature to Jerusalem, since it was the view of the committee members that its proper place was in the Jewish national home.

This view was not without controversy, however. The position of the occupation authorities was that all the looted material should be returned to its countries of origin. But it was unthinkable for most Jews that the books and manuscripts should be sent back to Poland, Lithuania, or Germany, where the communal institutions that had housed them had been destroyed, along with most of their Jews. Yet if they were not returned to their countries of origin, where should they go? The American Jewish Joint Distribution Committee (the Joint), represented by the historian Koppel Pinson, aimed to bring these stolen materials to the United States, at least initially to the Library of Congress, while British Jews also asserted their desire to acquire materials. YIVO, the research institute for east European Jewry that had relocated from Vilna to New York, sent Lucy Dawidowicz, who would later become well known as a historian of the Holocaust, to retrieve materials that the Nazis had plundered during their occupation of Lithuania. An umbrella committee under the name Jewish Cultural Reconstruction (JCR) was eventually formed in 1947 under the leadership of the historian Salo W. Baron, to coordinate all these efforts. Baron hired Arendt to lead the JCR's work in Germany. So a number of prominent Jewish intellectuals were involved in the recovery of looted cultural materials. At times, these various Jewish organizations worked in concert with one another, united by the urgent need to save the Jewish materials before they disappeared into the hands of indifferent European regimes, but at other times they worked in competition with one another.

Before the formation of the JCR, there was no obvious mechanism to coordinate these efforts. On January 24, 1946,

the Hebrew University committee decided to send two representatives to Europe to make a survey of the materials and see
which might be brought to Jerusalem. Not surprisingly, the
committee chose Scholem, whose knowledge of Jewish books
was unsurpassed, as one of the two. The other was the head of
the National Library, Avraham Yaari. Even before their departure in April, though, Scholem and Yaari came into conflict.
Although they were supposed to have equal authority, Yaari did
not have an academic appointment, so Scholem demanded that
he, as a full professor, be given veto power if they disagreed.
Despite an attempt by Judah L. Magnes, the president of the
Hebrew University, to mediate, Scholem was inflexible. It is
rather dispiriting to read the correspondence between Scholem and Magnes, in which Scholem magnifies petty issues into
major disputes and inflates his academic status. The dispute
between the two continued after they arrived in Paris on April
14, but Yaari, fed up with dealing with Scholem and frustrated
by the delays in getting into Germany, returned to Jerusalem
on May 15. Scholem was now on his own.

It was not possible to enter Germany without a visa from
the American authorities, and this was not forthcoming, possibly blocked by the Joint, which was supposed to be assisting
them. Scholem wrote to Stephen S. Wise, the American Zionist leader, as well as to Magnes, to urge intervention at the highest levels in Washington. While he waited impatiently for weeks
in Paris, he occupied himself by giving lectures to young Jews,
both French and refugees, on the cultural situation in the Land
of Israel. He saw himself as a *shaliach*, a Zionist emissary, whose
role was not only to rescue books but also to rescue people.
This was his first experience as a full-fledged agent of Zionism,
albeit through the Hebrew University, and it clearly brought
him, an inveterate dissenter, closer to the official movement.

While he cooled his heels in Paris, he received the devastating news that his mother, Betty, had died in Australia. He set down his reaction in his diary on May 17, 1946:

> Yesterday evening I got word that Mother died on May 5 just as we were touring Versailles! . . . I've been waiting for this moment for several (!) weeks and yet I still feel utterly petrified all the way to my heart. I don't know—what a feeling of awful petrification, of growing abandonment that makes it impossible for me to figure out my place in the world. Mother was a more important factor in my life in recent years than earlier. Her image became much clearer when she passed seventy . . . and I became even more connected to her soul in a number of ways. Her sufferings in Australia brought her closer to us, and her courage surprised us. I had an easygoing mother who did not demand to interfere and knew how to take care of herself with great wisdom. Those things that distanced me from her in earlier years, thirty years ago, have vanished into nothingness.[2]

If several years earlier Scholem had felt that his youth had come to an end, Betty's death brought this feeling home with a vengeance. He was no longer the rebellious young man whom his mother had to rein in with gentle, often witty, reproaches. And Betty's death, together with those of Werner Scholem and Walter Benjamin, finally spelled the end of his personal ties to Germany.

While he waited for his visa, he made a trip to Zurich between May 24 and June 5. Here his mood took a turn for the better. In Zurich he made the acquaintance of a circle of the followers of the psychologist Carl Gustav Jung. This encounter was to be of decisive importance because it led several years later to a long-term association with the annual Jungian-inspired Eranos Conferences in Ascona, Switzerland. He also met with Jung himself and had a cordial and interesting conversation with the great psychologist, although he was on his guard because of reports of Jung's earlier sympathy for Nazism. Scholem's Zurich friends defended Jung, but Scholem was not entirely convinced until the liberal German rabbi Leo Baeck told him that Jung had personally expressed remorse over his earlier political sentiments. Nevertheless, there are those who wonder at the ease with which Scholem, always so skeptical of the good intentions of Germans, accepted Baeck's reassurance about Jung.

From Zurich, he went to Prague, Bratislava, and Vienna in search of looted books, a venture that lasted most of June. Hugo Bergman had preceded him to Prague and had already reported on the trove of materials there. In Prague he met the historian Otto Muneles, who before World War I had journeyed to Galicia, where he became a Hasid of the Rebbe of Belz and later served as the head of the burial society in Prague. During the Holocaust, his wife and two children were murdered, and he was forced by the Nazis to work sorting pillaged books in the Theresienstadt Ghetto. After the war, he continued this work in Prague, now for the purpose of rescuing the books for the survivors. Muneles left a profound impression on Scholem. He was a man whose faith had been utterly destroyed and who had embraced the rabbinic statement of heresy: "There is no justice and there is no judge." From an obituary Scholem wrote after his death in 1967, it becomes clear that this encounter was perhaps the earliest and most shocking that Scholem had with a survivor of the Holocaust: "You had the impression that even in his veins the blood had frozen."[3] But with Muneles's aid, he was able to assemble a good account of the stolen books and manuscripts in Prague and to begin the process of transferring some of them to Jerusalem.

Finally, with the intercession of the Joint, which continued to play an ambiguous role throughout his mission, Scholem received permission to enter Germany on June 24, 1946, and arrived on July 1. He went "undercover" as an educational officer who was supposed to lecture to the refugees in the Displaced Persons camps. In this capacity he needed to wear an American army uniform and was provided with a driver and a jeep (a photograph of the forty-eight-year-old professor in an ill-fitting American army uniform is an incongruous sight). He did, in fact, visit a number of camps, where, as in Paris, he gave talks on the Zionist Yishuv, one of them, for the first time, in Yiddish! His reaction to his meetings with survivors was mixed. On one hand, as with his encounter with Otto Muneles, he was profoundly shaken by their experiences. But he also found them so different from his image of utopian Zionists that he feared the effect they would have on the Yishuv if and when they came. As we have seen, the Zion of his dreams was not primarily meant as a refuge.

Scholem took up residence in Frankfurt, half of which was destroyed. He commuted to Offenbach, where he set to work examining the well-organized piles of books and documents. The warehouse housed the Rothschild Library from Frankfurt and other collections from around Germany. At its height, it contained some 1.5 million books, but many of them had already been sent back to their places of origin by the time Scholem arrived. He lamented that he should have arrived in April, as had been originally planned. During his stay in Germany, which lasted until nearly the end of August, he also traveled to Heidelberg, Munich, and Berlin. In Munich, where he still retained some connections from his student days, he tried to arrange for a rare manuscript of the Talmud to be donated to the Hebrew University, but he was not successful.

The visit to Berlin at the beginning of August was particularly difficult. On August 2, he went to find the family apartments on Friedrichsgracht and Neue Grünstrasse, but as he wrote in his diary, "*Everything* is destroyed!! The inner city— *dead.*"[4] He was clearly shaken to realize that the city of his childhood was no more. He went for Friday evening services to the Oranienburgerstrasse synagogue, which was also partly destroyed, and noted how strange it was to celebrate Shabbat in Berlin after a fourteen-year absence. Some days later, he was involved in an automobile accident that did nothing to improve his mood.

While in Offenbach, Scholem worked with a young American Jewish chaplain, Herbert Friedman. Together they packed five boxes with especially valuable materials. The American authorities, possibly under pressure from American Jewish leaders, prohibited the export of the boxes to Palestine. Scholem returned to Jerusalem in late August without them, but in early January 1947, Friedman smuggled the boxes out of Germany to France and from there to Antwerp, where he stowed them with the library of the Zionist leader Chaim Weizmann, which was en route to Palestine. The plot came to light after the boxes had already arrived in Jerusalem, and Scholem was accused of conspiring with Friedman to steal valuable books and manuscripts from U.S. custody. An article in the army newspaper *Stars and Stripes* estimated their value at $3 million. Scholem hastened to respond that the real value could not have been more than $10,000 and that he was ignorant of Friedman's escapade, which had been hatched more than four months after his departure from Germany.

It is hard to know where the truth lies here. In the chaos of postwar Germany, theft of looted books was hardly unknown, and, in any case, Scholem certainly believed that the five boxes—as well as all the other stolen materials—belonged to the Jewish people, and that the Hebrew University was their proper trustee. To take such materials, far from constituting theft, was more properly to restore them to their rightful owners or, since most of their owners had been murdered, to the nation to which, for Zionists, all Jews belonged. Nonetheless, he might not have actually conspired with Friedman in this dramatic heist. Either way, Scholem the bibliophile found that the Shoah of the Jewish books provided a singular way for him to connect to the Shoah of the Jewish people.

Although Scholem's trip to Europe in 1946 was his most

intensive effort to rescue books, he continued to be involved as the deputy chair, with Hannah Arendt as secretary, with the Jewish Cultural Reconstruction. Despite the initial distrust between Scholem and the Americans, he came quickly to realize that it was more important to rescue the books before they disappeared into foreign hands than to win them only for the Yishuv. A common front with the Americans, who, after all, were friends and colleagues, now seemed essential. Tensions did not entirely vanish, however, as later letters between Scholem and Arendt attest.

When he returned to Jerusalem at the end of August 1946, he was exhausted both physically and mentally. According to his own testimony and that of Fania, he seems to have suffered an emotional collapse: unable to work and peripatetically moving from one bed to another in his apartment. An inveterate socializer under normal circumstances, he received barely any visitors. This depression—the diagnosis seems apposite here—lasted nearly a year. It is hard to diagnose its cause. Certainly, Scholem's firsthand encounter with the effects of the Holocaust had to have been traumatic, as was the encounter with the ruins of Germany. But in light of his state of mind during the war, his reaction to his 1946 trip appears to be the culmination of a longer crisis.

On December 5, 1947, by now recovered, Scholem celebrated his fiftieth birthday. His students—and at this point he had something like a dozen of them—staged a celebration. Joseph Weiss, who had come to Palestine from Hungary in 1940, gave the most memorable speech, which was published later in the daily *Haaretz*. He pointed out the contradiction between Scholem's personality, which reveled in "dialectical negations and paradoxical affirmations," and his seemingly dry scholarship. Weiss tried to resolve this contradiction by arguing that their teacher camouflaged his true metaphysical commitments, which were by definition esoteric. It would seem, said Weiss, that Scholem was drawn to his esoteric subject by his own desire to keep his true motives hidden.[5]

Weiss surely identified something essential in Scholem as a historian of Jewish mysticism: the paradox of a seemingly secular scholar immersing himself with such passion in the most arcane religious texts. As should now be abundantly clear, the power of Scholem's scholarship lay in his ability to make it urgently important to modern readers by conveying the urgent importance that he himself felt. And he recognized that Weiss was right on target. In a letter to Hugo and Escha Bergman, who were in Sweden at the time, he reported on Weiss's chutzpah with approval: in discerning that Scholem did indeed have an esoteric metaphysical agenda, his student had learned something crucial from his teacher.

The relationship between Scholem and Weiss was, in fact, one of the most important for both of them. Weiss had a highly sensitive temperament, and he would find it impossible to live in the pressure cooker of the new State of Israel. Despite his Zionist commitment, Scholem was sympathetic to Weiss's dilemma and worked to find Weiss a fellowship in Britain or America. However, when Weiss submitted his dissertation from England, Scholem refused to accept it, considering its last chapter incomprehensible and lacking in scholarly foundation. Nevertheless, their epistolary relationship continued. Weiss wrote to Scholem using an elevated, rabbinic diction that at times became tongue in cheek. And Scholem responded, always supportively. Weiss planned to write a biography of Scholem modeled on Nathan Sternhartz's biography of his master, the Hasidic rebbe Nahman of Bratslav, which is composed of a string of anecdotes. Weiss was profoundly influenced by Rabbi Nahman, about whom he wrote several seminal articles. Like Nahman's disciple, Weiss collected anecdotes about Scholem and wrote them down on scraps of paper. The scraps, however, remained scraps, and the book was never published.

In 1966, Weiss manifested symptoms of flagrant schizophrenia and, in 1969, committed suicide. His death was shattering for Scholem, who at a memorial half a year later spoke of Weiss as his favorite student. It might not be too speculative to suggest that Weiss was the closest Scholem ever had to a son. Later insinuations that Scholem had driven Weiss to suicide by not accepting his dissertation are belied by the letters, which reveal a very different story, characterized by intimacy and paternal concern.

Scholem's letter to Hugo and Escha Bergman of 1947 also conveyed his thanks to Hugo for an essay dedicated to Scholem on the occasion of his fiftieth birthday in which Bergman, possibly referring to the last sentence of *Major Trends in Jewish Mysticism*, called on Scholem to take up the mantle of prophet in addition to that of professor. Scholem responded that he no longer believed in prophecy, and he satirized Martin Buber for posing in the phony mantle of the prophet Elijah. He was probably referring to the testimony that Buber and Judah Magnes gave to the U.N. Special Commission on Palestine, at which the two, representing the Ichud group, had argued for a binational state. Even Magnes, wrote Scholem, "whose honesty clearly far exceeds that of Buber," seemed to have given himself over to flights of illusion. Scholem obviously thought a binational state in Palestine had become impossible by late 1947.[6]

By the time he wrote to the Bergmans, the U.N. General Assembly had already voted to partition Palestine, a civil war between the Jews and Arabs had broken out, and sniping had become a daily occurrence on the "seam line" in Jerusalem between the two communities. By the spring of 1948, Jerusalem was under siege, cut off from the coastal plain and enduring food shortages as well as attacks on civilians. Scholem was to spend the months of the siege in Jerusalem, and he even noted that fact on a manuscript of lectures on Hasidism that he delivered in New York in 1949. In his diary from the period, he inserted his identification card for the Civil Guard, so it seems that he did not remain holed up in his study during the momentous events of Israel's War of Independence. He was also drafted by the Haganah (the Jewish military force) to prevent the plunder of books. As he put it amusingly, "Which meant that I prevented myself from taking part in the corresponding looting."[7]

But he was also engaged in a project with contemporary ramifications that he published in the year of the war: a piece of detective work into the origins of the Star of David as a Jewish symbol. Here was the historian taking up the role of debunker of a historical myth. As opposed to what everyone commonly believed, he argued, the Star of David had appeared only infrequently as a Jewish symbol before the nineteenth century. It was primarily a magical symbol used on amulets. (It is a reflection of Scholem's view of the Kabbalah that Kabbalistic magic—called "practical Kabbalah"—was not considered essentially Jewish, as was "theosophical" Kabbalah.) The Prague community was possibly the first to adopt the Star as a Jewish symbol in the sixteenth century, perhaps even earlier. From there, it spread to other central European Jewish communities.

The Star seems to have acquired messianic significance in the Sabbatian movement and its aftermath, as, of course, it did much later in Franz Rosenzweig's *Star of Redemption*. In the nineteenth century, Jews eager to prove how similar they were to their Christian neighbors, used it to adorn their synagogues. When the Zionists put the six-pointed star on their flag, they were merely adopting for nationalist purposes what had earlier stood for assimilation. But the symbol for them served the subtle function of pointing to the future—and thus to secular redemption—rather than to past glories, since its association with King David was purely legendary.

In his argument, Scholem was leveling a hidden critique of the relationship of Zionism to Jewish history just as the movement had succeeded in winning a state: its cardinal symbol was less historical than its members thought. The Star of David was, in Scholem's telling, an "empty symbol." It acquired real meaning not when the German Reformers put it on their synagogues or when the Zionists put it on their flag but when the Nazis made the Jews wear it as an emblem of degradation:

> The yellow Jewish star, as a sign of exclusion and ultimately of annihilation, has accompanied the Jews on their path of humiliation and horror, of battle and heroic resistance. Under this sign they were murdered; under this sign they came to Israel. If there is a fertile soil of historical experience from which symbols draw their meaning, it would seem to be given here. . . . [T]he sign which in our own days has been sanctified by suffering and dread has become worthy of illuminating the path to life and reconstruction. Before ascending, the path led down into the abyss; there the symbol received its ultimate humiliation and there it won its greatness.[8]

Only out of the horror of the Holocaust had the symbol paradoxically become its opposite, a badge of pride. In these scant lines—and almost nowhere else—did Scholem give the most powerful expression to his feelings about the Holocaust and its connection to the State of Israel. And it is doubly striking that he published this essay in the same place, *Luah ha-Aretz*, in which a few years earlier he had published his cry of despair over the state of Jewish Studies. He seemed to believe that just as Lurianic Kabbalah and Sabbatianism were responses to the expulsion from Spain, so a myth of redemption was necessary in modern times in response to the destruction of European Jewry. Just as Shabbatai Zvi had descended into the abyss of antinomianism, so the Jewish people had descended into the abyss of genocide in order to be resurrected. The State of Israel, while not the messianic redemption, was thus a fitting answer to the greatest catastrophe of Jewish history.

For Scholem, the creation of the first Jewish state in two

thousand years aroused ambivalent feelings. It was a necessary response to the Holocaust, but he worried that it would not always have positive consequences. In an interview after his death, Fania Scholem reported that he said at the time that the Jewish people would pay a high price for a state won under the circumstances of the time. To have experienced in such a short space both the Holocaust and the creation of the state was perhaps more than any people could bear. Because now all the resources of the Jews had to go into defense, the spiritual role of Israel would have to suffer. And it is hardly necessary to add that for Scholem, the true task of Zionism was spiritual: the cultural renewal of the Jewish people. Yet there can be little doubt that he was deeply moved by the drama of renewed Jewish sovereignty. Shortly after the war, he and Fania officially changed their names, as did many Israelis of the time. The new Hebrew state now formally recognized him as Gershom.

With the end of the War of Independence, Scholem turned his full attention back to his research. In 1949, he delivered a second series of lectures, on Hasidism, at the Jewish Institute of Religion in New York and on the way back to Israel participated for the first time in the Eranos Conference in Ascona, Switzerland. This marked the beginning of yearly journeys to Ascona, trips that allowed him also to vacation in some of his favorite Alpine landscapes. He would give twenty-nine lectures there between 1949 and 1979. The Eranos Conferences gave him the opportunity to present his work in German. In an address in 1974 upon receiving the Literary Prize of the Bavarian Academy of Arts, Scholem spoke of his shock on encountering the German language in 1946 after the Nazis had so degraded it. He noted that the Eranos Conferences allowed him to "once again express myself properly in the German language without submitting to the provocation originating in that same shock."[9]

Although the Eranos Conferences were initiated by followers of Jung in 1933—and Jung participated in them until the early 1950s—they were hardly "Jungian." Instead, they included a wide array of intellectuals from different disciplines, including the history of religions; Mircea Eliade, the founder of the "Chicago School" of History of Religions was a central figure. (Eliade had been a member of the Romanian fascist Iron Guard in the 1930s, news of which in the 1970s created a crisis, not unlike his earlier discomfort with Jung, for Scholem, who had befriended the historian of religion.) Scholem became an important participant in this cosmopolitan circle of intellectuals, but in a diary entry in 1952, he noted with chagrin that the participants were interested in him more as a "Berlin" intellectual than as an Israeli. Eranos also offered him the opportunity to develop his ideas in a comparative context beyond his immediate field, which led to presentations such as "Kabbalah and Myth," "The Historical Development of the *Shekhinah*," and "The Messianic Idea in Judaism."

In 1951 he recorded a surprising visit in his diary. Ben Zion Dinur, his historian colleague at the Hebrew University who was serving as Israel's first minister of education, had come to propose that Scholem accept an appointment as the next president of the Hebrew University. Judah Magnes, the founding president, had died of a heart attack in 1948. A long discussion between the two ensued, but Scholem refused the offer. As he wrote, he had no patience for idle chitchat with wealthy donors and feared that his evident boredom would undermine his effectiveness. He was undoubtedly correct about why he might not be the right man for the job, but Dinur's proposition is clear evidence of the stature that Scholem had acquired not only in his own field but in the university generally.

If the 1940s were a time of despair and depression, Scholem seems to have recovered his footing by the 1950s. At long last, he was able to make great progress on the delayed study of Sabbatianism. In early 1957, he published a two-volume biography of the mystical Messiah with Am Oved. This massive work was limited to the Sabbatian movement during the Messiah's lifetime; the volume about the movement after his death never materialized, even though Scholem was to publish many excerpts from it in the form of lengthy articles.

Sabbatai Sevi (to use the spelling of the enlarged 1973 English translation) was an instant sensation in Israel. For those who had not read—or could not read—the chapter on Sabbatianism in *Major Trends in Jewish Mysticism*, the biography presented for the first time the whole complex and tragic story of the Messiah from Izmir. Here, Scholem expanded on his suggestion in *Major Trends* that Shabbatai Zvi suffered from bipolar disorder or manic depression, quoting a variety of sources. In a lengthy introduction, he advanced his argument that the proximate cause of the great messianic movement was not something external to Jewish history, such as the Chmielnicki massacres of 1648–1649, but rather ideas internal to Judaism and, more specifically, the Kabbalah. The seventeenth-century dissemination of Luria's sixteenth-century teachings, which refocused Kabbalah on redemption rather than creation, created the intellectual ferment whose result was the Sabbatian movement. For Scholem, it was ideas ultimately that moved history.

Scholem's biography of Shabbatai Zvi cemented his reputation, which had been building for decades, as perhaps the preeminent historian of the Jews. The book was bold, passionately written, and deeply researched, reading like a detective novel (Scholem's favorite leisure reading). Building on his earlier work, it advanced the highly original argument that a movement seen by many as marginal and unimportant was, in fact, the central drama in Jewish history on the doorstep of the modern world. Scholem's painstaking assembly of the widest range of sources was intended to demonstrate how the Sabbatian movement during Shabbatai's life encompassed the whole Jewish world, from Yemen in the south to Morocco in the west, Amsterdam in the north, and Poland to the east. From his prison cell in Gallipoli, Shabbatai Zvi and his immediate retinue conducted a propaganda campaign throughout the Ottoman Empire and beyond to create a truly national movement of redemption. And in the last pages of his long book, Scholem turned from the biography of Shabbatai Zvi to the memory of the movement in stirring language that should now be familiar:

> The Sabbatian legend is the historical form in which the person of Sabbatai Sevi affected later generations. . . . A longing for redemption through the mystical power of holiness, combined with a nightmarish awareness of demonic force, invested this legend with a sense of mystery and tragedy, present even in the versions of the non-Sabbatians trying to recount the story of the great messianic revival that shook a whole people. . . . Was it not a great opportunity missed, rather than a big lie? A victory of the hostile powers rather than the collapse of a vain thing? . . . The legend of the great actor and imposter, and the legend of the elect whose mission ended in failure, together form the legend of Sabbatai Sevi as it lives in the memory of the Jewish people.[10]

For all these reasons, the book excited not only admiration but also opposition. Chief among the opponents was Baruch Kurzweil, an Orthodox professor of Hebrew literature at Bar-Ilan University. Although Scholem had crossed swords with any number of critics over the years, his controversy with Kurzweil was undoubtedly the bitterest as well as the one with the highest stakes. Over a period of ten years starting in 1958, Kurzweil leveled a series of attacks that aimed to turn Scholem into the arch-demon of secular Zionism. Scholem presented himself as an objective historian, charged Kurzweil, but in fact he identified with the Sabbatians by creating a subjective, historical narrative that placed Sabbatianism at the center of Jewish history. Kurzweil averred that Scholem had succumbed to a belief in "demonic irrationalism" and that his research on Sabbatianism was "a grandiose and dangerous attempt to bestow a secular interpretation of Judaism."[11] Scholem had become not only the historian of the messianic movement but also its advocate, since he embraced Sabbatianism for its nihilism. More or less accepting Scholem's interpretation, Kurzweil argued that secular modernity, including Zionism, was the long-term product of the Sabbatian revolt against rabbinic authority. Far from foreign imports, and here Kurzweil agreed with Scholem, these modern movements derived from an internal Jewish source.

In this way, wrote Kurzweil, Scholem undermined the definition of what constitutes Jewishness, which, for Kurzweil was rabbinic law and biblical ethics. If Sabbatianism was as legitimately Jewish as these older traditions, then Judaism lacked any essential meaning. Scholem wanted the heretics to be counted as "kosher" Jews. Even worse, by embracing Sabbatian nihilism, Scholem was linking it to modern movements of myth that rejected the Jewish idea of God. Here, Kurzweil specifically referred to Jung's celebration of myth and the unconscious. Scholem, he said, was nothing but a Jewish mouthpiece for Jung, who, as we have seen, had associations with Nazism. In short, Kurzweil drew a direct line between Sabbatianism, modern secularism, Jung, and Nazism. By serving as the thread to connect all of these movements, Scholem had allied himself with the devil and embraced the demonic.

Kurzweil's frontal attack on Scholem was part of his larger battle against all forms of Jewish secularism and especially against modern Jewish historians, starting with those of the nineteenth century and including Scholem and his colleagues at the Hebrew University. (Sitting at the new Bar-Ilan University, Kurzweil sometimes sounded as if he had a chip on his shoulder because he did not have a position in Jerusalem.) He echoed and even quoted Scholem's 1944 essay on the Science of Judaism, but included Scholem in the list of offenders. However, where Scholem had upbraided his colleagues for leaving the "demonic" out of their picture of Jewish history, Kurzweil turned the tables and argued that they had all *included* the demonic (that is, secularism) and that this was their sin. With Scholem, the heretical potential in all the earlier historians had become actual.

In his attack on Scholem as the modern apologist for Sabbatianism, Kurzweil was reenacting the anti-Sabbatian polemics of the seventeenth and eighteenth centuries. Moses Hagiz, Jacob Sasportas, and Jacob Emden, rabbinic authorities of the time, had conducted heresy-hunting campaigns against both explicit and covert Sabbatians. Kurzweil took up the same cudgels against Scholem, as if the messianic movement had now morphed into secular Zionism, with Scholem hiding his true Sabbatian identity behind the guise of an "objective" historian, just as earlier Sabbatians had disguised themselves as rabbinic Jews. In his argument for incorporating such heretical movements as Sabbatianism as legitimate expressions of Jewish history, Scholem had become a heretic himself.

Kurzweil was the most extreme critic of Scholem, although at the same time Scholem's colleague Zvi Werblowsky wrote a similar review of *Sabbatai Sevi*, claiming that Scholem and his students were sympathetic to the Sabbatians. Werblowsky, however, worked closely with Scholem; he translated the biography for publication in English. After Scholem's death, the Israeli philosopher Eliezer Schweid would unleash a similar attack.

As we have already had occasion to note, however, Scholem's attitude toward Sabbatianism was more complicated than these critics allowed. Yes, he was fascinated by this movement of heresy and believed strongly that it was a crucial force in Jewish history; to ignore it meant to ignore the role that the demonic played. His view of history included all the competing forces: rational and irrational, philosophical and mythic, legal and antinomian. As opposed to Kurzweil, he was not prepared to expel the heretics. But at the same time, as his politics demonstrate, he was equally worried about the effect the demonic

might have on the Jews, possibly destroying Zionism by turning Jewish renewal into apocalyptic destruction. The dialectic
of history, which he found so compelling, was also extraordinarily dangerous.

Scholem never responded publicly to Kurzweil, although
his archive contains some correspondence between them. He did
not recognize himself in Kurzweil's angry portrait. Kurzweil's
attempt to connect him to Nazism via Jung was particularly offensive, as well as irresponsible. As we have seen, Scholem satisfied himself that Jung had atoned for his earlier sympathies for
Nazism, and, in any case, the two men crossed paths only once,
at the Eranos Conference in 1952. Although he occasionally
used a Jungian term like "archetype," his fascination with myth
—one of Jung's important contributions to psychoanalysis—
predated any knowledge of Jung by several decades (he owed it
much more to Martin Buber). Scholem was not a Jungian, and
his participation in the Eranos Conferences was a thin reed on
which to hang an association with Nazism.

Nevertheless, aspects of Kurzweil's critique are worth taking seriously. The problem, not of objectivity but of the identification of a historian with his sources, was one that Scholem
wrestled with in his own mind. He was not a Kabbalist, but he
found compelling resonance between the Kabbalah's theology
and his own modern meditations on God and revelation. He
did not believe in divine revelation at Mount Sinai, but he believed that God worked through the literary tradition. He was
not a Sabbatian, but he found in the Sabbatians' desire for national redemption and for revolt against a decaying world inspiration for his own revolt. In fact, Scholem's historical work
remains so powerful, even decades after his death, because of
the interplay between his scholarship and questions that modern Jews face.

Although he did not address Kurzweil directly, a highly
unusual publication of his shortly after Kurzweil's review of the

Shabbatai Zvi biography can be read as a kind of response. This was a contribution to a Festschrift for Daniel Brody, whose publishing house in Zurich brought out many of Scholem's German writings in the decade and a half after the war. To a certain extent, "burying" a publication in a Festschrift was a way of indicating some ambivalence about it, but Scholem did allow it to be included later in one of the volumes of his collected German essays under the title *Judaica*. Scholem titled his contribution to the Brody volume "Ten Unhistorical Aphorisms About the Kabbalah." In writing in this laconic form, he was harking back to the ninety-five theses he wrote in his youth and dedicated to Walter Benjamin. He was also no doubt alluding to Benjamin's own last writing from 1940, his "On the Concept of History," which is organized in the form of ten theses. And, of course, in compiling ten aphorisms, rather than some other number, he was alluding to the Kabbalists' ten sefirot: his aphorisms would share something with the Kabbalah, even though he was not a Kabbalist.

The first aphorism deals directly with the irony of writing the history (or philology, as he calls it in the aphorism) of the Kabbalah. The historian deals with the "veil of fog" that surrounds his subject, that is, its historical residue rather than its essence.[12] But this is also the problem of the Kabbalist: he transmits what can be known of God but not the ineffable and unknowable essence of God. *Kabbalah* means "tradition" in Hebrew, but the Kabbalist transmits something that can never be transmitted since it lies beyond language. And this, too, is the problem of the historian, who can never recover the immediate truth of the past, but only the truth as it has been refracted through centuries of the literary tradition. Scholem thus played with the ironic similarity between the secular historian and the Kabbalist: both seek to uncover a hidden truth, although for the first that truth is in history, while for the second it is God.

In the tenth aphorism, he returned, twenty years later, to

what he wrote in the 1937 birthday letter to Salman Schocken. A hundred years before Kafka, he notes, the Frankist from Prague Jonas Wehle wrote a never-published manuscript in which he attempted to formulate heretical messianism in the language of the Enlightenment. Wehle raised the question of whether paradise had not lost more with the expulsion of Adam and Eve than had human beings themselves. Could it be that some "sympathy of souls" connected Wehle with Kafka, whose own writing Scholem had earlier called "heretical Kabbalah" on "the border between religion and nihilism"?[13] Since Scholem identified so strongly with Kafka, we would not be in error in assuming a "sympathy of souls" between Scholem himself and the Frankist Jonas Wehle. Again, Scholem was no Sabbatian or Frankist, but he definitely felt a kinship with those who searched for religious meaning at the outer limits of religion.

A publication from the next year gave him the opportunity to address some of these questions from a historical—as opposed to the "unhistorical"—perspective. In 1959, he gave his annual lecture at the Eranos Conference, titled "Toward an Understanding of the Messianic Idea in Judaism" (like most of his lectures, this one was first published in German in the *Eranos Yearbook*). The essay is one of Scholem's most capacious and synthesizing, ranging far beyond the Kabbalah back to the Bible and forward to modern times. He posited that Judaism has three attitudes toward the world: conservative (the reign of halakhah, or Jewish Law), restorative (restoring the ancient Kingdom of David with its temple and sacrifices), and utopian (resurrection of the dead, eternal peace, and so on). The messianic idea is made up of the dialectical interplay among all three.

One radical type of utopian messianism is apocalyptic, the belief in a catastrophic rupture in history in which the world as we know it would end. He says about the apocalyptic: "From the point of view of the *Halakhah*, to be sure, Judaism appears as a well-ordered house, and it is a profound truth that a well-ordered house is a dangerous thing. Something of Messianic apocalypticism penetrates into this house; perhaps I can best describe it as a kind of anarchic breeze." Scholem would seem to be endorsing apocalyptic movements like Sabbatianism as just such an "anarchic breeze." Yet a closer look at his argument reveals something different: "I would say that the great men of *Halakhah* are completely entwined in the realm of popular apocalypticism when they come to speak of redemption."[14] In other words, the very "anarchic breeze" so necessary to revive a conservative tradition is part of that tradition and not a foreign or heretical infection. And so Scholem should be understood as a champion not *only* of the heretical but rather of a tradition that is at once conservative and revolutionary.

He concluded the essay with a reflection on "the price demanded by Messianism." To live the messianic idea means to live "a life lived in deferment," rather than a life lived in the present moment. Because the Jews have lived such a deferred life, they have discharged the tension from time to time in movements of messianic redemption:

> Little wonder that overtones of Messianism have accompanied the modern Jewish readiness for irrevocable action in the concrete realm, when it set out on the utopian return to Zion. . . . Born of the horror and destruction that was Jewish history in our generation, it is bound to history itself and not to meta-history; it has not given itself up totally to Messianism. Whether or not Jewish history will be able to endure this entry into the concrete realm without perishing in the crisis of the Messianic claim which has virtually been conjured up—that is the question which out of his great and dangerous past the Jew of this age poses to his present and to his future.[15]

This is one of the most stirring passages in all of Scholem's oeuvre and it is a summation of his thinking about Zionism and messianism going back to the 1920s. Zionism is not a messianic movement, even as it borrows so much of its energy from the messianic tradition. Where messianism reaches for unattainable "meta-history," Zionism acts within the "concrete realm." But because it borrows so much of its hope from messianism, it risks falling into the same abyss as Sabbatianism and destroying everything it sought to create. The Holocaust, which might be the very spark that ignites such an apocalyptic catastrophe, could also be the ground for building an enduring edifice within history.

9

The Sage of Jerusalem

In 1958, shortly after his sixtieth birthday, Gershom Scholem was awarded the Israel Prize, the Jewish state's highest accolade. It was an award for a lifetime of scholarship, but it was perhaps no coincidence that it came only a year after the publication of his most controversial work, *Sabbatai Sevi*. Despite—or perhaps because of—the radical implications of his work, by the beginning of the 1960s, Scholem had become that rare luminary in the scholarly firmament: a public intellectual who spoke with authority beyond his field of expertise. He was now sought after to make statements on affairs of the day. He was also widely seen as an almost oracular voice on all matters Jewish, expressing a viewpoint that was at once Zionist and secular yet deeply steeped in Jewish history.

But the years had not dulled his sharp tongue or curbed his zest for polemics. In 1962, he received an invitation from Manfred Schloesser to contribute to a volume in honor of the German Jewish writer Margarete Susman. The theme of the volume, wrote Schloesser, was to be the "German-Jewish dialogue." On December 18, Scholem wrote back to Schloesser in high dudgeon. There was no such thing as a "German-Jewish dialogue," he thundered. It was really a one-sided dialogue, in which the Jewish supplicant never received an answer, an unrequited love affair of the Jews for German culture (we recall that he had already made this point in virtually the same terms in 1939 in response to Hannah Arendt's book on Rahel Varnhagen). The only Germans who took this "dialogue" seriously were the anti-Semites, and they, of course, had a violent idea of how to end it.

Although Scholem never mentioned him by name, he may have had in mind Martin Buber's notion of dialogue, which Buber articulated in *I and Thou* in 1923. The true kind of dialogue, in which one partner sees the full humanity of the other, was precisely what was missing between Germans and Jews. Scholem published his reply to Schloesser in the Susman Festschrift and afterward independently as "Against the Myth of the German-Jewish Dialogue." He later expanded it into a long lecture and essay, "Jews and Germans." Tellingly, he wrote these essays in German and published them in German venues: his intended audience was German rather than Jewish, which meant that in the process of rejecting the dialogue he was actually renewing it, if on different terms. And we might say that Scholem's many writings in German after the war, as well as his frequent lectures in Germany, were all intended to create a dialogue with the Germans on a new basis. While he judged the German nation as a whole guilty for the crimes of the Nazis, he nevertheless believed that there were many individuals innocent of these crimes who might provide the basis for this new dialogue.

Scholem's critique of the idea of a Jewish–German symbiosis or dialogue came simultaneously with the capture, trial, and execution of Adolf Eichmann, and it is probable that the connection was not coincidental. A short article that he wrote against capital punishment for Eichmann made this clear. Unlike those, such as Martin Buber, who opposed the death penalty on principle, Scholem made a different argument: the German people might see the execution of Eichmann as expiation for their sins and a way of providing closure to the Holocaust. For Scholem, the wound had to be kept open if there were to be any hope of future dialogue between Jews and Germans, since only on the basis of Germany accepting its guilt could there be anything to discuss.

The Eichmann affair started on May 11, 1960, when Israeli secret agents apprehended Eichmann, one of the key functionaries in the Holocaust, near his home in Argentina and spirited him away to Israel. On May 22, Israel's prime minister, David Ben-Gurion, electrified the country with his announcement to the Knesset that Eichmann was in Israel and would stand trial for his role in the destruction of the European Jews. The trial opened in Jerusalem nearly a year later, on April 11, 1961.

The *New Yorker* commissioned Hannah Arendt to cover the trial, although she was only present for a few weeks of the proceedings. While in Jerusalem, she reconnected with old friends from Germany, but Scholem was away on a research trip and they missed each other. Perhaps had they been able to discuss Arendt's initial impressions of the trial, matters might have turned out differently. But in the event, Arendt published a series of articles and then turned them into a book in 1963 under the title *Eichmann in Jerusalem: A Report on the Banality of Evil.* The book excited a controversy that still reverberates more than a half-century later. Arendt blasted David Ben-Gurion—an old nemesis of hers—for staging a show trial that aimed to tell the whole story of Holocaust, beyond Eichmann's more limited role. She leveled criticism at the Judenräte, the Jewish councils forced by the Nazis to do their bidding. And she portrayed Eichmann himself as "banal," his evil more a crime of thoughtlessness than of pathological anti-Semitism.

When Scholem received the book, he exploded. He wrote Arendt a scathing letter, questioning her condemnation of the Jewish councils and arguing that no one could pass judgment about their behavior under conditions of extreme terror. He took particular exception to her sarcastic tone, charging that she lacked *ahavat yisrael* (love of Israel). Arendt responded by insisting that she loved no particular people—Germans, Americans, or Jews—but only her friends. She reminded Scholem that she had never thought of herself as anything but a Jew, a biological given like her gender.

Since gender plays virtually no role in Arendt's philosophy, one might be tempted to conclude that Jewishness was also immaterial to her, which would explain her lack of ahavat yisrael. However, in her *Origins of Totalitarianism*, the book that made her reputation more than a decade earlier, as well as in the book on Rahel Varnhagen and numerous essays over the years, Arendt grounded her historical and political analysis squarely in Jewish life in the modern world. It was the experience of Jewish refugees, for example, that forced the world to confront the collapse of the nation-state. The Jewish condition was at the very heart of Arendt's writing, even if her gender was not. Perhaps she did not love the Jewish people, but she was certainly obsessed with them. And, conversely, while Scholem obviously identified with the Jewish people and its fate, his attitude, going back to his youth, toward those many Jews with whom he disagreed could hardly be called "love of Israel." In short, the debate about ahavat yisrael, over which so much scholarly ink has been spilled, may be a red herring.

It was certainly true that Arendt's sharp tone toward various Jewish authorities, from David Ben-Gurion to the leaders of the Nazi-appointed Jewish councils, was often uncharitably hostile and reflected an inability to walk in their shoes. (Her hostility to Jewish leaders was long-standing and had not started with the Eichmann book.) But even if Scholem was correct that it was too soon to render historical judgment on those who had to confront the Nazi terror, Arendt's willingness to offer a sharp critique of the official Jewish leadership was something Scholem, at least in his youth, would have applauded. And he remained highly critical of Ben-Gurion's statism and realpolitik well into the 1960s. Now, however, he saw Arendt's hostility to the way the Israelis tried Eichmann as a demonstration of her lack of understanding of the relationship between the Jewish state and the Holocaust.

One aspect of the debate between Scholem and Arendt has drawn less attention than it deserves. Scholem pointed out that in subtitling her book "A Report on the Banality of Evil," Arendt was renouncing the idea of "radical evil," which had played an important role in *The Origins of Totalitarianism*. Arendt responded that she had indeed decided that there was a kind of bureaucratic evil that was essential to understanding the crime of genocide. Here was a place where Scholem's own research pointed in a different direction: he believed in the existence of the demonic, the source of what Arendt had called radical evil. If the demonic in the case of Sabbatianism had produced a nihilistic revolt against rabbinic law, in the case of the Nazis it gave rise to mass murder. No amount of intellectual somersaults over "thoughtlessness" could conceal this eruption of the demonic. While the demonic in Scholem's view—as well as in the view of the Kabbalah—was a dialectical product of the divine, its origins in God by no means lessened its malevolence or destructive power.

Scholem and Arendt recognized that their epistolary exchange was of great intellectual importance, and they agreed to publish it in both German—the language of the letters—and English. Although a tremendous amount of writing has swirled around Arendt's Eichmann book over the years, the Scholem-Arendt exchange remains seminal and was recognized as such at the time. But the bitterness of the exchange persisted. Arendt broke off communications. When Scholem was on his way to New York in 1964, he wrote to her in the hopes of breaking through her silence and setting up a meeting. Evidently still deeply wounded, she again failed to respond. The final letter in their correspondence was thus from him, and for the last decade or so of Arendt's life (she died in 1975) an unbridgeable chasm separated the two.

In fact, even before the Eichmann trial, Arendt's private view of Scholem had become critical. In 1957, she wrote her impressions of Scholem to her friend Kurt Blumenfeld, who had warned her to beware of Scholem: "He [Scholem] is highly intelligent but not really clever. In addition, he is self-absorbed. . . . He fundamentally thinks that: the center of the world is Israel; the center of Israel is Jerusalem; the center of Jerusalem is the university; the center of the university is—Scholem. And the worst thing is that he seriously thinks that the world has a center."[1] Arendt here ironically adapted a saying of the Hasidic master Nahman of Bratslav that may apply to the Messiah, putting Scholem instead in the center. Despite—or perhaps because of—their friendship, she equated what she viewed as his narcissism with his Zionism.

Five years after the Eichmann controversy, Scholem returned to what he perceived as Arendt's arrogance in a private response to an Arendt essay on Walter Benjamin. Arendt had flippantly said that Benjamin was prepared to learn Hebrew when the Zionists promised him three hundred German marks or, later, dialectical materialism when the Marxists offered him a thousand French francs. Noting that Arendt had once been a half-Communist and, at other times, a Zionist, Scholem could not understand how she spoke "from her sovereign height" so disparagingly of two movements she had once endorsed.[2] Needless to say, he rejected out of hand her characterization of Benjamin's motives (although she might not have been totally off the mark).

There was something deeply tragic about this polemic: two friends, who came from similar backgrounds and had both come to Zionism in rebellion against German Jewish assimilation, were now driven apart by what should have united them. Scholem accused Arendt of having been infected by ideas of the German left, but he surely knew, as Arendt reminded him, that her intellectual roots were in German philosophy, as were his. They both defined their Zionism in utopian terms. But Scholem's years living in Israel necessarily distanced him from Arendt, who did not share the profound existential experiences of Israel's War of Independence and struggles to form a new society composed of immigrants and survivors. Arendt could not fully understand how all of these experiences shaped Scholem's response to the Eichmann trial and rendered him hostile to what he perceived as Arendt's airy intellectual exercise. In the end, the overbearing personalities of both these intellectuals, as well as their different life experiences, got the better of their friendship and destroyed it.

Side by side with this very public falling-out with Arendt came a new set of polemics against Scholem's old nemesis, Martin Buber. Buber and Scholem had by now been colleagues at the Hebrew University since 1938, and relations between them were generally quite collegial. Nevertheless, in 1961, Scholem let loose in the American magazine *Commentary* with an attack on Buber's interpretation of Hasidism. In a nutshell, he criticized Buber's understanding of the eighteenth-century Pietistic movement as ahistorical, based on Hasidic tales rather than on the more theoretical Hasidic sermons. He charged that Buber had projected his own existentialist philosophy on a movement whose core theology actually renounced the world, rather than, as Buber argued, affirmed it. Whereas Buber thought that "worshipping through the material" meant that the Hasidim made the everyday sacred, Scholem contended that the phrase actually meant the opposite: to "annihilate" the material world.[3]

When Buber, deeply wounded by what he regarded as Scholem's profound misunderstanding of his work, responded to this devastating critique two years later, Scholem's private reaction was scornful. He wrote to Theodor Adorno: "Three weeks ago, in the *Neue Zürcher Zeitung*, old Buber published a rejoinder—the lamentable response of a helpless blabberer—to my criticism of his Hasidic interpretations." Two years later, on June 20, 1965, he again wrote to Adorno, this time reporting on Buber's funeral a week earlier. Scholem had been asked to say a few words of eulogy. He admitted to Adorno that he was reluctant to speak lest he utter "a bald-face lie." Fortunately, Fania had provided him with three "talking points" which allowed him to squeak by without revealing his real feelings about his deceased colleague.[4] And three years after Buber's death, Scholem wrote to George Lichtheim that the first time he saw a Jew with a picture of Jesus on the wall was when he visited Buber in the Zehlendorf neighborhood of Berlin during the First World War. The tone of the letter makes it clear that he had viewed it then—as he continued to view it—with a measure of contempt.

The year after Buber's death, Scholem chose to devote his Eranos lecture to "Buber's Conception of Judaism," which is less overtly critical than the earlier essay on Buber's interpretation of Hasidism. Scholem starts out by explaining Buber's attraction—as a kind of Jewish heretic—for young, assimilated central European Jews of the early twentieth century. But he then levels a devastating observation about "the almost total lack of influence of Buber in the Jewish world, which contrasts strangely with his recognition among non-Jews."[5] Whatever Buber's attraction might have been earlier, by the post–World War II era, at least in Scholem's eyes, he had ceased to matter much to Jews.

As to their disagreement over Hasidism, Scholem recounts a meeting with Buber in 1943 in which he presented to the older man his critique of Buber's interpretation of Hasidism. Buber responded: "If what you are now saying were right, my dear Scholem, then I would have worked on Hasidism absolutely in vain, because in that case, Hasidism does not *interest* me at all."[6] A more telling contrast between a philosopher and a historian cannot be imagined.

Scholem's critique of Buber continued to rankle even after Buber's death. Grete Schaeder, a Buber disciple who had published *The Hebrew Humanism of Martin Buber* in 1966, wrote to Scholem that she was so distraught about his attack on Buber's interpretation of Hasidism that she was not able to bring herself to meet him. She makes clear how hurt Buber had been by Scholem's earlier words. Scholem answered Schaeder with a historical reflection on his struggles with Buber in his youth and concluded that, had he drawn on his unpublished youthful writings (most probably from his diary), he would have formulated his essay even more sharply.

Why did Scholem feel compelled to attack Buber repeatedly both in public and in private in the years immediately before and after Buber's death? It is noteworthy that in his unpublished English lectures on Hasidism of 1949, he was far less critical of Buber. But in a 1958 letter to the Swiss Jewish philosopher Hermann Levin Goldschmidt, he criticized Buber for his unhistorical interpretation of Hasidism and for his view that the Hasidim continued the philosophy of Baruch Spinoza. So by the late 1950s, Scholem had returned to the sharply critical view of Buber that had characterized his youth.

We have the sense that Scholem was completing some unfinished business—both scholarly and psychological—in the two articles that framed Buber's death in 1965. For Scholem, Buber was a lifelong foil, the embodiment of an approach to Jewish mysticism that Scholem had to conquer in order to rule. In 1933, he had praised Buber to the university authorities as the greatest expert in the world in the field of religious philosophy.

Buber might teach comparative religion, but he, Scholem, would dominate the discipline of Judaica. Yet he was not content to leave his youthful Buber complex in the past. Perhaps Buber remained a voice of reproach, the ghost of Scholem's own earlier Erlebnis enthusiasm, and the essays of the 1960s represented a kind of return of the repressed, a desire to settle accounts with a figure who remained both mentor and antagonist. Moreover, Buber was enjoying a renaissance in the 1960s, particularly in Germany and the United States. If Scholem saw himself as *the* representative of authentic Judaism, then Buber's renewed fame might have provoked him to revive the polemics of a half-century earlier.

However, in 1977, when Scholem came to write his memoir *From Berlin to Jerusalem*, he recounted his early meetings with Buber in far more irenic terms than were actually accurate. He concluded the passage on Buber by saying that even though he "later had great and far-reaching differences of opinion with Buber" and "I could not be blind to his weaknesses . . . I always greatly respected him—even revered him—as a person. . . . He was totally undogmatic and had an open mind toward different opinions."[7] It was almost as if he now regretted his harsh criticism of a decade earlier, if not also his criticisms from the World War I period. Certainly, he could not say of himself that he was "totally undogmatic and had an open mind toward different opinions."

These contradictory views of Buber bear witness to the role the older man played throughout Scholem's life. On some level, Scholem understood that without Buber, there would have been no Scholem, since it was Buber's passionate argument for the role of myth in Judaism that had influenced Scholem in his youth. It might not be an exaggeration to say that the intellectual support he could never win from his father he sought from Buber. But this desire for approval from the older man simultaneously provoked stormy rebellion, for Buber was a figure with whom Scholem continued to wrestle, even as he eclipsed his erstwhile rebbe as the greatest scholar of Jewish Studies in the twentieth century.

Buber may also have been on his mind when he delivered another Eranos lecture in 1963, "Tradition and Commentary as Religious Categories in Judaism" (the English version of this lecture was published under the title "Revelation and Tradition as Religious Categories in Judaism"). Here, too, he returned to themes from his youth, when he had searched for his own definition of Judaism against Buber's mysticism of experience. We recall that at that time he contrasted the idea of tradition with Buber's Judaism based on the experience of divine revelation. A decade and a half later, in his review of Hans-Joachim Schoeps's book, he came back to tradition as the medium through which the voice of revelation is refracted and given meaning. In a letter to Theodor Adorno, Scholem explicitly connected the Schoeps review to his Eranos lecture, which often borrowed from the earlier work word for word.

The Eranos lecture appears on the face of it to be an analysis of rabbinic and Kabbalistic texts rather than a statement of Scholem's own belief. Scholem brings in a number of famous texts that demonstrate how the rabbis allowed for a startling range of interpretations of biblical revelation, including interpretations contrary to the Bible's own meaning. Tradition encompasses an infinitude of interpretations, no matter how contradictory, in which every position a rabbinic authority announces has its grounding in the revelation at Sinai. Yet this seemingly scholarly account does little to conceal Scholem's own views. As he wrote in the 1937 birthday letter to Salman Schocken, he believed that Franz Kafka's writings had a "halo of the canonical" probably because they were open to an infinite number of readings.[8] Without passing judgment on whether Scholem was right in describing historical Judaism as involving an "anarchy" of interpretations, we must recognize that the philosophy he found in the sources from the tradition closely matched his own philosophy of Judaism.

As the sage of Jerusalem, Scholem was frequently called upon to offer political commentary, especially about Zionism and the State of Israel. We have seen that after the rise of Nazism, he withdrew increasingly from the political arena. Disillusionment certainly played a role. In 1961, Geula Cohen sent him her memoir of her years in Lehi, the Jewish underground known also as the Stern Gang. In the 1940s, Cohen had been the radio broadcaster and newsletter editor for this splinter group, which engaged in terrorism and also flirted with messianic ideas. Cohen had studied with Scholem, and he responded with a kind of paternal warmth, even as he disagreed vehemently with her right-wing politics.

Cohen's book caused him to reflect on the critical decisions that had confronted everyone in the years before the establishment of the state. While not denying that war or even terrorism might in certain circumstances be justified, he nevertheless found Cohen's ideology "quite repugnant." He too had had his dreams, although they were not the same as hers: "Even today my dreams do not conjure up the Kingdom and the heroism that enthralled you and your friends. But history makes equal fun of both your dream and mine. For the victory was not the one we hoped to see."[9] The State of Israel was not the messianic kingdom that Cohen desired, but neither had it produced the renewal of Judaism that Scholem had pursued since his youth.

Yet Scholem had not lost his belief in the dialectic of history, what the philosopher G. W. F. Hegel, whom he quotes, called "the ruse of reason." In 1965, he responded to the receipt of Georges Friedmann's *End of the Jewish People?* Friedmann was a French sociologist who had won some notoriety for his argument that the State of Israel was creating a nation that was no longer Jewish and, as such, was contributing to the demise of the Jewish people. Scholem's response was telling. He disagreed with Friedmann but confessed that "the Israeli nation, which has separated itself from the Jewish people, is marching toward its ruin." Nevertheless, where Friedmann had gone wrong was to "underestimate the tremendous power of reconstituting historical memory through dialectical swings of the pendulum." This swing of the historical pendulum would come as the result of a crisis that Scholem believed could be overcome by "the creative power of the Jewish genius, however indefinable."[10]

In his letter to Friedmann, we find in a nutshell Scholem's dialectical philosophy. He knew when he set out on his life's journey from Berlin to Jerusalem that Zionism would provoke a crisis of Jewish culture and identity, but he had faith that the forces unleashed by the Jewish national movement would also provide the solution to this crisis. His meditation in 1926 on the apocalyptic dangers inherent in the revived Hebrew language and his fears of the messianic nationalism of the Revisionists from the same period continued to haunt him. But he also believed that these same forces, properly harnessed, could dialectically produce a Jewish renaissance. And his reference to "the tremendous power of reconstituting historical memory" must surely refer to his own scholarly project.

Although no longer as politically active as he had been in the 1920s and early 1930s, Scholem paid keen attention to political developments and, from time to time, took part in public debates. In 1965, for example, he signed a statement in favor of the Mapai (Labor) Party of Levi Eshkol. The elections of that year included a new party, Rafi, that David Ben-Gurion had assembled with a number of younger politicians, such as the former general Moshe Dayan. Scholem's old hostility to Ben-Gurion's statism and aggressive foreign policy must have informed his decision to speak out with others against Ben-Gurion's challenge to the Labor Party, which Ben-Gurion had led for decades before splitting from it. The statement, almost certainly not written by Scholem, warns against Ben-Gurion's leadership, which it characterizes as a danger to Israel's democracy.

Scholem was abroad during the Six-Day War on a mission for the Israeli Embassy in London, but he was in Israel during the tense weeks before hostilities commenced. Within months after Israel's sweeping victory, an intense public debate began, which has not ended to this day, about what to do with the conquered territories. A group of intellectuals and political leaders, including members of the Labor Party, as well as more right-wing Zionists, formed in July 1967 under the banner of "Movement for a Greater Israel," by which they meant annexation of the territories. In August, Scholem, together with a long list of other intellectuals, artists, and writers, signed an opposing statement with the headline "Security and Peace, Yes—Annexation, No." The statement argued that the Six-Day War was a justified war of self-defense but that annexation of the territories would constitute "a danger to the Jewish image of the state, to its humanistic and democratic character, or to both."[11] The goal of Israeli policy must be first and foremost the pursuit of peace and the avoidance of creating obstacles to that goal.

In the years after the 1967 war, Scholem, by now one of Israel's most famous intellectuals, was increasingly called upon to defend his country in world public opinion. Journalists beat a path to his door on Abarbanel Street, and he was also frequently interviewed when he traveled abroad. While he was forthright in his criticism, especially at home, of Israel's occupation of the territories seized in the war, when it came to attacks from those outside the country on Israel's right to defend itself and, more broadly, on Zionism, he was equally forthright in defense of his country. Even if he had had his doubts when he came to Palestine about establishing a Jewish state, he had little doubt later that the state had every right to exist. On October 17, 1973, while the Yom Kippur War was still raging, he signed a letter to the *New York Times* with twenty other liberal professors from the Hebrew University that excoriated the Arab countries for their refusal to recognize Israel's existence and their perfidious attempt to destroy it.

From time to time, he also expressed himself on domestic matters. The recurrent debate over "who is a Jew?" arose from Israel's Law of Return, which guaranteed immediate citizenship to Jews. But how should the state define those to whom the law pertained? Should it be the halakhic definition (a Jew is the child of a Jewish mother or a convert) or the Nazi definition (a Jew is someone who has one Jewish grandparent)? Who should control conversion? In 1970, these unsettled questions again came in front of the Knesset, generating considerable controversy both within Israel and among diaspora Jews. In March 1970, Scholem spoke to a convention of American Reform rabbis meeting in Jerusalem on the subject. Addressing his audience as a historian rather than a rabbi, he asserted that Judaism is a "living and undefined organism. It is a phenomenon which changes and is transformed in the course of its history."[12] In the Middle Ages, those who disagreed with the rabbis were either punished or left the Jewish fold. When the rabbis lost their power in the modern world, those who disagreed with them could remain Jews and define Jewishness their own way. We are not surprised to learn that he rejected any dogmatic definition of a Jew, preferring instead an open, one might even say anarchistic, definition.

In his talk Scholem mentioned a moving example of this new freedom from his own family. We recall that his brother Werner had married Emmy, a non-Jewish German woman, much to the outrage of their father. Many years after the Holocaust, one of Werner's daughters, who because her mother was not Jewish could not be considered halakhically Jewish, returned to Germany and asked the Jewish community of Berlin to accept her. They did so since she was the daughter of a Jewish father and she wished to be counted among them. He might have also mentioned that Emmy herself returned to Germany and was accepted by the Jewish community of Hannover to live in the Jewish retirement home. Scholem retained a warm relationship with his brother's widow throughout her life and visited her on trips to Germany.

These examples from his family demonstrate how capacious was Scholem's definition of Jewishness, grounded as it was in a profoundly secular sensibility. And he held that such a broad definition was made possible by Zionism: "With the realization of Zionism, the fountains of the great deep of our historical being have welled up, releasing new forces within us. Our acceptance of our own history as a realm within which our roots grow is permeated with the conviction that the Jews, following the shattering catastrophe of our times, are entitled to define themselves according to their own needs and impulses; and that Jewish identity is not a fixed and static but a dynamic and even dialectical thing."[13]

In 1980, Scholem gave one of his last interviews, this time in English, to the *New York Review of Books*. Titled "The Threat of Messianism," it recapitulated in language and themes many of his long-standing preoccupations. But it also broke new ground in terms of Israeli politics. In 1974, religious Zionists had formed the Gush Emunim (Bloc of the Faithful), which, based on a messianic ideology, aimed to establish settlements in the occupied territories. With the election of the right-wing leader Menachem Begin, the settlement enterprise acquired strong government backing, and the number of Israelis living in the territories accelerated. Asked how he would characterize this settlement movement, Scholem was adamant: "They are like the Sabbatians. Like the Sabbatians, their messianic program can only lead to disaster. In the seventeenth century, of course, the failure of Sabbatianism had only spiritual consequences; it led to a breakdown of Jewish belief. Today, the consequences of such messianism are also political and that is a great danger."[14] Here he was closing a circle. Just as he had warned in the 1920s that the Revisionists were modern Sabbatians whose messianism threatened the very existence of Zionism, so, half a century later, their religious stepchildren constituted an existential threat. If not checked, these messianists would exact a high price. This was the cautionary tale his historical studies of Jewish messianism moved him to tell.

Having retired in 1965, Scholem was free to travel, and he did so with relish, holding visiting professorships in Switzerland, the United States, and Germany. He developed deep friendships with German intellectuals such as the philosopher Jürgen Habermas whose home in Starnberg, near Munich, he visited frequently, commenting humorously on Frau Habermas's cooking and spoiling their two daughters with pralines. He later took Habermas and his wife on an extensive tour of Jerusalem and other places in Israel.

He continued to publish prodigiously. He closed another circle by returning to the subject he first conceived in 1919 for his dissertation: the linguistic theory of the Kabbalah. And he continued in hot pursuit of the theme he announced in his "Redemption Through Sin" essay: the subterranean linkages between the vestiges of Sabbatianism and the Jewish Enlightenment. One of the most thrilling of these adventures was the strange career of Moses Dobruschka, a Frankist, who took part in the French Revolution under the name of Junius Frey and was guillotined during the Terror. Although his friend and colleague Jacob Katz wrote a trenchant critique of Scholem's dialectical theory of the way religious heresy turned into secular enlightenment, he was not dissuaded.

In the last decade of his life, he also turned to memoir. In 1975, he published his book on Walter Benjamin with the subtitle "The Story of a Friendship." He made extensive use of letters and diaries from his personal archive, which was not yet available to the public. This book found an eager audience, for interest in Benjamin was just then beginning to take off, fueled also by Scholem's earlier work with Adorno in publishing Benjamin's correspondence, as well as by Hannah Arendt's publication of Benjamin's essays in English. *Walter Benjamin: The Story of a Friendship* is as revealing about Scholem as it is about Benjamin. Two years later, he turned to writing his own autobiography, which concludes in 1923, his first year in Palestine. *From Berlin to Jerusalem* became an instant hit, written in Scholem's customary vigorous German style and drawing rich portraits of individuals and events from his youth.

His spirit remained provocative and lively even in old age. And his wit and sense of the absurd remained equally keen, as did his fascination with religious fakery and humbug. A letter that he wrote in 1978 to a young scholar of Kabbalah, Daniel Matt, who had served as his teaching assistant at Boston University, is worth quoting at length for what it reveals about Scholem's playful manner. Matt had reported to Scholem on his trip to India and his visits to various gurus. Matt also inquired about Scholem's knowledge of 1960s folk music. Written with flair in English, Scholem's letter betrays the persistence of his Germanic syntax:

> My opinion of the swamis seems to be a little more reserved than yours. I smelled a rat in several of those whom I encountered. . . . I wonder how you could manage not to go the short way from Goa to Pondicherry, to the ashram of the most famous Jewess after the Holy Virgin, or whatever title you want to give to Maria, who, according to the latest pronouncements of the previous pope . . . was bodily transfigured into Heaven. Has the ashram of Miss Miriam Mizrachi of Marseilles—later Mrs. Richards, and a great pupil of the famous former terrorist transformed into a saint, who one day recognized her as being an avatar of the goddess Kali— not attracted you, or at least your Jewish pride? Or were you perhaps prevented from being so by some vicious thought

you heard from your former teacher Scholem? . . . Who was or is, Robert Zimmerman, called Bob Dylan? Being an old racist, please let me know if he is a Jew. . . . My receptivity to music is, alas, nothing; therefore I forgo the pleasure of listening to "Blonde on Blonde" or even the more seducing "Desire." The title "Highway 61" arouses no desire in me. Maybe I am too old for it.[15]

In old age as in youth, he was forever inquisitive and open—albeit with skepticism—to new ideas. When Matt informed him of new discoveries in the authorship of the *Zohar*, Scholem wondered in the same letter whether he might have missed something in his own scholarship, but, then again, noted that there were "new discoveries every day." He congratulated Matt and then said, slyly: "And may I express the hope that they will stand up to critical scrutinizing."[16]

At that beginning of a 1975 lecture, Scholem explained to the audience how he had somehow become attracted to the study of Kabbalah and could not find anyone to explain it to him: "So I had to grope my way by myself, which is called scholarship." Always eager to provoke the more staid members of the profession, when asked what new fields of Jewish Studies needed investigation, he answered without hesitation: "the history of Jewish criminals."[17]

In October 1981, he came to Berlin to participate in the opening of the Wissenschaftskolleg, the new German institute for advanced study, where he gave the inaugural lecture and was appointed a fellow for its first year. He was feted as one of the greatest living intellectuals born in Germany and, despite his earlier imprecations against the existence of a German–Jewish dialogue, he was clearly eager to participate in a new version of such a dialogue, with himself at its center.

However, he was not in good health. During the summer of 1981, he began to experience abdominal pain. Despite a two-week vacation in Sils Maria, in the Swiss Alps, the pain continued, and in September, he underwent tests in Zurich, where he was spending the month. Two polyps were removed from his colon, and he was given a tentative diagnosis of Paget's disease of the pelvis (a condition in which the bones thicken). In December, he fell and injured himself. He was forced to return to Israel. The trip, initially planned for just the winter holiday, now took an ominous turn as he was hospitalized in Jerusalem with worsening pain. The doctors were unable to come to a firm diagnosis, and his condition deteriorated (he may have developed a rare form of bone cancer as a result of the Paget's disease).

By the end of January 1982, he was too weak to continue work, and he wrote to Peter Wapnewski, the director of the Wissenschaftskolleg, that he would be unable to return to Berlin. Closing another circle, he asked for Kitty Steinschneider—whose friendship he had continued to cherish over the years—to be at his side. When he became too weak to answer his correspondence, she did so for him, writing to a German colleague that Professor Scholem was too ill to answer but should he return to health, he would surely meet with the colleague in Germany in the spring.

He did not return to health, and he died on February 21, 1982. He was buried in the Sanhedria cemetery of Jerusalem in the only property he owned in the Land of Israel. His tombstone refers to him not only as a researcher of the Kabbalah but also as "a man of the Third Aliya." This designation, usually applied to the pioneers who worked the land, may not be how we think of this Germanic scholar in his suit and tie. But it is certainly apt, for he, too, dug deep into arid soil to bring forth a world both strange and wondrous.

A Personal Epilogue

ALTHOUGH MANY DECADES have passed since Gershom Scholem's death in 1982, his image still looms large over the field of Jewish Studies and, indeed, over intellectual life generally. He is now widely regarded as one of the great thinkers of the twentieth century, in addition to one of its greatest Jewish historians. There have naturally been many critiques of various of his arguments, but, regardless of how convincing any of these might be, the power of his oeuvre remains, carried by its rhetorical passion and remarkable erudition. His greatest accomplishment—to make his esoteric subject crucially important to modern women and men—stands unchallenged.

When I was a college student in the early 1970s, I discovered Scholem's *Major Trends in Jewish Mysticism* and devoured it as one might a sacred text. Here, it seemed to me, was hidden the secret of how a secular historian might immerse himself in religious sources and find in them meaning for the modern world. Today, many years and a career later, I still find that Scholem provides a sterling model for how to write the history of Judaism.

Some years after I first read *Major Trends*, when searching for a topic on which to write a dissertation, I suggested to Jacob Katz, then a visiting professor at UCLA, that I might like to write about Scholem. His eyes lit up and he said, "No one in Jerusalem would dare to do such a thing, but everyone there will read it."

I was fortunate to have had a number of meetings with Professor Scholem, starting in 1975, when I interviewed him for the dissertation, later published as *Gershom Scholem: Kabbalah and Counter-History* (this was the first book-length study of Scholem's thought in what is now a small library of such studies). In our first meeting, he spoke virtually nonstop for four hours, an experience that cannot be captured on paper. He was clearly pleased that a young student from California wanted to write about him, or, more precisely, about his thought.

To write a biography of Scholem while he was still alive was impossible, since the diaries and most of the letters I have used here were not accessible at the time. (See the bibliographical note for what is now available in English.) In fact, I had not thought to write such a biography until I received an unexpected invitation from Steven J. Zipperstein, one of the co-editors of the Yale Jewish Lives series, to do so. One rarely has the opportunity that this invitation provided to return to one's earliest work late in a long career and see the subject with fresh eyes.

Following the publication of my first book, I saw Professor Scholem several more times. He appeared by surprise at an award ceremony for my book and delivered some ironic words of praise: "I read this book and to me it seemed more like a novel . . ." The last time I saw him was in the autumn of 1980, when my wife and I paid him and Fania a social call at his Jerusalem apartment, which had one of the most remarkable private libraries in the city, with books covering every inch of every wall except for the space where Klee's small painting *Angelus Novus* hung. We chatted about many subjects, but he seemed most exercised by the increasing encroachment of the religious in Jerusalem who were taking over venerable neighborhoods like Rehavia, the bastion of German- and other European-born Israelis. For a moment, he seemed not much different from any other European bourgeois Jew, and at that moment I was struck by a heretical thought: he had become his father.

And yet, of course, not his father, who never escaped the confines of the assimilated German Jewish culture of his age. For even if Gershom Scholem had shed the rebellions of his youth to become one of the most respected thinkers of his generation, he had done so by wagering on the improbable: leaving Germany for the barren hills of Judea and researching a subject widely considered disreputable. He won those improbable bets, leaving behind a flourishing Hebrew University and Hebrew culture, as well as a field of scholarship now recognized as central to the history of Judaism. His father would have been proud.

NOTES

Unless otherwise indicated, all translations from German and Hebrew sources are mine.

Chapter 1. Berlin Childhood

1. Quoted in David Clay Large, *Berlin* (New York: Basic, 2000), 17–18.

2. Quoted in Paul Mendes-Flohr and Jehuda Reinharz, *The Jew in the Modern World* (Oxford: Oxford University Press, 1995), 268.

3. Franz Kafka, *Dearest Father: Stories and Other Writings*, trans. Ernst Kaiser and Eithne Wilkins (New York: Schocken, 1954), 172.

4. Gershom Scholem, *Tagebücher nebst Aufsätzen und Entwürfen bis 1923*. 1. *Halbband: 1913–1917*; 2. *Halbband: 1917–1923* (Frankfurt: Jüdischer Verlag, 1995–2000), 1:9 (February 17, 1913).

5. Ibid., 1:1 (February 18, 1913).

6. Franz Kafka, *Letters to Friends, Family and Editors*, trans.

Richard and Clara Winston (New York: Schocken, 1977), 289 (to Max Brod, June 1921).

7. Scholem, *Tagebücher*, 1:24 (undated entry).

8. Gershom Scholem, *Briefe*, 3 vols. (Munich: C. H. Beck, 1994–1999), 1:6 (September 8, 1914); 1:9 (Werner Scholem to Gerhard Scholem, September 8, 1914).

9. Ibid., 1:6 (September 8, 1914).

10. Scholem, *Tagebücher*, 1:111–112 (January 27, 1915).

11. Ibid., 1:117 (May 22, 1915).

12. Ibid., 1:103 (May 8, 1915); 1:119 (May 22, 1915).

13. Ibid., 1:120 (capitalizations retained from the German for certain words for emphasis).

Chapter 2. The Abyss of War

1. David Clay Large, *Berlin* (New York: Basic, 2000), 122.

2. Gershom Scholem, "It Was the War," in David Biale, *Gershom Scholem: Kabbalah and Counter-History* (Cambridge, Mass.: Harvard University Press, 1979), 241n42. Copyright © 1979, 1982 by David Biale.

3. Gershom Scholem, *Tagebücher nebst Aufsätzen und Entwürfen bis 1923. 1. Halbband: 1913–1917; 2. Halbband: 1917–1923* (Frankfurt: Jüdischer Verlag, 1995–2000), 1:121 (June 22, 1915). © Jüdischer Verlag im Suhrkamp Verlag Frankfurt am Main 1995. All rights reserved by and controlled through Suhrkamp Verlag Berlin. The "Old-New Land" is a reference to Theodor Herzl's utopian Zionist novel.

4. Gershom Scholem, *From Berlin to Jerusalem*, trans. Harry Zohn (New York: Schocken, 1980), 72.

5. Story related to me independently by Michael Löwy and by Buber's longtime secretary and archivist, Margot Cohen.

6. Scholem, *Tagebücher*, 1:457 (December 21, 1916).

7. Ibid., 1:347 (August 1, 1916).

8. Ibid., 2:213 (no date); Gershom Scholem, *Briefe*, 3 vols. (Munich: C. H. Beck, 1994–1999), 1:55 (October 26, 1916).

9. Scholem, *Tagebücher*, 1:399 (September 10, 1916).

10. For Scholem's position in this paragraph and the next, see the letters from October 4 and 9, 1916, in Scholem, *Briefe*, 1:43–52; and Scholem, *Tagebücher*, 1:396–399 (September 10, 1916).

11. Scholem, *Tagebücher*, 1:58 (November 21, 1914).

12. Scholem, *Briefe*, 1:28 (April 1, 1916).

13. Ibid., 1:42 (July 17, 1916).

14. Ibid., 1:55 (October 26, 1916).

15. Ibid.; Scholem, *Tagebücher*, 1:416 (November 9, 1916).

16. Betty Scholem and Gershom Scholem, *Mutter und Sohn im Briefwechsel* (Munich: C. H. Beck, 1989), 13 (May 12, 1917), translated in Gershom Scholem, *A Life in Letters, 1914–1982*, ed. and trans. Anthony David Skinner (Cambridge: Harvard University Press, 2002), 41.

17. Scholem, *From Berlin to Jerusalem*, 91.

18. Scholem, *Briefe*, 1:77 (to Erich Brauer, July 15, 1917).

19. Ibid., 1:84 (to Aharon Heller, July 25, 1917); 1:93–94 (to Werner Kraft, August 11, 1917); 1:97 (to Heller, August 15, 1917).

20. Ibid., 1:95 (to Harry Heymann, August 14, 1917); Scholem, *From Berlin to Jerusalem*, 95.

21. Scholem, *Briefe*, 1:94 (August 11, 1917).

22. Scholem, *Tagebücher*, 2:61–63 (October 21, 1917); 2:70 (November 11, 1917).

Chapter 3. Scholem in Love

1. Gershom Scholem, *Tagebücher nebst Aufsätzen und Entwürfen bis 1923. 1. Halbband: 1913–1917; 2. Halbband: 1917–1923* (Frankfurt: Jüdischer Verlag, 1995–2000), 2:54 (October 15, 1917).

2. Ibid., 2:90–91 (December 5, 1917).

3. Ibid., 2:274 (July 23, 1918).

4. Gershom Scholem, *Walter Benjamin: The Story of a Friendship* (Philadelphia: Jewish Publication Society, 1981), 105–106.

5. Ibid., 130.

6. Ibid., 87, 95.

7. Scholem, *Tagebücher*, 2:58 (October 17, 1917).

8. Ibid., 2:75–76 (November 5, 1917).

9. Ibid., 2:300–306 (July 15, 1918).

10. Gershom Scholem, *Briefe*, 3 vols. (Munich: C. H. Beck, 1994–1999), 1:83 (July 17, 1917). Emphasis in the original.

11. Scholem, *Tagebücher*, 2:58 (October 17, 1917).

12. Scholem, *Briefe*, 1:340n2.

13. Ibid., 1:25–28 (February 4, 1916).

14. Scholem, *Tagebücher*, 2:46–47 (October 1, 1917); 2:52 (October 5, 1917).

15. Gershom Scholem, *From Berlin to Jerusalem*, trans. Harry Zohn (New York: Schocken, 1980), 73–74; Scholem, *Tagebücher*, 1:305 (June 10, 1916).

16. Scholem, *From Berlin to Jerusalem*, 100, 101.

17. Scholem, *Tagebücher*, 2:93 (December 18, 1917).

18. Ibid., 2:99 (no date).

19. Scholem, *Briefe*, 1:103 (to Aharon Heller, October 2, 1917).

20. Scholem, *Tagebücher*, 2:16 (May 17, 1917).

21. Ibid., 2:74 (November 4, 1917).

22. Ibid., 2:139 (February 24, 1918).

23. Ibid., 2:145 (March 1, 1918).

24. Scholem, *Briefe*, 1:374–375n1 (March 5, 1918).

25. Ibid., 1:142–144 (March 7, 1918).

26. Ibid., 1:375n4 (March 11, 1918).

27. Scholem, *Tagebücher*, 2:150 (March 14, 1918).

28. Gershom Scholem, *Briefe an Werner Kraft* (Frankfurt: Suhrkamp, 1985), 71 (March 14, 1918); Scholem, *Briefe*, 1:145–146 (to Aharon Heller, March 16, 1918); 146–148 (to Escha Burchhardt, March 24, 1918).

29. The poem has been published in the original with a translation in Gershom Scholem, *The Fullness of Time: Poems*, trans. Richard Sieburth (Jerusalem: Ibis, 2003), 54–55; Scholem, *Tageücher*, 2:398–399 (October 13, 1918); "To Grete," in Scholem, *Tagebücher*, 2:634–635 (June 10, 1920).

30. Gershom Scholem, *Von Berlin nach Jerusalem*, expanded edition based on the Hebrew edition (Frankfurt: Suhrkamp, 1997), 75.

31. Gershom Scholem, *A Life in Letters, 1914–1982*, ed. and

trans. Anthony David Skinner (Cambridge: Harvard University Press, 2002), 76–77 (June 23, 1918).

32. Scholem, *Briefe*, 1:157 (May 28, 1918).

33. Ibid., 1:166 (July 23, 1918); Scholem, *Tagebücher*, 2:409 (November 25, 1918).

34. Scholem, *Tagebücher*, 2:410 (November 26, 1918); 2:417 (December 18, 1918).

35. Ibid., 2:424 (December 25, 1918).

36. Ibid., 2:459 (June 21, 1919), translation from Anthony David Skinner, ed. and trans., *Lamentations of Youth: The Diaries of Gershom Scholem, 1913–1919* (Cambridge: Harvard University Press, 2008), 304.

37. Gershom Scholem, *On Jews and Judaism in Crisis: Selected Essays*, ed. Werner J. Dannhauser (New York: Schocken, 1976), 55–57.

Chapter 4. The Book of Brightness

1. Gershom Scholem, *Tagebücher nebst Aufsätzen und Entwürfen bis 1923. 1. Halbband: 1913–1917; 2. Halbband: 1917–1923* (Frankfurt: Jüdischer Verlag, 1995–2000), 1:444 (May 15, 1919).

2. Quoted in David Biale, *Gershom Scholem: Kabbalah and Counter-History* (Cambridge: Harvard University Press, 1979), 74–76.

3. Gershom Scholem, *A Life in Letters, 1914–1982*, ed. and trans. Anthony David Skinner (Cambridge: Harvard University Press, 2002), 108. © Gershom Scholem. © All rights reserved by and controlled through Suhrkamp Verlag Berlin.

4. Betty Scholem and Gershom Scholem, *Mutter und Sohn im Briefwechsel* (Munich: C. H. Beck, 1989), 58 (November 25, 1919), translated in Gershom Scholem, *A Life in Letters, 1914–1982*, ed. and trans. Anthony David Skinner (Cambridge: Harvard University Press, 2002), 108.

5. Scholem and Scholem, *Mutter und Sohn*, 59 (December 6, 1919), translated in Scholem, *Life in Letters*, 109. Translation slightly modified.

6. Scholem, *Life in Letters*, 117 (March 7, 1921).

7. Rosenzweig, letter to Rudolf Hallo (May 12, 1921), in Franz

Rosenzweig, *Briefe und Tagebücher*, ed. Rachel Rosenzweig and Edith Rosenzweig (The Hague: Martinus Nijhoff, 1979), 704. Emphasis in original.

8. Rosenzweig, *Briefe*, 482 (May 30, 1923).

9. Gershom Scholem, *Briefe*, 3 vols. (Munich: C. H. Beck, 1994–1999), 1:230 (to Ernst Simon, December 22, 1925). Emphasis in the original.

10. Gershom Scholem, *From Berlin to Jerusalem*, trans. Harry Zohn (New York: Schocken, 1980), 129–130.

11. Ibid.

12. Scholem, *Life in Letters*, 118–119 (incorrectly dated), translation revised based on Scholem and Scholem, *Mutter und Sohn*, 80–81 (December 3, 1921).

13. Scholem, *Life in Letters*, 112 (April 17, 1920).

Chapter 5. A University in Jerusalem

1. Gershom Scholem, *A Life in Letters, 1914–1982*, ed. and trans. Anthony David Skinner (Cambridge: Harvard University Press, 2002), 128 (November 1, 1923).

2. Ibid., 159 (January 31, 1928).

3. Gershom Scholem, *Briefe*, 3 vols. (Munich: C. H. Beck, 1994–1999), 1:230 (January 22, 1925).

4. Ibid., 1:233 (to Ernst Simon, May 12, 1926).

5. Ibid., 1:222 (to Werner Kraft, December 17, 1924).

6. Gershom Scholem, untitled manuscript (end of 1924), Gershom Scholem Archive (National Library, Jerusalem) 4* 1599.277.1.52.

7. Scholem, *Life in Letters*, 145 (to Ernst Simon, September 2, 1925).

8. Gershom Scholem, "The Despair of Victory," April 12, 1926, Scholem Archive 4* 1599.277.1.57.

9. Gershom Scholem, "From My Diary, 1926" (Hebrew), Scholem Archive 4* 1599.277.1.60.

10. Gershom Scholem, "Einige Bemerkungen über Hebräisch und Hebräischlernen," undated [1926?], Scholem Archive 4* 1599.277.1.25.

11. The article was first published in Stéphane Mosès, "Langage et sécularisation chez Gershom Scholem," *Archives de sciences sociales des religions* 60 (1985): 85–96. For the original German, see Michael Brocke, "Franz Rosenzweig und Gerhard Gershom Scholem," http://www.steinheim-institut.de/edocs/bpdf/michael _brocke-franz_rosenzweig_und_gerhard_gershom_scholem.pdf (accessed October 3, 2017).

12. My translation of Brocke, "Franz Rosenzweig und Gerhard Gershom Scholem," 21.

13. "Brit Shalom Society: Regulations" (Hebrew), *She'ifoteinu* 1, no. 1 (1927): 53.

14. Gershom Scholem,"Ist die Verstäundigung mit den Arabern gescheitert?" *Jüdische Rundschau* 33 (1928): 644.

15. Scholem Testimony on 1929 Events, Central Zionist Archives L59/115, quoted in Hillel Cohen, *Year Zero of Arab-Israeli Conflict: 1929*, trans. Haim Watzman (Waltham, Mass.; Brandeis University Press, 2015), 109–110.

16. Material Concerning Brit Shalom, Scholem Archive 4* 1599.07.253.2.

17. Gershom Scholem, "The Final Goal" (Hebrew), *She'ifoteinu* 2 (1930): 156.

18. Yehuda Burla, "The Covenant of Failure" (Hebrew), *Davar,* November 27, 1929; Gershom Scholem, "Three Sins of Brit Shalom" (Hebrew), *Davar,* December 12, 1929, 2.

19. Gershom Scholem, "Die Theologie des Sabbatianismus im Lichte Abraham Cardosos," in Scholem, *Judaica: Studien zur jüdischen Mystik*, 3 vols. (Frankfurt: Suhrkamp, 1968–1973), 1:146.

20. Gershom Scholem, *Walter Benjamin: The Story of a Friendship* (Philadelphia: Jewish Publication Society, 1981), 171–174.

21. *The Correspondence of Walter Benjamin and Gershom Scholem, 1932–1940*, ed. Gershom Scholem, trans. Gary Smith and Andre Lefevere (Cambridge: Harvard University Press, 1992), 173.

22. Gershom Scholem, "Franz Rosenzweig and His Book *The Star of Redemption*," trans. Paul Mendes-Flohr in Scholem, *On the Possibility of Jewish Mysticism in Our Time and Other Essays*, ed. Avraham Shapira (Philadelphia: Jewish Publication Society, 1997), 203.

23. Ibid., 205.

24. Gershom Scholem, "On the 1930 Edition of Rosenzweig's *Star of Redemption*," trans. Michael A. Meyer, in Scholem, *The Messianic Idea in Judaism and Other Essays in Jewish Spirituality* (New York: Schocken, 1971), 323. The essay originally appeared in the *Frankfurter Israelitisches Gemeindeblatt* 10 (1931): 15–17.

Chapter 6. Redemption Through Sin

1. Gershom Scholem, *A Life in Letters, 1914–1982*, ed. and trans. Anthony David Skinner (Cambridge: Harvard University Press, 2002), 199 (March 18, 1932).

2. Gershom Scholem, "Offener Brief an den Verfasser der Schrift, 'Jüdischer Glaube in dieser Zeit,'" *Bayerische Israelitsche Gemendezeitung*, August 15, 1932, 243. Reprinted in Gershom Scholem, *Briefe*, 3 vols. (Munich: C. H. Beck, 1994–1999), 1:466–471.

3. *The Correspondence of Walter Benjamin and Gershom Scholem, 1932–1940*, ed. Gershom Scholem, trans. Gary Smith and Andre Lefevre (Cambridge: Harvard University Press, 1992), 126 (July 17, 1934).

4. Gershom Scholem, *In the Fullness of Time*, trans. Richard Sieburth, ed. Steven Wasserstrom (Jerusalem: Ibis, 2003), 100 (translation revised). Reprinted by permission of Richard Sieburth.

5. Scholem, *Life in Letters*, 203 (November 20, 1932).

6. *Correspondence of Walter Benjamin and Gershom Scholem*, 29 (February 28, 1933).

7. Ibid., 44 (May 4, 1933).

8. Betty Scholem and Gershom Scholem, *Mutter und Sohn im Briefwechsel* (Munich: C. H. Beck, 1989), 298. See also Betty's response, ibid., 302.

9. *Correspondence of Walter Benjamin and Gershom Scholem*, 44 (May 4, 1933).

10. Hans (Shmuel) Sambursky, "The Crooked Giant," from Hans Jonas, *Memoirs*, trans. Krishna Winston, ed. Christian Wiese (Waltham, Mass.: Brandeis University Press, 2008), 88. Copyright © 2008 by Brandeis University Press. Reprinted with permission

of University Press of New England. Typographical error in line 4—"not" for "no"—corrected.

11. Escha Else Bergmann Archive (National Library, Jerusalem) 4* 1547.02.67. (The catalogue of the archive spells the last name "Bergmann.")

12. Gershom Scholem, note dated Wednesday night, February 15, 1934, Gershom Scholem Archive (National Library, Jerusalem) 4* 1599.01.2554; *Correspondence of Walter Benjamin and Gershom Scholem*, 122 (July 9, 1934).

13. Gershom Scholem, note to Kitty Steinschneider, September 12, 1934, Scholem Archive 4* 1599.01.2554.

14. Gershom Scholem, Diary (November 25, 1934), Scholem Archive 4* 1599.265.

15. Samuel Hugo Bergman, "Tagebücher" (October 21, 1935), Samuel Hugo Bergmann Archive (National Library, Jerusalem) 4* 1502.02.47. (The catalogue of the archive spells the last name "Bergmann.") I thank Enrico Lucca for sharing this material from Bergman's unpublished diaries.

16. *Correspondence of Walter Benjamin and Gershom Scholem*, 176–177 (April 19, 1936).

17. Scholem, *Life in Letters*, 277 (December 4, 1936).

18. *Correspondence of Walter Benjamin and Gershom Scholem*, 181 (June 6, 1936).

19. Ibid., 174 (June 20, 1934).

20. Gershom Scholem, "Redemption Through Sin," trans. Hillel Halkin, in Scholem, *The Messianic Idea in Judaism and Other Essays in Jewish Spirituality* (New York: Schocken, 1971), 140–141.

21. Ibid., 126–127. Translation slightly modified based on the Hebrew original.

22. Hans (Shmuel) Sambursky, "To Scholem," from Hans Jonas, *Memoirs*, trans. Krishna Winston, ed. Christian Wiese (Waltham, Mass.: Brandeis University Press, 2008), 88. Copyright © 2008 by Brandeis University Press. Reprinted with permission of University Press of New England. Translation modified based on German original.

Chapter 7. Kabbalah and Catastrophe

1. Gershom Scholem, *A Life in Letters, 1914–1982*, ed. and trans. Anthony David Skinner (Cambridge: Harvard University Press, 2002), 280 (July 10, 1937).

2. Gershom Scholem, *Major Trends in Jewish Mysticism*, 3rd rev. ed. (New York: Schocken, 1995), xxv.

3. Ibid., 37.

4. Ibid., 290, 293.

5. Ibid., 349–350.

6. Ibid., 350.

7. *The Correspondence of Walter Benjamin and Gershom Scholem, 1932–1940*, ed. Gershom Scholem, trans. Gary Smith and Andre Lefevre (Cambridge: Harvard University Press, 1992), 214 (March 25, 1938).

8. Ibid., 255–256 (June 30, 1939).

9. Ibid., 257.

10. Scholem, *Life in Letters*, 312 (July 17, 1941).

11. Gershom Scholem, "Tagebücher: Ende 1922 Juli 1934–Nov. 34; 1935–48," 65, Gershom Scholem Archive (National Library, Jerusalem) 4* 1599.265.22, translated into Hebrew and quoted in Noam Zadoff, *Mi-Berlin le-Yerushalayim u-ve-Hazarah: Gershom Scholem bein Yisrael ve-Germania* (Jerusalem: Carmel, 2015), 179.

12. Scholem, "Tagebücher," 74, quoted in Zadoff, *Mi-Berlin*, 197; Scholem, "Tagebücher," 79–80, quoted in Zadoff, *Mi-Berlin*, 197.

13. Gershom Scholem, will, July 14, 1943, Scholem Archive 4* 1599.02.8a.

14. *Luah Ha-Aretz* (Tel Aviv: Schocken, 1944–1945), 94.

15. Gershom Scholem, "Meditations on Jewish Studies" (Hebrew), *Devarim be-Go* (Tel Aviv: Am Oved, 1975), 396. An English translation that differs somewhat from mine can be found under the title "Reflections on Modern Jewish Studies" in Gershom Scholem, *On the Possibility of Mysticism in Our Time*, ed. Avraham Shapira, trans. Jonathan Chipman (Philadelphia: Jewish Publication Society, 1997), 51–71.

16. Scholem, "Meditations on Jewish Studies," 391.

17. Ibid., 399.

18. Ibid., 402.

Chapter 8. The Zionist Return to History

1. Gershom Scholem, *A Life in Letters, 1914–1982*, ed. and trans. Anthony David Skinner (Cambridge: Harvard University Press, 2002), 330 (January 28, 1946).

2. Gershom Scholem, "Mi-nisiyotai be-Shlihut be-Europa" (Diary), 15 (May 17, 1946), Gershom Scholem Archive (National Library, Jerusalem) 4* 1599.265.24.

3. Noam Zadoff, *Mi-Berlin Mi-Berlin le-Yerushalayim u-ve-Hazarah: Gershom Scholem bein Yisrael ve-Germania* (Jerusalem: Carmel, 2015), 224.

4. Scholem, "Mi-nisiyotai be-Shlihut be-Europa" (Diary), 45 (August 2, 1946). Emphasis in original.

5. Gershom Scholem and Joseph Weiss, *Halifat Mikhtavim*, ed. Noam Zadoff (Jerusalem: Carmel, 2012), 383–385; translation quoted in Anthony David Skinner, "Introduction," in *Lamentations of Youth: The Diaries of Gershom Scholem, 1913–1919*, trans. Anthony David Skinner (Cambridge, Mass.: Belknap, 2008), 4.

6. Scholem, *Life in Letters*, 341 (to Hugo and Escha Bergman, December 15, 1947).

7. Ibid., 356 (to Isaac Leo Seeligmann, August 3, 1948).

8. Gershom Scholem, "The Star of David: History of a Symbol," trans. Michael A. Meyer, in Scholem, *The Messianic Idea in Judaism and Other Essays in Jewish Spirituality* (New York: Schocken, 1971), 281.

9. Gershom Scholem, "My Way to Kabbalah," in Scholem, *On the Possibility of Jewish Mysticism in Our Time and Other Essays*, trans. Jonathan Chipman (Philadelphia: Jewish Publication Society, 1997), 24.

10. Gershom Scholem, *Sabbatai Sevi*, 2nd ed. (Princeton: Princeton University Press, 1973), 928–929.

11. Baruch Kurzweil, *Ba-Ma'avak al Arkhai ha-Yahadut* (Tel Aviv: Schocken, 1969), 134, 111.

12. Gershom Scholem, "Zehn unhistorische Sätze über die Kabbala," in Scholem, *Judaica: Studien zur jüdischen Mystik*, 3 vols. (Frankfurt: Suhrkamp, 1968–1973), 3:264.

13. Ibid. 3:271.

14. Gershom Scholem, "Toward an Understanding of the Messianic Idea in Judaism," trans. Michael A. Meyer, in Scholem, *Messianic Idea*, 21.

15. Ibid., 35–36.

Chapter 9. The Sage of Jerusalem

1. Hannah Arendt and Kurt Blumenfeld, *Die Korrespondenz* (Hamburg: Rotbuch, 1995), 174–175 (January 9, 1957).

2. Gershom Scholem, *A Life in Letters, 1914–1982*, ed. and trans. Anthony David Skinner (Cambridge: Harvard University Press, 2002), 433–434 (to Hans Paeschke, March 24, 1968).

3. Gershom Scholem, "Martin Buber's Interpretation of Hasidism," trans. Michael A. Meyer, in Scholem, *The Messianic Idea in Judaism* (New York: Schocken, 1971), 227–250; originally published as "Martin Buber's Hasidism," *Commentary* (October 1, 1961): 305–316.

4. Theodor W. Adorno and Gershom Scholem, *"Der liebe Gott wohnt im Detail": Briefwechsel, 1939–1969*, ed. Asaf Angermann (Frankfurt: Suhrkamp, 2015), 286 (April 22, 1963); 354–355 (June 20, 1965).

5. Gershom Scholem, "Martin Buber's Conception of Judaism," in *On Jews and Judaism in Crisis*, ed. Werner Dannhauser (New York: Schocken, 1976), 128.

6. Ibid., 167.

7. Gershom Scholem, *From Berlin to Jerusalem*, trans. Harry Zohn (New York: Schocken, 1980), 72.

8. Quoted in David Biale, *Gershom Scholem: Kabbalah and Counter-History* (Cambridge: Harvard University Press, 1979), 31.

9. Scholem, *Life in Letters*, 366–367 (December 15, 1961).

10. Ibid., 411–412 (July 18, 1965).

11. "Security and Peace, Yes—Annexation, No" (Hebrew), *Haaretz*, December 15, 1967, front page.

12. Gershom Scholem, "Who Is a Jew?" in Scholem, *On the Possibility of Jewish Mysticism in Our Time and Other Essays,* ed. Avraham Shapira, trans. Jonathan Chipman (Philadelphia: Jewish Publication Society, 1997), 93.

13. Ibid., 98–99.

14. David Biale, "The Threat of Messianism: An Interview with Gershom Scholem," *New York Review of Books* (August 14, 1980): 22.

15. Scholem, *Life in Letters,* 473–474 (July 20, 1978).

16. Ibid.

17. "Gershom Scholem—Conception of Tselem, the Astral Body in Jewish Mysticism," YouTube (accessed November 3, 2017); private conversation with the author.

SELECTED READINGS IN ENGLISH

FOR SCHOLEM'S BIOGRAPHY in English, the best source, although it does not treat Scholem's youth, is Noam Zadoff, *Gershom Scholem: From Berlin to Jerusalem and Back* (Waltham, Mass.: Brandeis University Press, 2017). Additional insights can be found in Amir Engel, *Gershom Scholem: An Intellectual Biography* (Chicago: Chicago University Press, 2017). A great deal of biographical material on Gershom Scholem can also be found in Mirjam Zadoff's biography of Scholem's brother Werner Scholem: *The Red Job: A Biography of Werner Scholem* (Philadelphia: University of Pennsylvania Press, 2017). A biography of all four Scholem brothers that gives a detailed social history of their background is Jay Howard Geller, *The Scholems: Gershom Scholem, His Family, and the Jewish Middle Class in Germany* (Ithaca: Cornell University Press, forthcoming). Finally, George Prochnik has written a detailed biography of Scholem interwoven with his own autobiography in *Stranger in a Strange Land: In Search of Gershom Scholem and Jerusalem* (New York: Other Press, 2016).

The first study of Scholem's philosophy of Jewish history is David Biale, *Gershom Scholem: Kabbalah and Counter-History* (Cambridge: Harvard University Press, 1979). An interpretation of Scholem's thought that compares him to other Weimar-era intellectuals is Benjamin Lazier, *God Interrupted: Heresy and the European Imagination Between the World Wars* (Princeton: Princeton University Press, 2008). On the intellectual relationship between Scholem and Walter Benjamin, especially their interpretations of Franz Kafka, see Robert Alter, *Necessary Angels: Tradition and Modernity in Kafka, Benjamin, and Scholem* (Cambridge: Harvard University Press, 1991). See also Eric Jacobson, *Metaphysics of the Profane: The Political Theology of Walter Benjamin and Gershom* Scholem (New York: Columbia University Press, 2003). For the way Scholem, Hannah Arendt, and Victor Klemperer confronted the upheavals of their time, see Steven Aschheim, *Scholem, Arendt, Klemperer: Intimate Chronicles in Turbulent Times* (Bloomington: Indiana University Press, 2001). On the historical evolution of Scholem's studies of Sabbatianism, see Yaacob Dweck, "Introduction to the Princeton Classics Edition," in Gershom Scholem, *Sabbatai Sevi: The Mystical Messiah, 1626–1676* (Princeton: Princeton University Press, 2016).

Scholem's two memoirs, written in the last decade of his life, are *Walter Benjamin: The Story of a Friendship* (Philadelphia: Jewish Publication Society, 1981) and *From Berlin to Jerusalem* (New York: Schocken, 1980). A translation of selections from his youthful diary is Anthony David Skinner, ed. and trans. *Lamentations of Youth: The Diaries of Gershom Scholem, 1913–1919* (Cambridge: Harvard University Press, 2008). Skinner has also translated selected letters from throughout Scholem's life in his edition of Scholem's *A Life in Letters, 1914–1982* (Cambridge: Harvard University Press, 2002). An English translation of Scholem's correspondence with Walter Benjamin in the 1930s can be found in *The Correspondence of Walter Benjamin and Gershom Scholem, 1932–1940*, ed. Gershom Scholem, trans. Gary Smith and Andre Lefevre (New York: Schocken, 1989).

Scholem's own writings on Kabbalah and other subjects in the field of Jewish Studies are too numerous to mention. Several collections are noteworthy: the volume containing "Redemption Through Sin" is *The Messianic Idea in Judaism and Other Essays in Jewish Spirituality* (New York: Schocken, 1971). The essay "Meditations on Jewish Studies" (under a different title) is in *On the Possibility of Jewish Mysticism in Our Time and Other Essays*, ed. Avraham Shapira, and trans. Jonathan Chipman (Philadelphia: Jewish Publication Society, 1997). A volume that contains some of Scholem's writings from his youth is *On Jews and Judaism in Crisis: Selected Essays*, ed. Werner J. Dannhauser (New York: Schocken, 1976). Scholem's two most important books are *Sabbatai Sevi*, trans. R. J. Zwi Werblowsky (Princeton: Princeton University Press, 2016), and *Major Trends in Jewish Mysticism* (New York: Schocken, 1995).

ACKNOWLEDGMENTS

MY FIRST THANKS go to Steven J. Zipperstein, co-editor of the Yale Jewish Lives series, who invited me to write this book, a project that I had entertained but dismissed in earlier years. Steve's friendship and intellectual companionship, going back to graduate school at UCLA, have been a great gift. He also provided some excellent critical interventions as the manuscript unfolded.

I am in the debt of the members of the Scholem Workshop (or, as we call it, the Scholemaniacs), which has met twice, first at Indiana University and then in Zurich, to discuss our common interests in writing Gershom Scholem's biography: Steven Aschheim, Amir Engel, Eric Jacobson, Andreas Kilcher, Shaul Magid, Daniel Weidner, Mirjam Zadoff, and Noam Zadoff. Noam has been particularly generous in sharing his knowledge of the Scholem corpus.

I was honored to be hosted by two institutions during the writing of the book: the Simon Dubnow Institute in Leipzig, Germany, in the summer of 2015 and YIVO at the Center for Jewish History in New York in the fall of 2016. I thank them for their support. I also thank the Scholem Library and the Scholem Archive at the Hebrew University in Jerusalem for several research visits to explore their holdings and for organizing a lecture in January 2017 on writing Scholem's biography.

A number of people either read versions of the manuscript and/or shared their views of the subject in conversation. I thank Asaf Angermann, Steven Aschheim, Rachel Biale, Jay Geller, Peter E. Gordon, Martin Jay, Enrico Lucca, Jonatan Meir, George Prochnik, Paul Reitter, Dan Schifrin, Naomi Seidman, Assaf Steinschneider, Mirjam Zadoff, and Noam Zadoff. A special thanks to Avraham Shapira for two long conversations and for sharing his extensive archive. I also thank Emilia Engelhardt for assistance in deciphering some of Scholem's more difficult German handwriting. Finally, this book has benefited greatly from Susan Laity's meticulous and thoughtful copyediting.

INDEX